The Reawakening of Myth

SELECTED WORKS BY BORIS NAD

Translated and Edited by Jafe Arnold and Zinka Brkić

2020

PRAV Publishing

www.pravpublishing.com
pravpublishing@protonmail.com

Copyright © 2020 Boris Nad

All rights reserved. No part of this book may be reproduced or distributed in any form or by any means, electronic or mechanical, including photocopying, recording, or by any information storage and retrieval, without permission in writing from the publisher.

Copy-edited by Lucas Griffin.

Cover image: "Issa and the Head of the Giant" by Nicholas Roerich, 1932, reproduced by permission of the Nicholas Roerich Museum in New York.

ISBN 978-1-952671-06-7 (*Paperback*)
ISBN 978-1-952671-07-4 (*Hardcover*)
ISBN 978-1-952671-08-1 (*Ebook*)

Table of Contents:

From the Publisher	7
Author's Preface	11

PART I: THE RETURN OF MYTH

1. The Return of Myth — 21

Myths of Hyperborea	23
The Oblivion and Speech of Being	47
The Return of Myth	57
The Androgyne	67
East and West	83
Mythical America	103
The Idea of the Center	113

2. Symbols of Hyperborea — 125

Ithaca	127
The Lions of Kalemegdan	129
One Dream	133
Hyperboreans	135
Iran	139
City of the Gods	141
Symbols of Hyperborea	147

3. Stories and Chronicles — 153

Odin	155
Achilles	159
Atlantis: The Kingdom of Shadows	161

Baghdad	171
Two Dreams	175
Pannonia	177
Barbaric Scythia	181
Dalmatia	187
Slavonia	189
America (The United States)	191
The Golden Fleece	197

PART II: A TALE OF AGARTHA

1. The Secret of Secrets	203
2. Descent into Agartha	249
3. Epilogue	315
Afterword: Sikorsky's Mission	342

PART III: SACRED HISTORY AND THE END OF THE WORLD (SELECTED ESSAYS)

Sacred History	355
Archy and Anarchy	377
The Antichrist	395
Post-Apocalypse: Technocracy and the Apocalypse	411
The War for the End of the World	425
Rome and Carthage	437
The Secret of the East and the Crisis of the Western World	445

From the Publisher

The Reawakening of Myth is the ultimate, perhaps unexpected result of the relatively isolated work of individuals who each happened to find themselves, at one point or another, involved with the mythical writings of Boris Nad. Whenever the selected works of such an exploratory, wide-ranging, and multi-genre author as Boris Nad are brought from one language into another, this development can hardly ever be reduced to the work - or significance - of one or two individuals. Accordingly, this book owes acknowledgements to an altogether plural translation front. The first work comprising this volume, *The Return of Myth*, was first published by Manticore Press in 2016 as an alternative English edition (abridged, rearranged, and featuring some other texts) of Mr. Nad's major 2010 Serbian work of the same title, *Povratak mita*. The first translation of the latter was owed to a whole host of contributors, namely, Zinka and Viktor Brkić, Vesna S. Disić, Zorana Lutovac, Ivana Ivanc, and Sofia and Aleksandar Stojić (the latter two also contributing "The Golden Fleece" to the edition here). The second part of this book, *A Tale of Agartha*, published in Serbian in 2017, was first translated by Zinka Brkić, who also contributed the translation of "The Antichrist" to the third part of the present volume. The third part, titled "Sacred History and the End of the World", includes texts which were left out of the previous English edition of *The Return of Myth* as well as other selected essays translated by myself. Taken together, all of the preceding translations were re-edited and, in more than a few places, re-translated by myself in collaboration with Mr. Nad for PRAV Publishing's *The Reawakening of Myth*. It is also worth pointing out that some of the texts included in this volume have never been published before in Serbian or English. It is our hope that *The Reawakening of Myth* can stand as the first volume of Boris Nad's selected writings in the English language, thus offering readers an unprecedented introduction to the works, worlds, and thoughts of this visionary Serbian author.

-*Jafe Arnold*
PRAV Publishing
25 October 2020

Author's Preface

The book before you now, *The Reawakening of Myth*, follows the line of two works: *The Return of Myth* and *The Awakening of Myth*. The first, *The Return of Myth*, was published in Serbia in 2010. The book originally entitled *The Awakening of Myth* was for various reasons re-titled by the publisher as *Towards the Post-History of the World* and published in Belgrade in 2013. *The Return of Myth* was quite voluminous, numbering over three hundred pages, consisting of several books of different literary genres and including a collection of poetry. The second book was a selection of essays exploring and touching upon diverse mythical *topoi*. At the risk of self-assurance, it could be said that in these latter books the author moved through altogether diverse fields - from sacred geography and sacred history to the history of art, from geopolitics to mythology, from the "Hyperborean theory" to technocracy, from the "idea of the center" and the notion that this center really represents something that is now lost, to the modern opposition between East and West. *Towards the Post-History of the World* ended with a survey of the Christian Apocalypse.

The fundamental idea of the author across these works is that today (unlike in prehistory or post-history) we live in a historical world, a world from which mythical forces have withdrawn - but never entirely. In a mysterious way, myth repeats itself in history whether we are conscious of it or not. Max Weber discerned that we live in a "disenchanted world" and that we are doomed to live in an "iron cage." This "way of life", which is a sign of moving away from the sacred and denying the very existence of the sacred, of which myth itself is an expression, is what constitutes the very foundation of the modern age. Yet this observation is only partially true: mythical forces do and indeed have withdrawn, but they also return and break back into the historical world, and always in an unexpected way. "De-mythologization" and "re-mythologization" are processes happening constantly, sometimes at the same time: some myths disappear only to be replaced by "new" ones (sometimes in the form of the "anti-myths" of the modern age). Such may be "new" in form but not in their content, which always belongs to the world of deeply rooted archetypes. One example of this is the beginning of the Christian era, when old myths came to be replaced by "new" myths about the Savior, in which theologians and the Church Fathers saw not myth but literal and veritable history and, indeed, the central event of history (as recorded and described in the Gospels). A new wave of de-mythologization began with the age of the Enlightenment, yet this "new age of reason", in which man in the very least claimed and seemed to have assumed divine authority and status, was itself "just a myth" - the myth of the "enlightened man", perhaps that of Prometheus, the "one who thinks fast", or more sinisterly, the myth of the Titans who assault Olympus (Heaven), the world of the gods, and the very "father of the gods and men" (Zeus).

In any case, speaking of the "return of myth" in modern times might seem to be an anachronism. In the "age of reason", after all, myth is relegated a very modest place: it can be the subject of (marginal) studies, an object of ridicule, contempt, or mockery as the "superstition" of "savages", as a mere attempt at an "explanation of the world", or simply a fun story from past times which, while not devoid of imagination and poetry, is basically just the "ravings of primitives." Reason is supposed to illuminate myth with its cold light. The essence of myth, however, escapes reason. Myth is neither history nor superstition, but timeless reality, a reality that perhaps "never happened at all or anywhere", but which is constantly repeated in history and, moreover, is a reality that determines and defines history. A myth does not need to have happened in the way in which it is described, and it actually never has happened that way, but it could have happened and it has happened to a certain degree. As Novalis remarked in one place: "Only that is true which has never happened anywhere."

The 20th century did not lack lucid and penetrating scholars of myth. Suffice it to mention but two here: the Romanian scholar and writer Mircea Eliade, who overcame the false dualism of the sacred vs. the profane, for "there is no profane existence", and the German writer Ernst Jünger, who constantly returned to thinking through the relationship between the mythical and historical world. Let us recall a few important points of reference from the first, Eliade. According to Eliade, images, symbols, and myths which have been forgotten or suppressed in the West since the 19th century reveal to us the most hidden modalities of human beings. The spiritual role of literary works in the modern age consists in the fact that they have preserved and transmitted many myths, albeit sometimes degraded. Eliade also pointed out the fact that the renewal of interest in symbolism and myth in Western Europe temporally coincided with the entry of Asian peoples onto the historical scene, beginning with the revolution of Sun Yat-sen. Moreover, we also owe to the 20th century the discovery that all "objective", "scientific" knowledge is, in reality, to quote Alexander Dugin, only "a particular variation of mythology", and that "development and progress have a cyclical character." In other words, progress - that invention of the moderns - is only illusory. Humanity, despite all the changes it has undergone, in essence "remains such as it has always been." The era of optimistic positivism and materialism has essentially ended: "In its place has come a new understanding of mythological constructs" and "the rehabilitation of those various disciplines and sciences that were too hastily classified as overcome and primitive."[1] This realization also collapses the sense of supremacism or skepticism toward the ancient heritage of mankind and the civilizations of the remote past (so-called prehistory). Our time is not privileged over the other eras of human history that preceded it. Rather, it would be the other way around: at hand is involution and impetuous spiritual decline. After all, we do not know the ancient past of mankind, or we do not know it to a sufficient extent, since "official history", as René Guénon noted, nowhere reaches beyond the last six thousand years, a span which is negligibly small compared to the total duration of man's existence on Earth. A dense darkness falls upon all the rest. In front of all of our attempts to know the distant past, a mysterious and impenetrable wall emerges. It is not accessible to "reason" (scientific knowledge), as the reach of "reason" (rational cognition and research) is altogether modest; reason has its clear limitations. Yet this does not mean that "reason" should be banished, just as the positivist age tried to do away with all those forces which it designated "irrational" and "things of the dead past." The above-mentioned German writer Jünger proposed a different and quite likely far more difficult and demanding approach: the simultaneous use of both optics, both angles of observation, "rational" and "irrational" methods of knowledge. The moon, for example, is at once a physical and cosmic body that is subject to scientific

---

[1] Alexander Dugin, *Misterii Evrazii* [*Mysteries of Eurasia*] (Moscow: Arktogeia, 1991).

observations and measurements, as well as a mythological fact or even metaphysical entity; the moon is not merely a dead object for scientific, "objective" knowledge which a scientist can approach "coldly" and without prejudice.

The author of this book is not a scientist or a scholar, but only a writer. This gives him greater freedom of accessibility, as well as frees him from the obligation of following scientific meticulousness. Myth, however, is a topos to which I, as a writer, have returned often. My first literary work published in my homeland was a short "epic-fantasy" novel entitled *The Feast of the Victor* (2005). Basically, this mythical story takes place at a point where different temporal and spatial perspectives intersect. In fact, this story, although prompted by immediate events (the war in the country called Yugoslavia), unfolds in a timeless place or "uchronia." This approach bears similarities to the one employed by Jünger in his short story *On the Marble Cliffs* (1939). This comparison, of course, concerns only approach, not the value of the literary work. My book *The Silent Gods* (2008), which was a collection of short stories, notes, and prose, and the collection of fantasy stories entitled *The Invisible Kingdom* (2016) were centered around mythical themes and my own variations of well-known mythical plots.

The book before readers now is a kind of selection of writings by which the author presents himself to the Anglophone public more completely than ever before. In fact, this book consists of three works, the first of which is the abridged English edition of *The Return of Myth*, originally published in 2016 in Melbourne, Australia by Manticore Press. This text was re-edited and partially re-translated for this occasion and appended with one previously untranslated text, "The Golden

Fleece." The second part is a short novel, *A Tale of Agartha*, i.e., a tale of the underground kingdom that has, for thousands of years, invisibly and mysteriously influenced events on the surface of the Earth, history and the world of people. This is one of the great myths of the East which the author approaches in a way characteristic of a writer: in the form of a fantasy tale. The third part of this book, "Sacred History and the End of the World", complements the first two, including texts which were left out of the previous English edition of *Return of Myth* as well as featuring other, previously untranslated and unpublished texts in which I approach related topics in an extremely free, essayistic way. These topics include, among others, the notion of sacred history, the appearance of the Antichrist and the Second Coming of Christ (which is of special importance to Eastern Christianity), and relations between East and West. The latter section is not only about the crisis of the West, but also the crisis into which Eastern societies (and civilizations) are evermore descending - crises which, without a doubt, have essentially the same spiritual root. Now more than ever before, it is necessary for East and West to come together in a rapprochement instead of, as has been the case over the course of the modern age (unlike in some earlier historical periods), moving further away and becoming more divided from one another. The first and necessary condition for this is that East and West come to know each other better and finally engage in dialogue (otherwise, they will only be at war).

Yet here, on the pages of this book, it is not East and West that meet, but above all, the reader and the writer. The writer's ambition is not to explain or interpret anything; he does not seek to persuade, but rather to ask questions, to simply speak about what is important to him with his own voice and following the flow of his own thoughts. It is not necessary for the reader and writer to always agree on everything, but it is necessary for there to be a certain affinity between them. It is disagreements and disputes that make dialogue desirable and possible. The role of the reader is no less demanding than that of the writer, as it is up to the reader to make the writer's work come to life again. If this book facilitates this even only on a symbolic level, then it will have fulfilled its purpose. After all, everything of importance happens first on the level of symbols, in the realm in which the spirit rules sovereignly, and only then causes consequences in the world which we so very clumsily call "material."

- Boris Nad
Serbia
August 2020

The Reawakening of Myth

PART I:

THE RETURN OF MYTH

The Return of Myth

MYTHS OF HYPERBOREA

Myths of Hyperborea, the land of the ancestors in the Far North, the land that lies "beyond the North Wind", are deeply embedded in the mythology and collective unconscious of nearly all Indo-European peoples (and indeed other peoples as well). This fact is of great importance even in and of itself, yet beyond the widespread prevalence of these myths there is the question of their meaning. If Hyperborean myths truly occupy such an important role in the collective unconscious of Indo-European peoples, then this is due to their meaning, their inner content. Myth for us is not a "fabricated story", superstition, or misunderstanding. Myth is a timeless reality which perhaps "never played itself out at any time or any place", but is constantly repeated in history, and, moreover, is a reality that determines and defines history.

The meanings of myths are numerous, and it is possible to interpret them in diverse ways. As a matter of course, they also have their literal, "naturalistic" meaning: every true myth is not exclusively a fantasy or work of the imagination; what is contained within them corresponds to certain concrete conditions in time and space on Earth. In other words, a myth did not need to have happened in the way it is described, and it may never have actually happened in that way, yet it could have happened, and it has happened or has been happening to a certain degree. "Only that is true which has not happened anytime and anywhere" (Novalis).

Hyperborean myths are not the only direct and clear evocations of a land of immortals in the Far North of the continent. In Russian fairy tales we have an example mentioning three brothers, of which the youngest was Ivan, who lived in a distant land where eternal darkness prevailed until Ivan killed the giant snake and set free the Sun – this is for us an obvious and clear explanation of the Arctic night, and hence the North, Hyperborea. Here Ivan repeats the archetypal undertaking of Indra, who killed the dragon Vritra to regain the Sun and liberate the celestial waters. Hyperborean myths also possess the quality of representing, similar to myths of Atlantis, remembrance of a real land, although this does not deplete their meanings. Yet compared to Atlantean myths, they are relatively narrowly localized in circumpolar areas: only there is it possible to search for their material traces and confirmation.

But, independently of their literal authenticity, the question at hand is primarily the archetypes of the North, which possess their own force and embody an almost separate reality. Independently of specific historical conditions, they can withdraw and resurrect anew with previously unforeseen force. There is no need to prove their particular attraction throughout the ages. They have easily found expression in myths, popular legends and folklore, fairy tales, fables, poetry, and local customs. We would perhaps be going too far if we even tried to enumerate their various forms and guises across diverse traditions. They have also been the topic of works of art, as well as, since more recent times, the subject of scientific studies which have in various ways lent them at least the illusion of scientific argumentation. Sometimes, though, we have the impression that the aim of such studies is not to set up new postulates, theories, or even scientific truth, but are simply an end in and of themselves.

Beyond the Eagles, Guardians of Gold

The oldest known reference regarding Hyperborean myth is the one found in Herodotus' *Histories*. Herodotus conveys to us the strange story of Aristeas of Proconnesus, who, following in the footsteps of Apollo, reached Issedonia. A cult and worship of Aristeas was established in Metapontum, and it was believed that he had spent seven years with Apollo in the land of the Hyperboreans. Here is the fabulous description which Herodotus owes to Aristeas, the author of the lost "*Arimaspea*" poem, which still attracts commentators and interpreters today: "beyond the Issedones lives a one-eyed race called the Arimaspians, beyond them there is the land of the gold-guarding griffins, and beyond them the Hyperboreans [whose land stretches] all the way to the sea."[2] There, according to Plutarch, the God of the Golden Age, Cronos, is dreaming in slumber. Indeed, Aristeas' description contains a clear memory of the Golden Age, of the primeval condition, of the "first and foremost of all countries", Hyperborea. However, when it comes to the name "*Arimasp(o)i*", Herodotus' etymology is obviously incorrect: it represents a typical case of Greek translations and interpretations of names in terms of sonority. "The illumination of the ancient Iranian lexis allows us to understand the proper interpretation of the meaning of the name '*Arimaspi*' - '*Aryannaaspa*' means 'Aryans who love horses.'"[3]

Aristeas followed the path of Apollo, for which he earned deification and cult-reverence. As for Apollo, it was believed

---

[2] Herodotus, *The Histories* IV:13 (trans. by Robin Waterfield; Oxford: Oxford University Press, 2008), p. 680.

[3] Dragoš Kalajić, "*Uvod u arktičku teoriju B.G. Tilaka*" [Introduction to the Arctic Theory of B.G. Tilak], in the 1987 Serbian edition of Tilak's *The Arctic Home in the Vedas*.

that he himself traveled each year to Hyperborea in a chariot pulled by swans. He no longer wanted to return and the Greeks were only able to lure him back with song. According to Diodorus Siculus, the Temple of Apollo, the sanctuary dedicated to the God of the Sun, was located in Hyperborea. In other words, the cult of Apollo originated in Hyperborea, from where it was brought to ancient Greece by the Achaeans.

From the Far North, the Hyperboreans sent votive gifts each year, from people to people, wrapped in wheat straw and sent from the Northernmost end of the Eurasian continent all the way down to Delos in the South. These votive gifts wrapped in wheat straw symbolized the eternity of a value, of a tradition passed on from people to people and from generation to generation. In remembrance of the death of Hyperborean girls who brought these gifts to Delos, Herodotus records, tradition dictated that "before they get married, the girls [of Delos] cut off a lock of hair, wind it around a spindle and put it on the tomb…and the Delian boys wind some of their hair around a twig and put it on the tomb as well."[4]

Ultima Thule Sole Nomen Habens

Ultima Thule is a late Hellenic and Roman variation of the Hyperborean myth. It is a land of eternal light in the Far North: "*Ultima Thule sole nomen habens.*" In the second half of the fourth century BC, Pytheas embarked on a voyage from his native Massalia (now called Marseilles) to the Far North of Europe. He named the last country which he saw *Ultima Thule* ("The Last Thule"). It has been recorded that Constantius Chlorus undertook a campaign to the British Isles to contemplate the "most sacred land, nearest to heaven."

---

4   Herodotus, *Histories* IV:34, p. 695.

The toponym *Tula* occurs in many Native American traditions as well: the center of the Toltec Empire was called Tula. Tula, "the land of eternal sunshine in the North", "near the great waters", was known to the mythologies of the Mayans, the Aztecs, and other tribes. According to legend, Native American tribes from Quiche (Central America) set off towards Tula, but it was found to be submerged in ice and darkness, without sunlight. In 1925, the Cuna people tried to establish an independent Republic of Tula by force.

Tula is a toponym which is extremely widespread in Eurasia, from Russia (e.g., the old city of Tula and Tulos Lake in Karelia) to Ukraine (Tulchyn) to France (Toulon or Toulouse). The meaning of the word, however, is preserved in the Russian and Serbian language, where the word *utuliti* has the meaning of "damping" and "concealing", and *tuliti* means "to lament", to cry long and deeply. It is the same with the meaning of the word Borea, the North Wind, which has an analogy in the Sanskrit *bhurati* as well as in Russian *buria* and Serbian *bura*, which mean "storm." But the name Apollo, as the Russian researcher Valery Demin says (citing Chertakov), has its roots in the word *opaliti* which, in Russian and Serbian, has the same meaning of "to set off", "to set on fire."

The Chariot Pulled by Swans

The meaning of the myth which Herodotus described is obvious: the Hyperborean North is the ancestral homeland, the primordial land of many peoples, including the Greeks. It is an ancient memory, a memory transposed onto land, and not a mere geographical description. The origin of the cult of Apollo is in the North. In the study *The Hand Bracelets and Cultural Identity of the Indo-Europeans*, Živojin Andrejić presents a remarkable finding from our soil, the so-called "statue from Dupljaja" (Dupljaja is a village near Vršac in northern Serbia):

> The emergence of the bird-like idol on a cart pulled by pond birds from Dupljaja near Vršac is of great significance. This image is undoubtedly connected with the myth of the Delphic Apollo who resides for six months in the land of the Hyperboreans, a distant and fog-covered region…and then spends the next six months in sunny Greece. This could therefore be the forerunner of Apollo Belenus, who is revered in our region as the god of the sun.

The origin of the cult of Apollo, therefore, should be sought not in the centers of Mycenaean culture, but far away from the Mediterranean altogether, and it should be sought only in the North. This is clearly the meaning of the customs of girls and boys from Delos cutting their hair, laying it on the graves, and the tradition of the gifts that are sent by the Hyperboreans each year from the Far North through the hands of different peoples down to the South of Europe. This was a pledge of fidelity to Hyperborean tradition.

Valery Demin cites Pausanias, an ancient writer in the second century whose work *Description of Hellas* states (X:V:8) that the first priest-prophet of the Temple of Apollo at Delphi was named *Olen, Oleny*, i.e. *"Jelen"* in Serbian. *"Jelen"* is a deer, which is unambiguously a Northern, Hyperborean symbol of the Sun. The Roman author Pliny the Elder also writes in his *Natural History* (*Historia Naturalis* IV:26) of the Hyperboreans as a very real population of the Arctic Circle connected with Hellas through the Hyperborean cult of Apollo.

The Temple of Apollo in Lapland

Russian archaeologists have discovered a Paleolithic archaeological site in Berezevskaya on the banks of the River Pechora, which has an estimated age of 40,000 to 20,000 years old. Their findings significantly change our understanding of settlements in the Northern circle during these ancient epochs. In 1922, Alexander Vasilyevich Barchenko and Alexander Kondyayin organized an archaeological expedition to the Kola Peninsula in Russia's Lapland, where, on the shores of Lake Seyd, there was an ancient temple of the Sami people. The name of the peninsula bears a clearly solar symbolism: it is the land of the Sun, the "sun wheel." There are many toponyms on this peninsula with typical Indo-European roots, such as *"ind"*, *"gang"*, and *"ram."* There are, for example, six rivers with the root *"ind-"* (Indoga, Indomanka, Indega, Indigirka and two rivers named Indiga; there is also Lake Ram(o), etc.)

"The results of this expedition", we read in the book *The Continuity of the Vinča Civilization: From Possible Hyperborean Roots to the Present* by Dragoljub Antić (Belgrade, 2004), "together with the data that inspired the research, were lost in the archives of the KGB, and the researchers themselves lost their lives in the following years." The same author informs us of the expeditions "Hyperborea '97" and "Hyperborea '98", organized by Valery Demin, which were also undertaken on the Kola Peninsula in Russian Lapland. Here they found labyrinths of pebbles, about five meters in diameter, stone pyramids, and a petroglyph with dimensions of about one hundred meters and a crucifix-like human contour chiseled into the rock. There also stands a distinct form of shrine (*seyd*), consisting of stacked stones with deer antlers. While in the past such were ubiquitous, now they are mostly found in remote areas, such as mountains.

The most interesting of all is the finding of the expedition "Hyperborea '97" in the Lovozerska tundra in the central part of the peninsula, located about 500 meters above Lake Seyd. The ruins of megalithic complexes discovered there, consisting of gigantic staircases, walls, and embankments, Demin deemed "ruins of Hyperborea" and drew a connection between them and Diodorus Siculus' account of the Temple of Apollo in Hyperborea.

With each passing day, new evidence confirms that the Far North was by no means a desolate land, even in such ancient eras. Many tumultuous events of proto-history are apparently related to it, about which we know very little. There is no doubt that new archaeological research will greatly, if not entirely, change the ideas that we hold today.

The Deer, the Mammoth, and Cattle

The Serbian scientist Milutin Milanković is the author of the most complete and to this day unequaled mathematical model explaining shifts in the ice ages and climate change on Earth. In his book *The Calendar of Earth's Past* (Belgrade-Zemun, 1926), we read the following: "During that one thousand years, some 9,500 before Christ, a slight heatwave rose over Northern Europe. During that millennium, the summer in the northernmost parts of Europe was unusually warm, and plants could thrive then which now cannot."

Similar conclusions were reached by the Russian scientist Lev Nikolayevich Gumilev as well, although in a quite different way, by analyzing the traditions of the steppe peoples of Eurasia. In the book *The Ethnosphere: Human and Natural History* (Moscow, 1993), Gumilev concludes that during the end of the last ice age (20,000 to 12,000 BC), Northern Siberia was home to a very rich steppe, not today's cold Taiga. This climatic peculiarity was conditioned by the existence of a stable anticyclone which, in turn, resulted in a very small amount of snowfall. Sufficient water was provided by the surrounding glaciers, whose melting created numerous rivers and lakes full of fish and birds. The steppes were grazed by herds of cattle, deer, mammoths and gazelles. This is the environment which raised the Indo-Europeans, creating the cult of the Sun, with its symbol, the deer, and the great importance of cattle, which for the Indo-Europeans symbolized prosperity.

With the end of the ice age in Northern Siberia, Northern Russia and Scandinavia, cyclones brought cold and moisture. The climate changed drastically. Fertile steppes were transformed into the cold Taiga, with ice and snow encroaching everywhere; huge herds of steppe animals moved south, and after them their hunters. Thus onset the great anabasis of the Indo-Europeans. Was this the same glaciation remembered in the old Iranian Avesta? Gumilev does not claim that the ancient inhabitants of the steppes were solely Indo-Europeans; their fate could be shared by the ancestors of many other races and ethnoi that we know today. But still, the most vivid memory of this has been preserved in the traditions of Indo-European peoples, and this became the subject of the extensive and ingenious study of Bal Gangadhar Tilak, *The Arctic Home in the Vedas*.

It must be said that Tilak's work provided the most complete and bold formulation of the "Hyperborean theory." He imparted this theory with exceptional scientific argumentation which has yet to be refuted - thus far, time has only worked in its favor, confirming in essence this author's conclusions and intuitions. The fact that authors involved in research on the ancestral homeland and origins of the Indo-Europeans regularly mention this book, even if only in footnotes without refuting or confirming it, ought to be seen as a sign of recognition of Tilak's genius. Tilak's *The Arctic Home in the Vedas* was published in the very beginning of the 20th century, in 1903. The significance of his theory has not waned since then, but has grown over the past hundred years and has, without a doubt, exerted great influence and inspired many to follow in the footsteps of researching the Arctic and the ancient heritage of the Indo-Europeans.

"The Most Ancient Testimonies left by Our Race"

Let us summarize Tilak's work in the briefest possible terms. We will dwell on his conclusions and outcomes, bypassing for the time being his otherwise very well-founded, complex, solid argumentation.

Tilak's considerations were based on what he calls "the most ancient testimonies left by our race", i.e., an analysis of the most ancient texts of the Indo-Europeans: the Vedas, the sacred books of Hinduism, and the Avesta, the sacred books of the Persians. Using the first and oldest chapter of the latter, *Vendidad*, Tilak writes his exegesis in the terms of astronomy, meteorology, geology, biology, archeology, paleontology, and comparative mythology.

The result is a significant shift in the estimated age of the Vedas, making them several millennia older. Tilak moved us back many thousands of years into the past, into the darkness of proto-history, where we witness the contours of a great Aryan culture which flourished in the circumpolar regions. It should be noted that Tilak, while interpreting the naturalistic aspects of the Vedic tradition, often does not dwell purely on them, but also highlights the basic, essential contents of the Indo-European tradition, such as the absolute dualism of light and darkness, summer and winter, long days and long nights:

> The evidence, cited in the foregoing chapters, mainly consists of direct passages from the Vedas and the Avesta, proving unmistakably that the poets of the Rig-Veda were acquainted with the climatic conditions witnessible only in the Arctic regions… A day or a night of six months, and a long continuous dawn of several days' duration with its revolving splendors, not to mention the unusually long Arctic day and night or a year of less than twelve months' sunshine, were all known to the Vedic bards, and have been described by them not mythologically or metaphorically but directly in plain and simple words, which, though misinterpreted so long, can, in the light thrown upon the question by recent scientific researches, be now rightly read and understood.[5]

The Aryan homeland, says Tilak, could only have been in the Far North, "for a continuous dawn of thirty days is possible only within a few degrees of the North Pole. But though the latitude of the original home can be thus ascertained more or less definitely, yet there is unfortunately nothing in these

---

5   Lokamanya Bal Gangadhar Tilak, *The Arctic Home in the Vedas, Being Also a New Key to the Interpretation of Many Vedic Texts and Legends* (Poona City: Tilak Bros, 1903), pp. 386-387.

traditions which will enable us to determine the longitude of the place…" However: "It is not unlikely that the primeval home was located to the north of Siberia rather than to the north of Russia or Scandinavia."[6]

The ancient Aryan homeland was destroyed by snow and ice, a glaciation of which there is unequivocal, clear and direct testimony in the *Vendidad*, and this happened more than 8,000 years before Christ; this was the beginning of the post-glacial era, the time of the Aryan migration, the beginning of their scattering across the Eurasian continent. We read in the *Vendidad*:

> The first of the good lands and countries which I, Ahura Mazda, created, was the Airyana Vaeja, by the Vanguhi Daitya. Thereupon came Angra Mainyu, who is all death, and he counter-created the serpent in the river and Winter, a work of the Daevas. There are ten winter months there, two summer months; and [even] those are cold for the waters, cold for the earth, cold for the trees. Winter falls there, the worst of all plagues.[7]

In *Fargard II* we find the beginning of the tale about the dispersion of the Aryans, when Ahura Mazda warns Yima: "Upon the material world the evil winters are about to fall, that shall bring the fierce, deadly frost; upon the material world the evil winters are about to fall, that shall make snow-flakes fall thick, even an aredvi deep on the highest tops of mountains."[8]

---

6   Ibid, p. 388.
7   *Vendidad, Fargard* I:1-3 (translated by James Darmesteter in *Sacred Books of the East*, 1880).
8   Ibid, *Fargard* II:22.

Atlantean Star Maps

Tilak is not the only one to have followed the footprints of Hyperborean myth. Although his discoveries in the scientific domain are the most spectacular and the most comprehensive, other authors before and after him have reached similar or even the same conclusions by following other paths and other, quite different optics and methods of cognition.

First and foremost, we should mention one French astronomer, the astronomer of the last French king. His name was Jean-Sylvain Bailly (1736-1793, guillotined). Like Tilak, he researched data based on the positions of the constellations mentioned in Vedic literature. Bailly's curiosity was spurred by ancient celestial maps brought to him by missionaries and travelers from India. These maps, Bailly claimed, could have arisen only in a field of precise observations from an area between 50 and 60 degrees of Northern latitude. He assumed that the observations were from "some unknown people" – Bailly called them Atlanteans – who migrated from the Far North to the South. The author found proof for his beliefs by exploring various strands of mythology. Here are his main conclusions: "Taken together, we note with amazement that all of these traditions, while often 'blurred' and confused, all strive toward the same goal, which places their origins in the North."

Bailly identified the "unknown people" as "Atlanteans": we will identify them as the Hyperboreans, since their homeland is placed "between 50 and 60 degrees latitude North", and "in areas around the North Pole", which is our main point of interest (the mythical Atlantis of Plato was reportedly located somewhere in the Northwest Atlantic). The latter is closely related to Hyperborea for authors such as René Guénon, but only as a secondary center of the polar tradition, and it is erroneous, even fatal, to see them as absolutely identical.

Man-Gods and Man-Beasts

Other authors have reached almost identical conclusions by different paths. For the purposes of this survey, we should mention, among all the others, the Frisian scholar Herman Wirth, whom the Russian author Alexander Dugin draws upon in his work *The Hyperborean Theory* (Moscow, 1992). Dwelling on the ideas of the so-called Traditionalist authors, such as René Guénon and Julius Evola, Dugin does not speak of scientific discoveries, theories, or "points of view", but rather "the universe of Herman Wirth."

It is not known to us the way in which Herman Wirth came to his knowledge, but it is perfectly clear that he did not gain such knowledge from following the ways of the orthodox science of his time. As we shall see, that is only of secondary importance. What is more important is the question of what Herman Wirth observed, what the true result of his work was. The fact that Wirth's works are sometimes described as fantastic does not diminish their importance – Wirth speaks of things which established science avoids or passes over. But here, we are first and foremost interested not so much in concrete historical facts as in the truth, the truth of myth.

The most important of Wirth's works was titled *The Emergence of Mankind* (*Der Aufgang der Menschheit*, 1928). In this book, as well as in his many others, Wirth developed his own concept of which the starting point is "Arctogaia", i.e. "Northern Land" or "Northern Earth", that is Hyperborea as the origin of humanity, but, above all, as the home of one unique human race and tradition which from the beginning appears in its complete – it would be better to say organic – form. During the following period, in the post-Arctic era, this tradition would be subject to distortion and perversion, but also mysterious re-appearances in more or less pure and original form. This tradition remains the main subject, the most important matter of the spiritual history of mankind.

The main bearer of this tradition, and therefore the main subject of history, is Arctic Man. The man of the North Pole was a representative of the Arctic race, a representative of god-men: the true children of God in the universe. The extreme nature of the Arctic polar environment fits him perfectly, with its almost absolute duality of light and darkness, life and death, heat and cold (the dark, cold, and death which occur during the Arctic winter).

Naturally and logically, insofar as God himself is dualistic, the Arctic proto-continent had its own complete opposite and counterweight, the proto-continent of the South, Gondwana. This is the country of night, of the tropics and the equator (not the South Pole), inhabited not by man-gods, as is the case in Arctogaia, but rather by man-beasts. The South is the demonic counterpart to the Arctic. Once upon a time, the two cultures lived completely separately without mutual interference (the Vedas remember this absence of interference). Sometime in the early quaternary, with the glaciations of Arctogaia, at the time when the Northern land started to freeze over and a small number of representatives of the Nordic race remained among the icebergs, Northern man started his journey from North to South. This led to confrontations, conflicts, and finally to mixing between these two types. Thus begins a period of gradual degradation of the Nordic tradition. Not only was there the freezing over of Arctogaia, but Gondwana also broke up into several continents, and the original North-South opposition was replaced by a new East-West opposition. Atlantis was then located in the North Atlantic and consisted of the remains of Arctogaia. The Eastern continent was the proto-continent of Eurasia.

Wirth then follows the complex migration paths of the Nordic race that gradually changed the appearance and ethnic composition of the population of Gondwana. The Atlantic cycle, roughly speaking, corresponds to the late Paleolithic, the Magdalenian period, 22,000 to 10,000 years before Christ.

From Archeological "Nowhere"

Cro-Magnon man appears out of archaeological "nowhere." His appearance is inexplicable from the standpoint of evolutionary doctrine. He is not the Nordic type that would only appear in a pure form later in history, in the Mesolithic and Neolithic, and whose discovery is quite difficult due to the distinct funerary practice of cremation instead of burial, which leaves no anthropological traces behind. The Aurignacian type represents a mixed subtype of the Nordic and the semi-animalian Gondwanan type which appeared not as a result of evolution but from the mixing of the Cro-Magnon with the Neanderthal type, the Neanderthals being descendants of the proto-race of Gondwana (man-apes, half-beasts). The first wave of migration of the Nordic type, the "man-gods", the Atlanteans, came from the North Atlantic and the Western Arctic. They left behind megalithic monuments, as well as the "North African, Arab, Assyrian, Southern Indian and oceanic

Atlanteans (the Amorites, Moors, Maori...)" in highly complex patterns and lines of migration, procreation, and settlements.

The second wave of migration of the Northern type was that of the people known as the Tuatha Dé Danann, who arrived in Ireland from the North. These were the actual Proto-Indo-Europeans, the Aryans, who, like the Cro-Magnons but later, in the late Neolithic, migrated southeast, across the Caucasus to India and Iran, where they either built the foci of purely Aryan civilizations (Iran, India) or became castes of spiritual teachers (Japan).

It was these main migration flows and racial intersections that Herman Wirth attempted to reconstruct. At the basis of his concept was a duality of two opposing fundamental principles, whose consequences are the human races themselves and their spiritual contents. Herman Wirth's ambition was to reveal the traces of the true history of humankind. His starting point was the Hyperborean myth, which Wirth developed in a grandiose manner, thus complementing the missing chapters in the history of mankind.

The Tradition that Always Existed

The French thinker, metaphysician, and "Traditionalist" or "Perennialist" René Guénon exerted a limited but very powerful, focused impact on intellectual circles with his concept of the "Primordial Tradition": the Tradition that has always existed and is divine by origin, but which has been obscured and lost, retreating gradually into the realm of hidden, secret knowledge and into complete oblivion in the final "dark age", which the Hindu tradition calls the Kali-Yuga and is known to European traditions as the "iron age", or in Christianity as the "End Times." Guénon's field of research, therefore, is not science but esotericism. Guénon himself refused to inform readers of the sources of his knowledge, emphasizing that his work is not about knowledge that can be acquired through books in libraries.

We will describe Guénon's idea of the "Primordial Tradition" here in only the most general terms, as briefly as possible, without dwelling on secondary "details." The Primordial Tradition has always existed. In many places, Guénon suggested that this tradition was polar, Hyperborean, and therefore of Indo-European origin. In its fullness, however, it existed only in the first Golden Age of mankind (which corresponds to the Hyperborean cycle), and in subsequent periods was subjected to regressive processes. The myths and legends of different peoples, religions, metaphysical doctrines, traditional symbols, and rituals are all fragments of this knowledge, adapted to new conditions or translated into popular language.

The Atlantic cycle of human history was secondary to that of Hyperborea. In one place, Guénon explicitly warns of the danger of identifying Atlantis with Hyperborea. The former is in the West, the latter is in the North. Both were destroyed by cataclysms, which was basically a consequence of the regressive and degrading pattern of history and time. The downward, regressive flow can be slowed down, but it cannot be changed until the beginning of a new cycle for humanity.

According to Guénon, the name "Thule" or "Tula" encountered in a variety of regions from Russia to Central America refers to a former "seat of spiritual power":

One must doubtless conclude that in some more or less remote age each of these regions was the seat of a spiritual power that was an emanation as it were of that of the primordial Tula...In Sanskrit, the word Tula means 'scales', and denotes more specifically the zodiacal sign of that name 'the Scales, or Libra]; there is however a Chinese tradition in which the heavenly Scales were originally the Great Bear. This point is of the greatest importance, for the symbolism attached to the Great Bear is naturally connected in the closest possible way to that of the Pole.[9]

And further: "But it is also necessary to distinguish the Atlantean *Tula* and the Hyperborean *Tula*, the latter then truly representing the original and supreme center...All the other 'sacred isles', which everywhere bear names of identical meaning, were only its images."[10]

Close to Guénon was another Traditionalist, the Italian Julius Evola, although it would be wrong to consider him Guénon's teacher or follower. Evola was, without a doubt, inspired by Guénon's works, but the two of them had significant differences. Evola presented his views most fully in his book *Revolt Against the Modern World*. Evola's worldview was characterized by an almost Manichaean order of dualism: on one side is the modern world, on the other are the values of the world of Tradition, which has its origin in the polar regions, at the North Pole, in Hyperborea. This is the true Golden Age, if not for all humanity, then at least for the Indo-Europeans. The original homeland of the Indo-Europeans is located at the Pole, in the circumpolar regions. With the cataclysm that beset Hyperborea began the long march of the Indo-Europeans

---

9   René Guénon, *The King of the World* (Hillsdale: Sophia Perennis, 2004), p. 63.
10 Ibid, pp. 62, 63.

through time and space, from the Far North to the South of the planet, from primordiality down the paths of perversion and decadence, through the Atlantic cycle, from prehistory to antiquity, from the Middle Ages all the way to our "modern age" that is the utter antithesis of Tradition. With this march began the degradation of man, from god or man-god to merely human and even lower, finally to the animalistic and demonic, to the dark abyss of the "modern era."

On the deepest level, this is a battle between two cosmic principles: on the one hand, the life-giving hierarchy of Order - Order equally supported and defended by men and Gods - and on the other the forces of chaos and entropy. This is also a struggle for sanctification, for the sacralization of Space (through ritual), against the forces of Time which destroy and devour it. It should be said that many of Evola's insights and brave intuitions were subsequently confirmed by the research of Georges Dumézil, such as on the tripartite ideology of the Indo-Europeans.

The Light from the North

We have seen that myths of Hyperborea are anything but dead and of the past. They are not a product of the imagination of classical writers, much less mere superstition from a distant era. Otto Muck, an admirer of another myth, that of Atlantis, attempted in the book *All About Atlantis* (*Alles über Atlantis*) to explain the myth of Hyperborea by recourse to fascinating natural phenomena that trigger the imagination of the viewer. Even if that was the whole truth about Hyperborea, still, such an environment would have over time attracted or created a certain type of people, naturally leading to the emergence of a corresponding race, ethnos, culture, and civilization.

Myths of Hyperborea still inspire a great number of researchers and thinkers. The North, the polar areas that once attracted tourists, today attract archaeologists and explorers of the past. This is not a sterile field of research: the archetypes of the North are still alive and effective today, they spur onward those who seek them in true spiritual adventure and discovery. Very slowly, with incomparably greater gravity than other regions and lands, the North reveals its deeply forbidden secrets. They belong to a much deeper past than others. Some indications confirm this: carbon-14 tests have shown that "the megalithic tombs of western Europe and the copper metallurgy of the Balkans are actually older than their supposed Mediterranean prototypes", and "not only copper metallurgy but also the attractive little sculptures of the Balkans were more than a millennium older than their supposed Aegean prototypes."[11] Is this not a roadmap for future researchers, a roadmap directing one to the North and not, as before, the South of the continent?

In the nineteenth century, archeology was sometimes guided by the principle *Ex Oriente Lux* ("Light from the East"). This principle has been replaced by a new one: Neolithic culture spread from the Northwest to the Southeast, from Western Europe and North Africa, through southern Arabia, to India and Oceania. Yet today the universally accepted assumption is that the oldest cradle of Mankind is Africa, and therefore the South.

There is no doubt that during the course of the Aryan migration, Negroid and Mongoloid populations already existed, and that the Aryans were foreigners, strangers on the

---

11   Colin Renfrew, "Carbon 14 and the Prehistory of Europe", *Scientific American* (1972).

Eurasian continent. Today, thanks to the zealous aspirers and heroes of the North, of the Pole, we must contemplate a new view, which gives all of the above a completely new and different place and significance. If the origins of humanity, or at least part of it – the Indo-European race –, lie in the North, then it is perfectly possible that migrations during the Neolithic period and afterwards proceeded from the Northwest and Northeast, crossing into the Balkans and the Middle East and creating centers of civilizations related to the cultures of Northern Europe and Eurasia.

Sooner or later, these suppositions will have to be proven or disproven by new ones. Research on the North is still in its infancy. Without a doubt, the myths of Hyperborea will pose a very powerful incentive. Nothing of the sort, after all, is to be found in connection to any other region or continent, with the exception of the ancient legend of the Atlanteans in the West. The origins and traditions of the Indo-Europeans (and perhaps even the whole of humanity), their ancestral homeland, the movement and migrations of peoples and races during what we call "prehistory", and ancient religion - all of this, we have seen, is closely tied to Hyperborean myths.

The Idea of the Center

In its final and highest sense, the Hyperborean myth represents the idea of the center. The center has a primarily metaphysical meaning: it is the center of both the intangible and the material world. It is a spatial and temporal center symbolized by "the first and best of all lands", Hyperborea, in whose center one finds the mythical Mount Meru which, again, has its own center at its peak. In temporal terms, this is the first and Golden Age, the ideal Beginning. For reintegration, metaphysical realization, which is nothing other than the "conquest of the Center", implies moving against the erosive flow of the current of time and history.

The center is immaterial, meta-geographical, suprahistorical and beyond time. It does not exist in the phenomenal world and therefore cannot be destroyed. It is a center that man needs to win but which is hidden, accessible only to the exceptional. Logically, therefore, it is symbolized by the North Pole: it is the "motionless place", unmovable, around which everything else revolves. The position of man at the center is like the "action of non-action." This immobility determines reality itself and its movement: in this sense, it is "more powerful than reality." He who possesses the center, possesses the rest of the circle, for everything is within its orbit.

Thus, in the phenomenal world, the conquest of the Pole (in the physical sense) has the potential value of being a metaphysical act. In Sanskrit, the word *Uttara* means "North" and also "noble land." Setting out for Hyperborea, towards the ideal homeland, gradually changes even the protagonist of Miloš Crnjanski's *Among the Hyperboreans*. In a world that is exterior-centric, he is the one who has his own center, timeless, invisible, and immaterial: "We are all tied to the polar landscapes, to the polar Sun...These icy lands are the aim of all peoples, and whoever peeks into this realm of ice becomes different. That community of dead researchers in the polar regions interests me the most. Why did they go there? Why have they changed?"

The god Apollo himself was the first to set off for (or return to) Hyperborea. He was followed by Aristeas, the author of the Arimaspian poems that are lost to us today. Crnjanski's hero, like many polar explorers, repeats this act. Just as do all who set out to reach Hyperborea today.

***

THE OBLIVION AND SPEECH OF BEING

In ancient Sparta, art was far from the center of public life. It had a secondary role and a primarily educational character. In fact, this is the case with many traditional cultures which shared a kind of cultural "minimalism." Works of art did not bear the stamp of individual authors, they did not express their personal aspirations, nor did they serve the curiosity of the artist. Yet this is not a matter of "stuntedness" of "primitive" forms of culture, as modern historians of art and culture believe, but rather a refusal to develop something of secondary importance (which would be the domain of culture, at least in its present meaning). Artistic expression was concise and self-sufficient without the need for self-interpretation and any further explanation.

Three Human Domains

When it comes to the development and capacities of man, and human beings in general, there are three areas in which they manifest. The first and lowest one is that of elemental forces, which corresponds to what modern science calls "primitive societies" (although here is not meant the primordial state, but a state of extreme degeneration of ancient cultures down to the point of veritable savagery). The second is the development of values that are commonly considered civilized with the corresponding forms of spirituality (those which first and foremost constitute culture and the arts in the modern understanding of the term). The third, and in fact primary and highest domain is truly superhuman, because it implies the development of human capacities beyond man himself and that which is merely human. It bears remarking that every civilization is only the horizontal development of the principle of this final and highest domain, and such development always results in the loss of the metaphysical dimension and tensions inherent to this domain. This was precisely the case with European society in the late Middle Ages and the early Renaissance. From the standpoint of the second domain, however, it is very difficult to distinguish between the first and the last, because both of them are opposed to the "human, all too human" and bear similarities, at least in their manifestations.

On the other hand, with regards to the presumed primitiveness and "stuntedness" of ancient cultures, we should bear in mind the observations of the Serbian writer Rastko Petrović, who in his 1924 *A Primitive Civilization that went Extinct* observed:

> In the caves used as the primitive habitats of the so-called cavemen there have been discovered rock drawings and ornaments which show the strange creative power and even stranger creative perception of those who created them. The movements of leaping animals - bison, deer, etc. - have been confirmed only in modern, scientific times with the latest photography, yet they show such precision in the eyes of these early artists that the belief that their visual power was much stronger than ours, which is primarily synthetic, is imposed by force. We are not able to observe a single movement separated from the movement that follows it, whereas for the cave dweller this was quite an ordinary experience. It has also been noticed that all the fragments of paintings are to be found in the great depths of caves, where it is completely dark, where we could work only with some artificial lighting, whereas there have been found no

remains or traces of smoke and soot that should be left there since both the torches and oil lamps of that time must have emitted smoke. Thus, they could see quite clearly in what for us, today's people, would be the dark, and they still felt the need to paint with dyes, for which ever stronger lighting is needed by the eye.

Art as an Instrument of the Oblivion of Being

In Athens, however, there was a real abundance of artistic creativity, and because of that it is possible to speak of a "blossoming of Athenian art." The target of Plato and Isocrates' criticism of free-thinking poets are the fantasies of a degraded culture. The skill of the Sophists consisted of making reasoned and representative statements, giving the illusion of free judgment, which was valued the same as it is today. Something similar occurred in philosophy during the twilight of the Roman Empire, when the idea of philosophy disintegrated and its subject became a variety of fields and objects compiled out of pure philosophy. The peak of this process was the period that we know as the Italian Renaissance, in which an abundance of artistic creation became the purpose and the goal itself, and that process continued on to become the idolatry of art and artistic creation.

In ancient Sparta, however, artists had no need at all to express tradition with works or to exteriorize its inner content: this implied that such was all the same and common knowledge to everyone. The prime function for such art was, therefore, educational, pedagogical. Wherever the function of art is organic, it finds its perfect form and expression, and there is no need for its further development. The artist is, on the contrary, forced to restrain his own imagination and individuality. Epic poetry, from the Vedas to Homer, from Homer to Filip Višnjić, has a set formula, using patterns which are not just stylistic embellishments, but are instead, as mentioned by Georges Dumézil, modes for transmitting a point of view, an ideology.

In other words, the spirit is subordinate to Being. It is subordinated to the higher principle, and there can therefore be no question of its autonomy. The free and autonomous spirit ultimately turns against being, subordinating being with corrosive dilemmas and doubts. Purely autonomous art – free from the demands of being – is turned against being by itself. Refusing to submit to a superior, it submits to an inferior. What used to be just a tool thus becomes an end in itself, the first and only goal. This shift in balance cannot occur without impacting the language of the epoch. When artists are focused on a purely formal plan, as well as rethinking questions of artistic creation, or transforming art into a means for their own psychological introspection, there can be only one result: the loss of the original meaning and purpose of art. Art, having lost its principle, becomes inferior, or even subhuman. In such a situation, art, as well as all domains of the spirit, is transformed into a frightening tautology which does not help man to perceive himself, but rather serves to distract him from himself. Art becomes a means of forgetting being.

The Disintegration of Meaning and Purpose

Language is the most perfect and most complete tool of human expression. However, the existence of different languages is likely the result of the dissolution of the original character and integrity of human beings, whereby a language became the means of expression of but one particular human type, one ethnos. But language itself is subject to development and can lead to the gradual degradation and dissolution of meaning. This perspective, of course, is different from that of modern science, which is based on the assumption that language evolves from primitive origins to stages of increasing complexity. In his study *The Indo-Europeans*, Jean Haudry dispelled this misconception:

> The existence of the complex sentence in Indo-European is frequently denied on the ground that subordinating conjunctions are everywhere recent in Indo-European languages, and its very absence held up as evidence of a primitive mental stage in which thought-processes were still very under-developed. This is a fallacy. The mechanism of subordination may be recent, but the process itself may well reach back into the remote past; above all, the latter is not the result of a creation ex nihilo presupposing intellectual progress, but of pre-existent textual structures and in particular of correlation. It is thus certain that the Indo-European were familiar with linguistic structures more complex than the clause, and we have no reason to believe them incapable of structured discourse or systematic thought.[12]

The Indo-Europeans have also been deemed incapable of abstract thought due to the fact that abstract nouns in Indo-European languages are gender specific entities, or gender ambiguous entities are neuter. But as Haudry warns, the illusion of an animistic vision of the world is based on a misunderstanding: "As for the animate nouns, nothing compels us to see them as the names of beings. If we do, we must

---

12   Jean Haudry, *The Indo-Europeans* (Washington D.C.: Scott-Townsend Publishers), p. 12.

postulate that Indo-European gender is totally motivated, which is the contrary of what can be observed in other languages."[13] Many connoisseurs of extinct languages, after all, profess the same feeling: ancient languages, starting with the classical ones, had a fullness of meaning and significations that makes them difficult to translate, or even untranslatable, into modern languages. In other words, they have an organic character which makes them different or largely different from all modern languages.

Here, then, is the process of the disintegration of meaning and purpose at work, confirming the rule that the older a language is, the greater the degree of its fullness and meaning. The words of ancient languages fully correspond to the signified. The meanings of the words of modern languages "fall away" from the signified. They resemble dead bodies in decay. In order to become truly expressive, modern languages must be "cleansed" of these deposits of meaning in decay, and words must be returned to their original meaning. This is something completely different from both the ruling rhetoric of the era, and the speech of the street from which many wrongly expect the renewal of artistic language. As Goethe wrote: "If you are looking, do not think that you are seeing." Paraphrasing Goethe's saying, today we could say: "If you are listening, do not think that you understand."

"Arrow Words"

The poet is the companion of heroes. Epic and myth belong to the heroic age of poetry. The warrior needs a poet to describe his deeds and preserve them in the memory of descendants. In aristocratic society, Jean Haudry wrote, "the

---
13   Ibid, p. 13.

poet is the lord's veritable partner, as without him the great deeds would soon be forgotten and neither praise nor blame would carry far."[14] Such are the songs that the bard's sing at the warrior's feasts. The legendary Nart people, according to Ossetian tradition, had a magic cauldron which allowed them to verify the truthfulness of words. On the other hand, according to Iranian tradition, when King Yima began to enjoy false and misleading words, he lost his warrior's glory (charisma). Indeed, in false and misleading words lies the true cause of decadence.

The ideal is, by contrast, true and correct words: only such words can strike the heart like arrows. In the Vedas we find mention of "words that touch the heart." If we follow the formulas that are transmitted from generation to generation, we achieve coherence and decency, which, again, does not exclude the inventiveness or inspiration of poets. Such poetry is understood as "technics", but at the same time it is "divine rage", "mania", a special state into which poets are spurred by the gods themselves. The Latin name for poets was *vātēs*, which is derived from the Latin root for "to breathe." Émile Benveniste, therefore, rightly speaks of an aristocratic style of Indo-European epic poetry.

The disintegration of aristocratic style was followed by the collapse of languages. Artistic language then became a matter of experimentation or psychological introspection on the part of the artist, the end result of which was the loss of coherent expression. The final outcome is monstrous contemporary and postmodern art, which ceases to be an expression of being and falls prey to personal phantasms.

---

14   Ibid, p. 18.

Language transforms into ravings, stories for idiots, automatic texts written by Surrealists whose results were, instead of the desired breakthrough in the unknown (as desired by Arthur Rimbaud), becoming what Louis Aragon deemed "deplorable nonsense." Wherever meaning and significance are missing, after all, illusions are good. They arise as a consequence of chance, such as from the random selection of the order of chapters by the reader himself (as the Serbian novelist Milorad Pavić suggests to his readers, which we can only conclude is precisely such an extreme case of the degradation of language and meaning). Missing meanings are also, with equal success, replaced by countless interpretations of works of art that are just as arbitrary and accidental as the illusion of such meaning imparted by the reader himself by mere mechanical choice. Epic poetry has no need for any (re-)interpretations or explanations; moreover, any attempt at a "new" or "different" interpretation falls away from it like diseased tissue from a healthy body, because such poetry is recited and represented as a model of clarity and meaning, and is therefore real.

With the disintegration of language and style, language becomes a central problem for the artist for whom art is not the goal in and of itself, but is instead a means for the expression of Being. Such art is subordinate to a higher principle. The same is true for language, which must be able to express the higher principles of Being. Such artists, moreover, face a new problem which was quite unknown to artists from earlier eras: content which was easily understood in previous times now has to manifest in a basically foreign, hostile environment. This requires the use of "words that act as arrows" and no longer conventional language and speech. It is no coincidence that these "arrow words" were evoked by Ernst Jünger in his novel *Heliopolis*:

> Going to hunt for words was the supreme competency of the archer, the shooter. Of course, this goal will never be attained: he was at one ideal point, a postulate, a limit. In all these transformations, his mission was to direct meaning towards the ineffable with words, towards exceptional harmonies with sounds, towards untouchable landscapes with marble, and to spark supernatural flashes with colors.

Being, Ethics, Ethnos, Language

It has long been observed that there are links between ethnos and ethics, ethics and being, being and ethnos, ethnos and language. Ideally, the spirit is subordinate to being and is not autonomous or free from being. Ethics is derived from being, not from speculation of the spirit. Ethics is not a product of speculation of the spirit, but, on the contrary, is the imperative of being itself. We can only agree with the position of Dragoš Kalajić, who in his book *The Stronghold* posited that the relationship between being and ethnos is something that "cannot be rationally broken down, but only seen": "Within the scope of our history, one veritable and lasting being cannot have any other definition than an ethnic one: all other determinations that change the modality of human beings belong to the categories of the transient and the contingent."

Language is the expression of Being. In modern philosophy, Martin Heidegger is the first and only one to have noticed the deep relationship between language and being. Heidegger began his "thinking through language" with the seemingly paradoxical tautology of "Language is language." He refuses to explain language in terms of anything else; in his opinion, all conventional approaches to language, from the grammatical and the linguistic to the logico-philosophical, miss the essence of language, its ontological dimension. Language itself, Heidegger reveals, speaks. Language is the speech of Being; in language and through language it is Being that speaks. The relationship of one people to Being is revealed through this people's language. We can add that the archaicness or antiquity of one language is its only true measure of closeness to being itself. Of all the modern Indo-European languages, the Serbian language shows the greatest affinity with Sanskrit in words and roots as well as grammatical and mental structures.

There is no need for Being to explain and articulate itself, because it is. Unlike morality, ethics is not a concept that is subject to development, but an order of Being, a commandment. Honor is not a matter for deliberation, it is not subject to proof. The meaning and purpose of traditional art is to transmit ethical content, and this content is closely tied to the ethnos. One language is suitable to convey certain content while others are not, or at least not to the same degree. Not all languages possess the same expressive power, but this is not a matter of the definition of superior and inferior, but of the complementary nature of their relation. The emergence of different *ethnoi* followed the disintegration and development of different languages out of a single proto-language (e.g. the Indo-European) as a consequence of the collapse of the original language, which was the most perfect and complete expression of Being.

***

THE RETURN OF MYTH

The contradictory processes of de-mythologization and re-mythologization were not unknown to ancient civilizations, in which old myths were sometimes destroyed (de-mythologization) and replaced with new myths (re-mythologization). In other words, the processes of de-mythologization and re-mythologization are mutually conditioned and dependent processes. They do not call into question the very foundation of traditional mythical associations; rather, they keep them eternally current and alive.

Myth for us – except in exceptional cases of extreme degradation and the secularization of tradition and culture – is not the fiction of primitives, superstition, or misunderstanding. Instead, myth is a very concise expression of the highest sacred truths and principles, which are "translated" into a specific language for worldly life to the extent that such is practically possible. Myth is sacred truth expressed in popular language. Wherever the preconditions for a myth's understanding disappear, the mythical content must be discarded for another to take its place.

Dangerous Intuitions

In traditional cultures, myth is also a great field of antitheses in which, as Johann Jakob Bachofen demonstrated in his work *Matriarchy*, two major and irreconcilable principles confront one another: the Uranic and the Chthonic, the patriarchal and the matriarchal. And this contrast is projected onto all modalities of state and social order, through to the arts and culture. With the advent of the Indo-Europeans, who represented patriarchal invaders on the soil of the old matriarchal Europe, began the struggle of these two opposite principles highlighted in Bachofen's study. In the examples provided, old matriarchal myths and cults turned patriarchal through the parallel and alternating processes of de-mythologization and re-mythologization. Traces of this struggle are also found in some mythic themes which, as Robert Graves interpreted in his book *Greek Myths*, can be understood as compressed religio-political history.

In Greece, by contrast, the process of de-mythologization reached its complete and radical peak after Xenophanes (565-470). This was not followed by any process of re-mythologization, it was the consequence of a total de-sacralization and profanation of culture, whose result was the extinguishing of the mythical and the awakening of historical consciousness, in which man ceases to see himself as mythical and instead begins to understand himself to be an historical being. This is a phenomenon that has analogies in two moments in history: the first was the process of de-mythologization brought by early Christianity.

For the first Christian theologians, myth was the opposite of the Gospel, and Jesus was an historical figure, whose historicity the Church Fathers proved and defended to the unbelieving. This was contrasted by the process of re-mythologization of the Middle Ages, which saw a whole series of revitalizations of ancient mythical content, often conflicting and irreconcilable, ranging from the Grail myths to the myth of Frederick II, eschatological myths in the era of the Crusades, and various millenarian myths. Such was, without a doubt, the re-actualization of mythical content and their "dangerous intuitions" which transcend their causes and serve as evidence of the very presence of mythical forces within the historical world, which no process of de-mythologization is capable of destroying or extinguishing.

The Consumer Mythology: The Midnight of History

Another example of the radical process of de-mythologization was that brought by the Enlightenment era to its peak in the "technological universe." This is the direct expression of the degradation and decline of modern man, who is no longer a mythical or historical being, but merely a "consumer" within the "consumerist and technocratic civilization", or simply an "appendix" to the technological universe. The heroic impulse of man as a mythical being, or even a historical being, was extinguished. The destructive forces of de-mythologization constantly purged and expunged mythical components from the domain of consumerist civilization and human memory in general, exterminating the "dangerous intuitions" harbored within them. Within the technological universe, which is only the final stage of the fall of (modern) man, the human horizon is finally closing, because here man has only one power and only one freedom: the power to spend and the freedom to buy and sell. This freedom and this power testify to the death of man (as known by myth and history), because within the universe of technology and the consumer civilization anything that transcends this "animal of consumption" simply cannot exist. "The death of art" spoken of by the historical avant-garde was simply a consequence of the death of man, first as a mythical being, then as a historical being.

Of course, the process of de-mythologization can never be completed for the simple reason that destruction does not touch the mythical forces themselves. They continue to appear and return through history, whether under the guise of the "historical" or as something opposed to history. This is also true for the one-dimensional universe of the technocratic utopia. As a result, in the consumer civilization real mythical components are replaced by mythical simulacra, by self-sown sub-cultural ideologies and the "myths" of the consumer mythology whose heroes are comic book figures such as Superman. But the exhaustion of the long and destructive processes of de-mythologization does not mean a return to mythical time. Ernst Jünger wrote in his *At the Wall of Time*:

> We are standing at the midnight of history, the clock has struck twelve and we look ahead into the darkness, where we see the contours of future things. This view is followed by fear and heavy premonition. Things we see or think that we can see still do not have a name, they are nameless. If we address them, we do not intuit them accurately and they escape the noose of our control. When we say peace, it could be war. Plans of happiness turn into murderous ones, often overnight.

In short: "Rough incursions, which in many places convert historical landscapes into elementary ones, hide subtle changes of a more aggressive kind."

At the Dawn of History

At the Wall of Time by the German author Ernst Jünger conveys much about the transition of myth into history, about the moment in which mythical consciousness is replaced by the historical. History, of course, has not existed as long as man has: historical consciousness rejects as non-historical the vast spaces and epochs of "pre-history", whole peoples, civilizations, and countries because "some person or some event must have very specific characteristics that would make them historical." The key to this transition, according to Jünger, is provided in the work of Herodotus, through which man today "passes as through a land illuminated by the rays of dawn":

> Before him (Herodotus) there was something else: mythical night. That night, however, was not darkness. It was more of a dream, and it knew of a different connection between people and events than that of historical consciousness and its selective forces. This brings rays of dawn into Herodotus' work. He stands on top of the mountain that separates day from night: not only are there two epochs, but also two types of epochs, two types of light.

In other words, what we call history is the moment of transition from one mode of existence to something quite different. This is the time of the shift of two cycles which we cannot identify with a change of historical epochs – the matter in question is a profound change in the very existence of man. The sacred in the manner of previous epochs retreats, ancient cults disappear, and in their place come religions which soon afterwards become historical or anti-historical, even when they trigger events and historical plots. The Crusades called by the Western Church deepened divisions and schisms and eventually gave birth to the Reformation, which began with religious enthusiasm and the desire to return to "biblical beginnings", only to end with a historical movement which opened the way for the unhampered development of industry and technology unconstrained by the norms of (Christian) tradition and free from human hopes and desires.

The Grimace of Horror

The historical world, the outlines of which we can find in Homer and which were shaped by Thucydides, reached its zenith somewhere at the end of the 19th and beginning of the 20th century with unclear boundaries in time and space. But upon clear consciousness of its laws and regulations, it started to collapse, and the vast edifice of history became unstable, signifying penetration by hitherto unknown, foreign forces. These forces have a Titanic, elementary character, first seen in technological disasters which claimed hundreds of thousands of victims and then in the cataclysmic events of the 20th century, in the world wars and revolutions in which millions were killed and crippled. The release of nuclear energy, radiation, and the environmental destruction that enormous areas were exposed to, the daily toll in blood, whether it was sacrificed to "progress" in peacetime conditions or as a direct consequence of military intervention and conflicts, represented something that emerged out of the framework established by the historical world.

Of course, history did not end there, as was expected by Marx or Fukuyama. Rather, what really became apparent is the acceleration of historical time, which condenses events and shortens the distances between key turning points of history. The point, however, is that those forces which we have called historical do not operate alone, and man's role in these events is fundamentally changing: he is no longer able to act on an equal footing with the gods, to follow them, oppose them, or even subdue them as is represented in myth. He is no longer an active participant in history guided by passions or his own will, as was still the case in the mature historical era. He now becomes the plaything of something unknown, involved in events that surpass him, against his will and outside of his ideas.

The expression of cheerful self-confidence is gradually replaced by a grimace of horror. Man, who until yesterday considered himself a sovereign and master, realizes his weakness. The means on which he relied to turn against his creator at the decisive moment prove powerless. Technological systems and social arrangements have their reverse side, their automatic features which do not restrain but encourage destruction, putting man in the position of a wizard's apprentice who frees forces which he is too immature to handle. Corruption, crime, violence, and terror are consequences rather than causes, and political responses, regardless of color and sign, do not offer solutions but increase disarray. If the hour of panic had not descended, man would have at least gained awareness of his own downfall.

All of this was unthinkable in the mature historical age, because man then was still ruled by himself, and thus history as well. History, therefore, could have no sense of direction other than the one given by man himself, his own deeds and thoughts. Each concept of the "meaning of history" was a concept of the emergence of man, whereas in the classical historical age man did not emerge but simply was. The question of the "meaning of history" was a meaningless question, and it is not found in the works of classical writers from Herodotus and beyond. The question of the "meaning of history", which is always found outside of man, becomes possible only when the focus of history shifts beyond man himself, whether into the sphere of social or technological relations.

Modern man discovers his weakness too late. But his collapse is not to be blamed on myth or history, but on none other than the weakness and cowardice of modern man. The world of "civilized values", and the historical world in general which he himself created, proves to be much weaker than we have been accustomed to believe - weaker structurally, spiritually, and ethically. At the first sign of alarm, it begins to collapse, thus revealing what is, in fact, modern man's inner readiness for capitulation.

This is the "midnight of history", which will soon be replaced by something different, and this moment is marked by the spread of Titanic forces demanding sacrifices of blood.

Towards Post-History: The Awakening of Myth

History, let us repeat, has not lasted as long as has man on Earth. But consciousness of this only occurs late within history, perhaps only at its end, when the boundaries of time and space change, on the one hand with the discovery of the distant past of man and lost civilizations, then the past of the planet and the cosmos, and on the other with the discovery of space, of the ocean depths, and the interior of the Earth through archaeological and geological layers in a virtually Vernean way. New perspectives cause dizziness. Pre-history and post-history gain in importance only when history becomes a crumbling edifice. Yet man's turn from history towards something that he is not yet able to define or see clearly now resembles escape.

In one way or another, the technological universe and the consumer civilization will come to an end, in the same way that the classical historical epoch ended with technocracy and totalitarian order in its complete form, which arose not out of courage or strength but out of cowardice, weakness, and fear. It is impossible to say how long this will take. It is also irrelevant whether this will happen due to internal attrition, overreach, disaster, or a combination of all these factors together. But in each of these cases, collapse is the consequence of man's inability to dwell within the historical world and to rule it as a sovereign-supreme being.

The return of myth, however, is not possible in the sense of a return to the state of "pre-history." Mythological forces remain present, just as they have been during the entire historical period, but they cannot establish the previous state for lack of the necessary preconditions. First and foremost, the "substrate", the fertile ground, is missing, as modern man is too weak in the spiritual, psychological, and even "physiological" senses.

Together with history, culture and its current meaning gradually disappears as well, remaining basically a mere instrument of social engineering. In the technocratic utopia, mass culture (as opposed to the culture of the historical period) is just one of the ways for the utopian fantasies and desires of the masses to be channeled. The elite culture, meanwhile, which constantly drifts between conformism and negation, between skepticism and denial, between skepticism and irony and back again to conformism, remains essentially a tool of de-mythologization and the suppression of the dangerous intuitions contained in myth, thus enabling more or less painless integration into the technological universe under the illusion of free will. The appearance and awakening of dangerous intuitions and dormant archetypes on the margins of the technocratic social mechanism creates a situation of conflict and leads to glitches in its functioning.

In the domains beyond the technocratic utopia, culture will need to take a more traditional role than the one it assumes under consumer civilization. The disintegration of the historical world in its final stage, which we are witnessing today, allows us to see something out of it.

For much of the historical period, culture was the privileged domain of sacred and mythical forces. This is one of the ways in which mythical forces can penetrate the world again - historically, realizing themselves in history, unlike in the technological universe where they usually manifest themselves through the uncontrolled elements of folkloric subcultures and are often distorted to the point of being unrecognizable simulacra of the mythical, not veritable expressions. Such testify more to the eternal and unquenched need of man for mythical content than they represent a sign of the real presence of the mythical.

In the post-technocratic era, culture will be very closely tied to re-mythologization under the sign of re-recognizing and re-awakening true mythical content, the revitalization and innovation of ancient and traditional forms instead of, as before, their exorcism. The meaning and purpose of de-mythologization, on the other hand, must be limited to its capacity in traditional societies: to the purification of degenerate, "folkloric" mythical forms so that in their place may come forms which veritably represent tradition.

***

THE ANDROGYNE

The myth of androgyny stems from a complex set of matriarchal beliefs and traditions. It is an eminently matriarchal symbol which cannot be understood outside of the complex of matriarchal beliefs and ideas. Indeed, no trace of the idea of androgyny is to be found in the oldest monuments of patriarchal, Uranic spirituality.

The oldest known formulation of this myth is found in Plato's *Symposium*, where Plato puts such a formulation in the mouth of Aristophanes. Yet we do not find traces of this idea in the most ancient layers of chthonic, matriarchal spirituality which knows only female deities. Its relatively late appearance in the soil of chthonic belief was a sign and consequence of the weakening of matriarchal cultures, their final defeat and collapse in the face of patriarchal values. Dragoš Kalajić writes in his *Map of (Anti-)Utopia*: "The formative principle of the myth of androgyny should be sought in the field of the historical and first great antithesis of the uranic and chthonic principles, in the field of conflict between the conquering Indo-Europeans and the indigenous civilization of the South of the Eurasian continent." We will examine the symbol of the androgyne exclusively from this and not any other metaphysical vantage point, since, in our opinion, it does not possess any substantial metaphysical content in and of itself.

Eros and sexuality are rooted in the deepest layers of being: such can only exist as male or as female. Sexuality is a primordial quality of being and not the property of secondary anatomical-physiological characteristics or purely biological functions. It is through man and woman that cosmic principles manifest themselves. These are the deepest foundations of the drama of love, which necessarily implies metaphysical tragedy, and this has nothing to do with the banal "quest for pleasure" of Freudianism. This romantic drama presupposes duality, the dyad, and these are differences which, inasmuch as possible, are sharpened to their extremes. In his famous work Weininger spoke of the Absolute Man and Absolute Woman, who, in different ways and always incompletely, are realized in each particular man and woman. The goal here cannot be to overcome differences but, on the contrary, to manifest these principles in their purity. The goal is rather the exaltation of this dualism to the extreme. The idea of androgyny, of bisexuality, is completely alien to Uranic spirituality in any form, as is nostalgia for any supposedly primordial, androgynous state.

The Attack on Heaven

It is to this very field of historical antithesis between the Uranic and Chthonic that the oldest androgynous cults belong, such as the cult of bearded Zeus depicted with six breasts revered in Labraunda in Caria, the Italic cult of "bald Venus", or that of bearded Aphrodite in Cyprus. Also androgynous is the god Dionysus, who is greeted in one of Aeschylus' fragments (fragment 31) with the following words: "Whence hails this woman-man? What is his country? What is his attire?" As Mircea Eliade noted in his *Mephistopheles and the Androgyne*: "Originally Dionysus was thought of as a stout, bearded being, doubly potent because of his double nature. Later, in the Hellenistic age, art made him effeminate."[15]

In this field of antitheses, the myth of the androgyne has, without a doubt, an "exterior", political function as a response

---

15   Mircea Eliade, *Mephistopheles and the Androgyne: Studies in Religious Myth and Symbol* (New York: Sheed and Ward, 1965).

on the part of the defeated matriarchal culture to the triumph of its conquerors. This function is confirmed by figures depicting the original Dionysus with prominent attributes of strength, allegedly "doubly potent because of his double nature." At the same time, this is an "inner" expression of crisis, a response to the weakening of matriarchal cultures likely caused or stoked by the same reason.

In Plato's *Symposium*, the androgynous myth is presented by the comedian Aristophanes in a manner that imbues the myth with a slightly ironic and humorous tone: Aristophanes does not represent the opinion of Plato himself, as is explained by his famous commentators, but rather Orphic ideas. This gentle irony is highlighted by the words that Aristophanes pronounces before his speech: "I'm not worried about saying something funny in my coming oration. That would be pure profit, and it comes with the territory of my Muse. What I'm worried about is that I might say something ridiculous."[16] The matriarchal origin and inspiration of the myth presented by Aristophanes is perfectly obvious, as Miloš N. Đurić wrote in his *Notes and Explanations to Plato's Symposium*: "Babylon is taken to be the cradle of such Orphic thoughts. Among the fragments of Babylonian prehistory can be found such stances that everything undivided [i.e. the original unity of matriarchal cults - B.N.] is designated as a woman, whom Baal cuts into two halves, heaven and earth..." The feminine principle here is primary. The priests of Astarte's cult were eunuchs. In some Mesopotamian cults and in the mysteries of Cybele, men castrated themselves to achieve the desired "transformation" into the feminine principle. In certain cults

---

[16] Plato, *Symposium* 189b in Plato, *Complete Works* (edited by John M. Cooper and D.S. Hutchinson; Cambridge: Hackett Publishing Company, 1997).

on Greek soil, goddesses were offered broken weapons, while the Amazons wielded Hyperborean sacred axes, the symbol of the patriarchal conquerors.

In other words, it is not just that the emphasis here falls on the feminine principle (and not at an equal distance between the two sexes), but the feminine principle is fully identified with Primordial Unity itself, which is attributed procreative power: in the oldest (matriarchal) theologies of pre-Aryan Greece, female deities give birth on their own. The Earth itself gives birth to starry night, just as Hera gives birth to Hephaestus and Typhon, who are also chthonic deities, on her own. But this is not the consequence of "Hera's androgyny" (*à la* Mircea Eliade), but rather of the presumed superiority of the feminine principle, which, as has already been said, was singularly ascribed the power of creation and procreation. In matriarchy, sons are considered apatores (without fathers) and *unilaterales* (born from only one side, i.e. the mother's).

Aristophanes presented another argument suggesting that androgyny is secondary to the feminine principle: "The male kind was originally an offspring of the sun, the female of the earth, and the one that combined both genders was an offspring of the moon, because the moon shares in both."[17] The "lunar" principle, however, is posterior, and its function is precisely to bridge the insurmountable, namely, that gap separating the matriarchal from the patriarchal, the Uranic from the Chthonic, Heaven from Earth. The very same version of the androgynous myth is presented in association with the rebellion of Ephialtes and Otus. The androgynes' "attack on Heaven", their attempt "to make an ascent to heaven

---

17 Ibid, 190b.

so as to attack the gods"[18], indicates that the true, concealed target of the myth of androgyny is the Uranic principle itself. Zeus, defending Olympus, cuts the androgynes in half, out of whom Uranic Apollo fashions the genders and thus negates bisexuality, while chthonic Hephaestus is given the power to "weld together and join" the genders into one.

Neither Greek nor Jew, Neither Male nor Female

Not only is androgyny completely alien to Uranic spirituality, but so is any sacralization of the sphere of sexuality (phallic cults are not patriarchal, but are the fruit of the matriarchal sacralization of sexuality). In Uranic spirituality, only that which belongs to the "luminous domains" of the intelligible world can be sacralized, not anything that "appears and disappears." The origin of the cult of Dionysus was Oriental, and its later spread marked the beginning of the twilight of the virile spirituality of the Hellenic world, just as the spread of androgynous motifs characterized the period of Roman decadence. Emperor Heliogabalus, the transvestite who came to Rome on a donkey and who introduced the phallic cult to Rome, a sign of the total inversion of patriarchal values, was also of Oriental origin. Myths of androgyny are undoubtedly of non-Indo-European origin, as their meaning is pronouncedly anti-patriarchal.

Christian teachings and traditions re-actualized this motif of androgyny: the Biblical Adam was originally androgynous, and Yahweh or Jehovah cut a piece of his body to create woman. John the Apostle saw androgyny as a sign of spiritual perfection, as in his *Epistle to the Galatians* 3:28, he says: "There is neither Jew nor Gentile, neither slave nor

---

18   Ibid, 190c.

free, nor is there male and female, for you are all one in Christ Jesus." This is not empty rhetoric, but a clear commitment to returning to the original androgyny or primordial unity, the Edenic state of Adam before the creation of Eve.

Various Gnostic and para-Christian teachings are even more explicit. In the Gnostic *Gospel of Thomas*, the following words are attributed to Jesus: "When you make the two into one…and when you make male and female into a single one, so that the male will not be male nor the female be female… then you will enter the kingdom." According to the Gospel of Philip (also one of the Gnostic Gospels), the separation of the sexes (the creation of Eve) is equated with the very principle of death: "Christ came to repair the split…and join the two and give them life who had died because of separation."[19]

Although these are not the canonical Gospels, they are clear testimony of the sources and environment in which Christianity originally developed: it grew upon the residue of matriarchal, predominantly Middle Eastern cults and teachings. The Christian tradition of Adam's androgyny provided the foundation for later understandings, such as that of the Irish mystic Johannes Scotus Eriugena, according to whom Christ became androgynous through the act of resurrection, uniting the genders in his own nature, so that "He was neither male nor female, although he was born and died as male." This Christian re-actualization can be considered in terms of the aforementioned historical "antithesis" between the Uranic and the Chthonic, the patriarchal and matriarchal. This was a period of decline for the patriarchal and the revenge of the matriarchal principle, a sort of anti-patriarchal

---

19   *The Gnostic Bible* (edited by Willis Barnstone and Marvin Meyer; Boston/London: Shambhala, 2011).

revolution. Christianity was originally characterized by such an extremely chthonic, matriarchal character, an aspect which would play a decisive role in the further history of the androgynous symbol and the ideology of matriarchy.

Subsequently, the medieval "correction" of original Christianity in the direction of patriarchal values and content still failed to completely suppress or repress open, distinctive matriarchal content. Beneath its seemingly patriarchal flow, Christianity is in fact a "mixed" religion, within which eminently matriarchal content survives in parallel, at times forming its underground and more or less hidden course, and at times in eschatological tensions that rise to the surface, as well as in teachings that straddle the border between dogma and heresy. Symbols, teachings, doctrines and ideologies are projected onto the "field of antithesis" of the two principles, and the awakening of ancient chthonic content and archetypes creates the history of their constant struggle.

The Hermetic Androgyne

Alchemical teachings constitute one of the "underground" flows of matriarchal content over the course of the Middle Ages. One of the names of the "philosophical stone" was Rebis (literally "two things"), the Hermetic androgyne being the "double matter." Rebis is born from the union of the Sun and the Moon or, in alchemical terms, Sulfur and Mercury. After all, androgynous doctrine is contained in one of the fundamental, earliest alchemical writings, the *Corpus Hermeticum*, according to which God possesses both sexes and, filled with their fertility, gives birth to everything he wants:

> *"You say then, Trismegistus, that God is bisexual?"*
> *"Yes, Asclepius; and not God alone, but all kinds of beings…"*[20]

Alchemical teachings inspired Jakob Böhme, who at times even borrowed the alchemists' terminology (this will be the case with many later authors who varied the myth of the androgyne). To Jakob Böhme we owe a famous variation of the Biblical myth of primordial androgyny. According to this German mystic, Adam's Fall is the result of a dream in which he fell in nature and, therefore, was degraded into a being of the earth. Watching animals mate, he succumbs to lust and God bestows him with sex, with which begins the separation of the sexes. Böhme compared this "disintegration" of the androgynous to the crucifixion of Christ.

The androgynous myth constitutes an essential element of many esoteric traditions, from alchemy to Kabbalah and from Rosicrucian teachings to the gnosis of operative Masonry. It should be noted that all these traditions are closely linked not only by doctrine, but also by their origination in the same, chthonic complex of beliefs, often sharing the same or similar content.

The myth of the androgyne is eschatological. Sexlessness or bisexuality are supposed to have marked the primordial, paradisal state to be restored by the reintegration of the human into Primordial Unity which ultimately transcends all dualism. Androgyny's merging with millenarian and chiliastic traditions, which made up part of original Christianity, occurred, for example, in the works of Ritter, who adopted the Joachimite idea of tripartite history. The first part of history, according to Ritter, is when "Man gave birth to Eve without

---

20 *Hermetica* (trans. by Walter Scott; Oxford: Clarendon Press, 1924), p. 333.

the help of woman", the second is "Christ born by a woman without the help of man", and the third, final, and supreme part will be when the androgyne gives birth to both: "both husband and wife will merge in one and the same splendor."

The Androgynous Utopia: The Paths of the Androgyne's Secularization

German Romanticism was characterized by a syncretism of all these traditions, but this syncretism was not arbitrary, insofar as all of them, as we have already noted, come from the same origin. In Friedrich Schlegel's treatise *About Diotima*, only the eschatological dimension is missing, by virtue of which this work does not fall into the domain of esoteric thought, but instead belongs to the domain of utopia. Schlegel rejected all existing practices and methods of upbringing and education, which he saw as the real cause of the division of gender, and proposed an education to overcome this divide and lead us to the desired androgyny.

In the revival of the motif of androgyny in German Romanticism, as well as in the decadence of the 19th century, we should recognize the very same esoteric influences: alchemical in the case of Ritter as well as Rosicrucian and Masonic doctrines which authors sometimes referenced explicitly. Joséphin Péladan, whose interpretations of the androgynous myth ranged from the bizarre to the comic, was the founder of a para-Masonic order whose name was the "Cabalistic Order of the Red Cross", and before him Honoré de Balzac was inspired in his *Séraphîta* by the teachings of Emanuel Swedenborg. The motif of androgyny also surfaces not only in the (para)-Christian mystics, but also in Christian theology itself, from the Catholic theologian Kaikhohen Kipgen, the author of *Gnosticism in Early Christianity*, who recognized androgynous entities in Christ, among believers and the clergy, to Orthodoxy and the eschatological thought of Berdyaev, who associated the resurrection of man with the "transfiguration of sexuality" and the "revelation of heavenly androgyny."

The development of the symbol of the androgyne, Mircea Eliade observed, cleared the way for the gradual degradation of symbols: from the metaphysical concept of destruction and the "reconciliation of opposites" through symbols of spiritual and existential fullness, to the idolatry of mere hermaphroditism with the "superabundance of erotic possibilities", down to the "morbid or even satanic hermaphroditism, in Aleister Crowley for example" of English decadence. According to Eliade:

> The androgyne is understood by decadent writers simply as a hermaphrodite in whom both sexes exist anatomically and physiologically... But the decadent writers did not know that the hermaphrodite represented in antiquity an ideal condition which men endeavored to achieve by spiritual means of initiative rites; but that if a child showed at birth any signs of hermaphroditism, it was killed by its own parents.[21]

The symbol of androgyny surfaced altogether frequently in 20th century works of art, in which, despite secularization, the esoteric meaning remains relatively preserved. Let us mention the work of Marcel Duchamp, who "transformed" da Vinci's Mona Lisa by drawing a beard and goatee on her, and the work of Man Ray, whose photography depicted Duchamp himself as a woman and whose title evokes the esoteric "mystical rose." André Breton spoke of "undertaking the

---
21   Eliade, *Mephistopheles and the Androgyne*.

reconstruction of the Primordial Androgyne" as essential to the Surrealist movement. Without a doubt, such rhetoric was borrowed from the esoteric tradition of Christian mysticism, but there is also no doubt that it was the Surrealist drift and flow of the "subconscious" that opened the door to these ancient matriarchal archetypes and telluric religiosity.

Like many other eschatological motifs, the androgynous symbol has followed the same direction of secularization, whereby eschatological symbols are translated into spatial and utopian ones, to the point that today it is possible to speak of an "androgynous utopia." The space of the androgynous utopia is the space of the human body itself. This includes scientific predictions on the future course of human evolution towards the "third sex" or the "evolution" of the male body into the female. But here we lose the original matriarchal religious content, wherein the androgyny symbolizes "the primordial totality", the state before creation, before and after each and every differentiation and duality.

The Promethean Moment of Androgyny

The sacred goal of androgyny is the *coincidentia oppositorum* (*à la* Nicholas of Cusa), which is an expression of the need to overcome duality and achieve the totalization of (fragmented) parts. It is also an expression of the inadequacy and insufficiency of man, or, in the words of Mircea Eliade, an expression of his "deep dissatisfaction with his actual situation, with what is called man's place in the world." "Man feels himself torn and separate. He often finds it difficult to properly explain to himself the nature of this separation, for sometimes he feels himself to be cut off from 'something' powerful, 'something' utterly other than himself, and at other times from an indefinable, timeless state, of which he has no precise memory."[22]

But this incompleteness and dissatisfaction with oneself and one's position in the world can only be the dissatisfaction and insufficiency of matriarchal, chthonic man, not the man of patriarchal, Uranic spirituality, for Uranic man stands in the central position: he stands at the center, which makes him integral, complete, and self-sufficient. He stands in the very center of the world, as a bridge between God (the gods) and creation (nature), between infinity and the infinitesimal, embodying and transmitting the Uranic principles of Light and Order. He is not something other than the Gods and therefore cannot be "inadequate", "torn" or "ambivalent." The *Brihadaranyaka Upanishad* states:

> Verily, in the beginning this world was Brahma. It knew only itself (atmanam): 'I am Brahma!' Therefore it became the All. Whoever of the gods became awakened to this, he indeed became fit... This is so now also. Whoever thus knows 'I am Brahma!' Becomes this All; even the gods have not power to prevent his becoming thus, for he becomes their self (atman). So whoever worships another divinity [than his Self], thinking 'He is one and I another,' he knows not. He is like a sacrificial animal for the gods. Verily, indeed, as many animals would be of service to a man, even so each single person is of service to the gods.[23]

The Order and Light that show themselves in creation are at once reflections of the Order and Light that make up the inner content of man, and are reflected in the mirror of nature (the creation of God).

---

22 Ibid.
23 *Brihadaranyaka Upanishad* I:4:10, *The Thirteen Principal Upanishads* (trans. by Robert Hume; Oxford: Oxford University Press, 1921).

Androgynous symbolism is an expression of the aspiration to overcome the inner insufficiency and dichotomy of matriarchal man through re-integrating with the supposedly superior feminine principle from which man, whether by his own wrongdoing (whether "sin" or the fall) or by the will of the gods, has been permanently detached. Again, in all myths of the androgyne, the focal point is not some presumed middle ground between the two sexes, but the female principle. This represents a stepping out of the natural order, an attack on the established order, or, as Plato's Aristophanes said, "an attack on the Gods themselves." This is what Julius Evola in his *Metaphysics of Sex* called the "Promethean moment" of androgyny. Zeus cut the androgynes in half and Apollo restored established order to the cosmos by rearranging the masculine and feminine genders. It is no coincidence that this role of re-ordering fell to none other than Uranic Apollo - he who is self-sufficient, absolute, and born without a mother.

Evoking the "Promethean moment", another fundamental difference between Uranic and Chthonic spirituality is revealed to us. "The tradition that gave form to the myth of Prometheus and the Giants is also that of the Heraclean ideal"; unlike the Titans, however, Heracles accomplishes this, he is granted immortality, and yet he attains this "not as a violator of duty but rather as an ally of the Olympians."[24] In other words, it is not about the goal, but about the way of achieving it: Hercules won immortality and a place on Mount Olympus as a god without violating the order inherent in the cosmos. Such a mistake committed by the Titans and the androgynes is made by Prometheus, who chooses between the Olympian (the Uranic,

---

24 Julius Evola, *Eros and the Mysteries of Love: The Metaphysics of Sex* (Rochester: Inner Traditions, 1991).

the heavenly) and the human (the chthonic, the terrestrial) the latter, thus closing himself off from the path of transcending the human towards the divine. "Instead of the Olympian principle of being, he seeks the 'new', the fickle, cunning, sly, and vile; he wants to deceive Olympus. But his deception draws the laugh of Olympus, brings misery to the human race, and his place is taken by his foolish brother Epimetheus" (Dragoš Kalajić, *Map of (Anti-)Utopia*). The consequence of such violation of order was the punishment which Zeus dealt him.

Modern Androgyny

The androgyne remains a prominent symbol of the modern age, despite the fact that the vast majority of people are not aware of its profound meaning. Moreover, the power of this archetype lies not in understanding and consciousness, but, on the contrary, in the deep roots and in the archaic structures of the "collective unconscious." "Archaic" here does not mean something deficient or backwards, but the strength of the archetype. Of course, it should be borne in mind that this power manifests itself only through the corresponding chthonic psychology, and that its power over Uranic psychology is null and void. Uranic psychology, however, can only be possessed by elites, while the sensibility of the masses is telluric, matriarchal, and chthonic.

The fields in which this symbol manifests today are practically endless: from popular culture to the sphere of "elite" art, from modern science to contemporary esoterica, reflecting the truth that modern culture is indeed matriarchal, filled with the latter's symbols and figures. Among all of these symbols, the androgyne occupies the central place in our time. The degradation of symbols of which Eliade spoke is not an obstacle, but a precondition for mass distribution. The inability of modern man to understand androgyny as anything other than physical hermaphroditism is only one aspect of his general inability to rise above the category of appearance, of his inability to privilege the categories of the intelligible over the categories of the sensory world.

Androgyny is, at its core, the ideology of the "equality of male and female." The same goes for homosexuality as well as the softness of modern man who evermore devalues his focal point down to the mere sexual plane, the sphere of the erotic, and professes his own "sensuality." True manifestations of virility and true womanhood become extremely rare, almost borderline cases in modern culture. The fact that the differences between the sexes are being reduced down to the final, physical, anatomic level has led many to conclude that "the human of the future will be bisexual" (Umberto Veronesi). Indeed, this prediction has already been realized today, as the vast majority of men and women already live, think, and even dream of looking like hermaphrodites.

After all, as we have said, for us the symbol of the androgyne does not possess the eminently metaphysical meaning and significance proper to the masculine and feminine principles or the archetypes of the Absolute Man and Absolute Woman. Its significance is largely exhausted in other, much more inferior areas than the metaphysical sphere. These "blurred motions" of the chthonic soul give birth to utopian passions, tensions, and expectations. This is the domain of history, its movements and contingencies.

***

EAST AND WEST

The concepts of East and West elude any definition. This does not mean that they are devoid of any factual basis. Moreover, they are an undeniable political reality and their antagonism constitutes one of the main motifs of modern politics. There is no doubt that East and West have a basis in history, although, as noted above, their importance should not be overestimated.

Just like North and South, East and West are nodal points of history which determine its axis. Themselves not subject to definitions, they nevertheless define and determine history, and history takes place in the relations vested by them. There are four corners of the world and four cycles of time which flow downwards in a course of progressive degeneration.

North and South, meanwhile, have a much greater significance. This is evident from the earliest times. The migration of peoples and races, sacred geography and toponymy, and the role which these directions fulfill in the traditions and legends of diverse peoples, most of all the Indo-Europeans, unequivocally confirm this. The importance of the North-South axis may be obscured or suppressed, as it has been in our epoch, but it does not become less of a reality or significance. The North-South axis remains the vertical axis of history and sacred geography. The dualism of East and West, on the contrary, only possesses modest significance and meaning. It arose later in human history than the former axis of North and South. At best, this division belongs to history and its contingencies, whereas the dualism of North and South is prehistoric, or rather supra-historical and meta-historical. In his study "The Planetary Tension Between

Orient and Occident and the Opposition Between Land and Sea", Carl Schmitt noted:

> Yet the conflict between Orient and Occident is not a (bi) polar one. Earth has a North and South Pole, but not an East and West one. Geographically speaking, in our terraqueous globe the East / West opposition is fluid and indeterminate; it merely represents 'the ebb and flow of a little night and a little day.'[25]

Drang nach Osten

The East-West axis is determined by the daily path of the Sun. Peoples who have entered the historical scene have moved in this very same direction (from East to West, not the other way around). Does this trajectory, as the great English geographer Mackinder thought, alongside many others, represent the main trajectory of history, its "geographical pivot?" No doubt can touch this, for clashes between East and West constitute a very old and important theme of history, a motif which, after all, has repeated itself constantly. Constant threat from the East – embodied by nomadic peoples such as the Scythians, Huns or Goths – corresponds to attempts by the West to subdue the East, or to colonize it. Along with wars, missionaries also went East, bringing with them not only a new religion, but also political and imperial ideas.

The very same questions, although renamed in different terms – that is to say translated into a new language – have projected themselves all the way up to our age. Standing in contrast to the small peninsula in the West of the continent,

---

25 Carl Schmitt, "The Planetary Tension Between Orient and Occident and the Opposition Between Land and Sea", *Política común 5: Carl Schmitt and the Early Modern World* (University of Michigan: 2014).

that is to cities and urban civilization, is the immeasurable space of the steppes and plains. Today this is the former Soviet East, and above all Russia. Hitler's "Drang nach Osten" had its immediate predecessor in the campaign of Napoleon Bonaparte as well as the same outcome: apparent triumph followed by disaster. Defeat was the consequence of the impossibility of controlling such an enormous space which, however, did not pose any problem to the indigenous population. The plot of the great battles between East and West may always be the same, but the actors are always new, whether the Greeks against the Persians, the Romans against the Scythians and Sarmatians, the Germans against the Slavs, or even earlier: the Danaans against Troy. But the significance of this topic should not be overestimated, much less absolutized (as in the manner of Mackinder and his influential followers), for such would prevent us from gaining insight into other, no less important axes of history, such as that linking North and South. The ancient Achaeans came from the North and North-East (not the West) and were originally pastoralists and "haters of cities", similar to the Vedic Aryans who conquered the Indian subcontinent and destroyed the ancient urban and mercantile Dravidian civilization.

Yet East and West nevertheless remain vague terms that elude precise definition and closer determinations. The lines which separate them become less clear the deeper we go into the past. Dravidian Mohenjo-Daro was "more Western" than Sparta, and Mycenaean culture was "more Eastern" than Troy. The same is true for the La Tène (Celtic) culture in relation to Rome. Nor in the work of Herodotus, who had the ambition of describing the "earliest contacts of East and West" and explaining the causes of their differing ways, did borders yet have the sturdiness which they would gain in later periods: they separated the known from the unknown rather than East from West. One of these borders was formed by the Ister River (the Danube), which divided Thrace from the land of the Scythian Sygynnes, that Scythia that "extends nearly as far as the land of the Eneti on the Adriatic." "But the land beyond the Ister seems to be vast and desolate" and "according to the Thracians, the land beyond the Ister is infested by bees, and that is why it is impossible to travel further inland."[26] Nevertheless, Herodotus clearly looked toward the East, its tribes, peoples and customs, much more than many subsequent authors. His work remains exemplary, but we are still far from being able to interpret it entirely.

A Wall of "Mutual Fear and High Mountains"

Tacitus, on the contrary, avoided Sarmatia and described to Rome a hostile and barbarous Germania which, in his words, was "separated from Sarmatia and Dacia by mutual fear and high mountains." Priscus, who crossed the Danube and entered the land of the Limiganates (now the Banat and Bačka) to visit the court of Atilla, also entered into unknown territory. Similar to Tacitus, who often did not distinguish Gaul from Germania and could not say whether the Veneti (ancestors of the Slavs) should be counted as Germanic or Sarmatian, Priscus does not know what language the local population speaks. The wall of "mutual fear" here is even stronger and more impenetrable than in Tacitus. It is also noteworthy that Priscus was on a diplomatic mission: writing about the Huns, he was speaking of the enemy. Is his account of Atilla's funeral, for instance, which he described

---

26 Herodotus, *Histories* V:9-10.

as accompanied by rituals of unsurpassed barbarity, truly an impartial eyewitness report, or a real example of the political propaganda of the time?

Even stronger than the limes that divided the "civilized" from the "barbarians" was the border established by faith. The schism into Western and Eastern Christianity remains deeper than that which would split the Western world, as the Protestant heresy originated within the Catholic Church.

Attempts to interpret the divide between East and West in political terms, in ways of governance and law - which is not only characteristic of our time, but was also typical of certain Hellenic historians - is equally as unsustainable today as it was during the Peloponnesian wars. The tyrants of the ancient world, like the emperors of late Rome or certain princes in the period of the Italian Renaissance, would in such a case fall under the notion of unadulterated Oriental despotism. Nor did Sparta correspond to the democratic ideal, and this did not prevent Plato from admiring it and placing its aristocratic arrangement higher than Athenian democracy. We would also have to ignore other entire historical epochs, such as the European Middle Ages or the totalitarian regimes of the twentieth century. The Scythians, on the other hand, if we are to believe the accounts of Greek writers, lived more freely than the Greeks, and an example of a democracy much purer than that established by the trading republics of the Mediterranean can be found in the Slavic institution of assemblies.

Mackinder was certainly neither the first nor the last to attempt to attribute racial coloration to the conflict between East and West. "The Scythians of the Homeric and Herodotian accounts, drinking the milk of mares, obviously practised the same arts of life, and were probably of the same race as the later inhabitants of the steppe."[27] Mackinder contrasted these "slant-eyed hordes of Asiatic horsemen without ideals" to the white dolichocephalic men of the West, North, and South of Europe. "European civilization is, in a very real sense, the outcome of the secular struggle against Asiatic invasion", and the result of this millennial-long fight are the cities of Western culture and modern urban civilization in general. The Scythians, however, contrary to what Mackinder believed, were not at all "slant-eyed", but pureblooded Indo-Europeans, while the Goths and Huns were motley alliances of the most different races, ethnoi, and peoples. Moreover, urban civilizations existed long before the invasions of the Huns or Scythians, and even before the Indo-European migrations. Their traces can be found in the Danube region of Europe, in Dravidian India, and also in the Mediterranean in the old Iberian and Cretan civilizations. All of these disappeared under the conquest of the white and dolichocephalic Indo-Europeans. Memory of this is preserved in Homer's story of the Trojan War.

Countries that Sink in the Evening Light

We all know what the East is. Luxurious palaces, ornate temples, inaccessible lands like Tibet or wild, harsh Mongolia, and the cities of Baghdad and Babylon, dotted with minarets and golden gates, narrow streets and bazaars teeming with dark-skinned merchants and slant-eyed strangers.

The East appears before our eyes in ancient splendor described by Herodotus, both a historian and a traveler, and then by many other explorers, such as Marco Polo, Ferdynand Antoni Ossendowski and Alexandra David-Néel. Vast deserts

---

27 Sir Halford J. Mackinder, *Democratic Ideals and Reality* (1919).

and oases where caravans stopped, high mountains and endless plains, the homeland of warrior-horsemen and those who ride camels. This is a world that never ceases to amaze and evoke horrors and kings, sorcerers and conquering hordes. It also never ceases to arouse fear and suspicion. Today this East is one that has been ravaged, but it is still the East, the one remembered that until recently created fabulous empires and formed armies that flooded everything in their wake, such as those of Darius, Attila, and Genghis Khan.

The West, by contrast, emerges in a different light. The West is the home of the city-republics and principalities of small, coastal countries that sink in the evening light of Iberia, the Western and Eastern Mediterranean, and the British Isles. Shallow seas and narrow gorges, ridges and ravines where the fate of armies was decided in a single moment, in decisive battles, such as the Battle of Thermopylae. This is a colorful, narrow region that created a powerful fleet which it used to conquer the seas. This West has its own prehistory, mostly forgotten, with the ancient port of Cadiz in Iberia and the many other cities and trading colonies of Mediterranean civilization whose traces can still be found today. Carthage was their prototype, and the civilizations of Crete and old Iberia as well. This West should not be equated with Europe which, from the earliest times, had a central position. For the Hellenes, "Europe" was the world north of Greece and the Mediterranean excluding Hellas. "Europe" was the lands of the hinterland trading colonies inhabited by "barbarian" peoples - the Scythians, the Germanics, and the Celts. Europe was the continent that stands opposite of the Atlantic and the Mediterranean. The Hellenic "West" had little in common with the civilization that would emerge in modern times and christened itself with this name. In Herodotus' time, "the West" simply referred to the countries west of Persia, Egypt, and Mesopotamia.

The true West is that which grew up with the era of overseas travel, with Christopher Columbus, Amerigo Vespucci, Vasco da Gama, and Magellan. The consequence of their discoveries was the creation of a new world entirely oriented towards seas and oceans and primarily consisting of Iberia (Spain and Portugal), Britain, and the North American "island." The complete reorientation from Land to Sea which neither Portugal nor Spain could accomplish succeeded in England sometime in the early 17th century. The West then spread rapidly to almost an entire hemisphere, across the Atlantic and all the countries surrounding it, thus constituting a real opposite and often open enemy of continental Europe. Their antipode and counterweight, the ancient East, which very quickly lost its former significance in the distribution of power, became easy prey for colonizers and sailors from the West. Thalassocratic and mercantile empire once again took shape in the West, this time of truly planetary dimensions and significance. It should come as no surprise that within only a few centuries this West would attempt to create the first global civilization, a civilization that wished to spread itself throughout the whole world despite racial, ethnic, and cultural differences.

The Planetary War of Sea against Land

In his above-mentioned study on the confrontation between East and West, Carl Schmitt evoked a certain historical example:

In July 1812, as Napoleon advanced upon Moscow, Goethe addressed the Empress Marie Louise in a panegyric poem, in reality a hymn to her husband, the French Emperor: "*What once confounded the multitude was revolved by one / That upon which centuries had meditated in darkness.*" Under the global aspect of land and sea, the poet continues:

He encompassed it in the diaphanous light of the spirit
Emptying out all that was extraneous
Only land and sea have here solidity...

In this way, Goethe - a typical representative of the West during the summer of 1812 - advocated for the order of Land and against that of the Sea.

The history of the planetary clash between East and West, according to Schmitt, can in all of its volume be reduced to the basic dualism of elements: Soil and Water, Land and Sea. The planetary war of Sea against Land is the key to the centuries-old confrontation between East and West. But it should be borne in mind that this tension is neither polar nor static: in Goethe's time, France was the West and Land (in other words, representative of the continental West), whereas today it is, like almost all of Western Europe, Sea.

All other attempts to explain the distinction between East and West, whether political or cultural, have shown themselves to be of quite conditional and limited value. One of these is basing the differences between East and West on iconographic terms (in the sense of the "iconography of space" of Jean Gottmann), whence differences arise over images: the East traditionally acts as an opponent of visual representation, images, and icons, whereas the West is their defender.

Goethe, in Schmitt's words, was "a typical representative of the West" in 1812 on the side of Napoleon: "The German poet hoped that the West would continue meaning the order of Land and that Napoleon, like a new Alexander, would advance as far as the coast. Thus would emerge '*Terra firme*, with all its rights.'"

Overall, Schmitt observed: "Rising above the peaks of world history we witness the disputes of great powers struggling against one another in a war of the elements, land and sea. At least that is how historians of the wars between Sparta and Athens or between Rome and Carthage saw it." If once upon a time these conflicts were limited to the Mediterranean region, then the so-called modern age gave this struggle a completely new quality, introducing into the battle against World Land something greater than the civilization of Sea: the civilization of Ocean (there is a conceptual difference between the two). A typical example of such an Ocean civilization is England since the beginning of overseas conquests or, in today's time, the United States of America, which also bases its power on the domination of the World Ocean.

With these considerations, Carl Schmitt was continuing the ideas of the great English geographer Mackinder, who spoke of a war of Sea against "Heartland", the very heart of which is Russia. In fact, the very formula "War of Sea against Land" belongs to the French Admiral Castex who thus sought to summarize the basic motif of world history. It should be said that at stake here is not simply a "form of power" - every state, every civilization bases its power on the development of one of these two principles - but above all two fundamental aspects of human existence. These are two mutually exclusive modes of human existence on Earth.

The principle of Sea (or Ocean), in the end, symbolizes the element of variability, instability, and chaos, while the principle of Land, on the contrary, is stasis, immutability, Order. The symbol of man's existence at sea is the Ship, while the symbol of man's existence on land is the House, the Home. From the principle of Sea is derived the principle of technology "freed from all the norms of tradition" (Arnold Toynbee). The centuries-old War of Sea against Land, however, is not something anachronistic. Schmitt predicted that the confrontation between Land and Sea (as Ocean) would reach its final world-historical phase once humanity has mastered the entire planet.

The very same principles, finally, might be further developed once humanity enters the space era: future cosmic civilizations will be built either on island trade, "mercantile empires", or on the principle of man's static existence on Earth, on which are built great continental empires. The difference separating one from the other would thus be that which separates Home and Ship.

God Makes Kings

One might think that it is justified to equate tellurocratic empires with telluric, chthonic civilizations in the sense in which these concepts were developed by Johann Jakob Bachofen. However, this is not true: developing on Land, tellurocratic empires are based precisely on the idea of triumph over the elemental, the terrestrial, the earthen. At their very core lies the idea of Space - Space that is arranged and consecrated, sacralized - and their principle is therefore more Uranic and celestial than it is chthonic. Hence the fact that all the great tellurocratic empires represented sacralized wholes (as is evidenced by such notions as Holy Russia or the Holy Roman Empire of the German Nation). On this rests the ancient belief that royal lineages originate from the gods themselves. Joseph de Maistre wrote:

> God makes kings in the literal sense. He prepares royal races; maturing them under a cloud which conceals their origin. They appear at length crowned with glory and honour; they take their places; and this is the most certain sign of their legitimacy. The truth is, that they arise as it were of themselves, without violence on the one part, and without marked deliberation on the other: it is a species of magnificent tranquillity, not easy to express. Legitimate usurpation would seem to me to be the most appropriate expression (if not too bold) to characterize these kinds of origins, which time hastens to consecrate.[28]

All of this does not apply to thalassocracy, in which there is no trace of the sacred authority of the state. The trade-based republics of the Mediterranean, as well as the North American republics, remain completely profane creations governed by the rationale and interests of those who are, in essence, equal among themselves. Tellurocracies are, in their ultimate meaning, Space that is sacralized, consecrated, whereas thalassocracy is of Time, with its dynamism, variability, impermanence. The ideal type of the latter is the mercantile republic, whereas the ideal form of tellurocracy is the empire based on the sacred authority of the state and its ruler. The sacred principle itself is

---

28 Joseph de Maistre, *Essai sur le Principe Générateur des Constitutions Politiques et des Autres Institutions Humaines* [*Essay on the Generative Principle of Political Constitutions and other Human Institutions*] (1809).

personified in the ruler; he is the object not only of reverence but literally of worship as the chosen one of God himself, as God's Anointed One.

The elements of Land and Sea, after all, have always been experienced qualitatively differently. Spoken in the language of myth, "after land and sea were separated from one another, man was assigned to land as a viable space. The ocean remained seen as something dangerous and bad", to which Schmitt added: "We may refer here to Karl Barth's commentary on the first chapter of Genesis (in book 3, chapter 1 of Church Dogmatics), and content ourselves with showing how it would require an extraordinary impulse for human beings to overcome their ancient religious fear of the sea." This, indeed, is also testified by the Biblical Book of Genesis.

"Battles Waged Among Men"

The same author also cited the thought written by the clairvoyant child-poet Arthur Rimbaud: "Spiritual combat is more brutal than battles among men." The opposition between these two modes of human existence on Earth - maritime and terrestrial - is absolute and uncompromising. Nothing else equivalent exists in nature: it would be absurd to speak of the existence of hostilities between sea and land animals. Rabbi Isaac Abravanel described a struggle between Leviathan (the sea monster) and Behemoth (the land beast), but this is but a mythical transposition of this struggle waged among humans, between two opposing and irreconcilable modes of human existence and, finally, between the two principles upon which states and civilizations are built: "Behemoth strives to tear Leviathan apart with his horns or teeth, while

Leviathan keeps shut the land animal's muzzle and nose so that he cannot eat or breathe."

The conflict between East against West, Land and Sea, and Continent and Ocean can reach truly frightening intensity: this dualism was at the core of the 20th century's great World Wars and revolutions. But the opposition between East and West remains a horizontal axis of history, whereas there is, on the other end, the vertical axis represented by North and South. The importance of this axis, as has already been said, can be suppressed or obscured, but it does not lose its relevance. Overall, unlike that between East and West, the conflict between North and South is polar; underneath it, in its essence, over all its series of changes and metamorphoses, lies the same tension, the eternal return of the same. It is here, in Schmitt's words, that the "Nomos of the Earth" is shaped, just as the tension between Land and Sea is the natural, objective content in which the Nomos takes form.

The confrontation between East and West can assume different forms over the course of history. Today, we can agree with the statement of Dragoš Kalajić in his book *Stronghold*, the antagonism of East and West has in our time acquired the meaning of an antagonism between the world of Tradition and the world of Anti-Tradition:

> In the highest forms of the East we recognize what are indeed the last remnants of Indo-European civilization. Historically, it is in these geographical areas that the last configurations of Indo-European content have been expressed…and by virtue of this these contents have for the longest time resisted the contaminating forces of Anti-Tradition of the modern world.

It is from here that we enter the domain of an antagonism which, unlike that between East and West, is not historical but meta-historical, one that is not produced or conditioned by history but rather creates history itself, which is not its object but its subject. This is, of course, the antagonism between North and South, which qualitatively and hierarchically precedes that between East and West.

The Sacred Side of the World, the Nearest to Heaven

Above and beyond the historical world, in darkness, rest the archaic landscapes of the North in "eternal" ice. The North is, for all Indo-European peoples, the land of the ancestors, the lost ancestral homeland. Everything, Virgil wrote, comes to us from those Northern peoples, from the Hyperboreans. For all of the peoples of Indo-European origins and tradition, whether conscious of this or not, the North has a primordial, central significance. The North, even in the new age of modernity, has its own, completely different destiny. This is confirmed by the rise of the Russian Empire, then the Soviet Union, and now the Russian Federation. Russia, indeed, as Emil Cioran lucidly observed in his *History and Utopia*, is not East but North:

> She [Russia] gives a singular impression of space and of claustration, of immensity and of suffocation, of the North in short, but of a special North, one irreducible to our analyses, a North marked by a sleep and a hop that makes us tremble, by a night rich in explosions, by a dawn we shall remember. No Mediterranean transparency and gratuitousness in these Hyperboreans whose past, like their present, seems to belong to a different duration from ours. Facing the West's fragility and renown, they experience an embarrassment, the consequence of

their belated awakening and of their unemployed vigor: this is the inferiority complex of the strong.[29]

Upon the North shines a completely different light than that which falls on the so-called historical world. It is difficult to say whether it is the darkness of winter night or the light of polar dawn. It has no history in the true sense of the word, and its ancient past remains shrouded in a veil of secrecy. We ought to look at the description of the North presented to us, for example, by Adam of Bremen (1075) or in the *Brief History of Norway* from the thirteenth century, which speaks of long-living and archaic peoples, mermaids and wizards, Scylla and Chabrydis, and a terrible whirlwind that marked the end of the world north of the Icelandic coasts. Below them was the wild variegation of the South: the Africa called Libya in Herodotus' time to which Roman legions would be sent. Generally speaking, the North is the sacred side of the world, the side "nearest to heaven", whereas the South is its demonic antipode.

Since the earliest times, peoples from the North have migrated, conquered, and resettled in the direction of the South and its warm seas. They shaped an important period of the (proto-)history of the Indo-European peoples, whose last chapters were written with colonial conquests. But until the new age of modernity, these conquests never extended particularly far south. They encompassed only one narrow strip of the African coast, de facto bypassing Arabia and the southern part of the Indian subcontinent.

The North is, let us repeat, the origin and ancestral homeland of the Indo-European peoples. It is from here, the

---

[29] E.M. Cioran, *History and Utopia* (New York: Arcade Publishing, 1987), p. 32.

Far North, the circumpolar regions, that the ancient Proto-Indo-European migrations proceeded south. The Old Iranian Avesta, the sacred book of the Mazdeans, remembers the Northern "Aryan Paradise", *Airyana Vaejo*, which was ruined by glaciation, and speaks of 15 different countries through which the paths of dispersion subsequently proceeded. This list of countries, as noted by Tilak in his famous study The Arctic Home in the Vedas, is undoubtedly authentic, for, among other things, "the old Persian and Greek names in the above table [comparing the Iranian names] are taken from the inscriptions of the Achaemenian kings and the works of Greek writers after the overthrow of the Achaemenid dynasty by Alexander the Great."[30]

"Nec Plus Ultra"

It is justifiable, however, to pose the following question: did the epoch of modern geographical discoveries and overseas conquests not bring peripheral regions such as the North American continent into the consciousness and history of the peoples of Eurasia? Was their existence unknown much earlier, before the Renaissance and Middle Ages, in the Old Age or even prehistory? And if this knowledge was not common, then did it gradually retreat into the spheres of the unconscious and/or esoteric knowledge?

Not only wars but contacts have existed between East and West since the earliest times. We find memory of this in ancient legends and myths, such as the myth of Atlantis recorded by Plato. Plato spoke very clearly of an "'entire continent on the other side, which surrounds that real sea beyond"[31], which

---

30   Tilak, *Arctic Home in the Vedas*, p. 335.
31   Plato, *Timaeus*, 25a in Plato, *Complete Works*.

might very well be recognized to be the American continent. Memory of the Northern ancestral homeland survived not only in the Greek myth of Hyperborea, but also in the related myths of other Indo-European peoples, and not only them. However, it is not always possible to accurately distinguish between "real" and symbolic continents, lands, and cities mentioned in sacred texts, from the Vedas to the Bible. In sacred texts, the sacred and earthly planes, physical and sacred geography, physics and metaphysics constantly intersect. But, overall, these fabulous lands are not the product of mere fantasy: rather, the matter is one of a fragile memory for which it is still necessary to find the appropriate keys.

In the traditions of many European peoples, we find mentions of a "Green Land" and "Land of the Dead" somewhere in the West. This is "some kind of semi-material world resembling the Greek Hades or Hebrew Sheol. This is the country of dusk and dawn in which there is no escape for mortals and which only the initiated can reach."[32] René Guénon claimed that the symbol "$", which today represents the financial emblem of America, is in fact a simplified version of a sacred seal whose meaning can be translated as "*nec plus ultra*", that is literally "no further." This inscription originally referred to the ban on sailing beyond the Pillars of Hercules and navigations in the direction of the inhuman worlds in the West.

Connections between the Vikings and the North American continent have today been archaeologically proven. Settling in Labrador and Newfoundland, the old Vikings interbred with the natives and left behind descendants in

---

32   Alexander Dugin, *Mysteries of Eurasia*.

the likes of the North American Mandan Indians. Jacques de Mahieu put forth an altogether well-founded hypothesis on contacts between the Vikings and the Inca civilization. It would not be without grounds to presume that the Phoenician sailors who prevented other peoples from navigating beyond the Pillars of Hercules knew of the existence of the American continent, and maintained more or less permanent ties with it. America, the continent in the Far West of the world, must have been known to Eurasian peoples since the most ancient, proto-historical times, and traces of this knowledge can be found in some of their oldest legends and myths.

***

MYTHICAL AMERICA

Historical events cannot be explained solely by the conscious intentions of their protagonists, nor exclusively by their personal characteristics and traits, even though the psychological structure of an important historical actor and their ideas or philosophical dispositions are indeed of no small significance. Apart from factors which are purely quantitative and quantifiable (economic, sociological, etc.), historical events are always influenced by far subtler and more delicate modes of reality which are no less real, even if they elude physical perception, as they affect quality rather than quantity. This also applies to many other spheres of human activity that are more ordinary than the sphere of politics. On many occasions, an "abstract" idea, concept, or myth has sealed the fate of entire peoples or civilizations (the Incas, for instance, thought the Spanish conquistadors to be White Gods). And political ideologies themselves, after all, belong to a quite distinctive reality that is largely independent of any individual. Indeed, they are often capable of subjugating whole peoples and "absorbing" any individual.

On an even deeper level, political realities are deeply rooted in the unconscious, in forgotten and deeply repressed archetypes. The activation of these archetypes – usually abruptly and unexpectedly – can provoke eruptive breakthroughs of the unimaginable in the depths of collective unconscious and its suppressed energies, both of individuals and entire peoples, all the more so if these archetypes elude consciousness. One example of such sudden intrusion is exhibited by Germany in the time of National Socialism. Several studies into the "metaphysics of history" have suggested that on this occasion it was the archetype of Wotan, the ancient pagan deity of the old Germanic peoples, that was awakened in the character of the German leader (of course, in distorted, pathological form, which was a consequence of long, artificial repression).

We can conclude, however, that it is precisely for these reasons that any political analysis which is not limited to strictly rational and empirical points is relevant. Political analysis must strive to encompass one political phenomenon in its entirety, always taking into account spiritual, religious, deep psychological, or symbolic-geographical factors.

The Secret of American Prestige

America today is a major geopolitical force. It is a model to which, whether intentionally or not, modern societies conform, to the point that it becomes the paradigm of modernity itself. This is the secret of American prestige. But behind the illusion of an ultramodern and ultra-rational society oriented exclusively towards dry rationalism, in which everything is subordinated to "business" and the economy, and its relentless activism, the outlines of an almost mythical continent can still be seen. This image has an almost magnetic force in the face of which few people can remain indifferent, provoking at times repulsion and at others a desire to imitate in the devilish circles of Americanism and anti-Americanism. This paradox simply cannot be rationally explained.

The Myth of America

The myth of America or "mythical America" really exists. On the most elementary level, this fact is recognizable to almost every inhabitant of the planet, instinctively as some still vague and unclear feeling. On a case-by-case basis, it becomes more obvious: mythical America can be seen in its symbols and "icons", in its celluloid canvases, in the profiles of its cities, and in the enormous empty spaces of the "New World." This finds expression in the "myths" and strange ideology of this country. Elsewhere, we have discussed the identification of America with the post-apocalyptic "New Jerusalem" and the "New Earth" of the Apocalypse, which found its foundation in extreme forms of Protestant (Puritan) religiosity.[33] In this chapter, we will once again turn to a less explicit but no less important explanation: America is equatable to the mythical Atlantis. It is to this subconscious correspondence that America owes a considerable part of its present prestige and glamour.

America or Atlantis?

Linking America with the lost Atlantis is natural and even inevitable – this takes place on both the unconscious and conscious level simultaneously, among Americans themselves and those peoples who submit to the new colonizers from the West. This is also testified by the ease with which terms take root that would otherwise make no sense, such as the "Atlantic community" as a synonym for "Euro-America", "Euro-Atlantic integration" or even the very name of the North Atlantic military alliance. Furthermore, "Atlanticism" is the generally accepted term for all those geopolitical doctrines pursued by the contemporary United States. "Atlanticism" is also a hallmark of the "imperial" mentality, the psycho-ideology of thalassocratic, mercantile and colonial powers which, since ancient times, have been linked to the Atlantic Ocean. From the Atlantic to Atlantis, however, on the symbolic level, there is

---

33 See "The War for the End of the World" in Part III of this volume.

only a single step, because the Northern area of this ocean was actually the space of the mythical Atlantis.

This symbolic identification is undoubted, yet America is not ancient Atlantis (the Western paleo-continent), but a continent that, even in prehistoric times, must have been located west of it. Nor are today's Americans the mythical Atlanteans mentioned by Plato. The description which the Greek philosopher provides is perfectly clear: he spoke of an "entire continent on the other side, which surrounds that real sea beyond"[34] - a land which is recognizable today as the American continent, located west of the Atlantean islands.

The Myth of Atlantis

Let us recall, in the most basic outlines, the myth of Atlantis, which, according to legend, was to be found in old, prehistoric times somewhere in the North Atlantic, west of the Pillars of Hercules, today's Strait of Gibraltar. Roughly speaking, Atlantis sank ten thousand years ago in a geological cataclysm that befell humanity. One of the most important testimonials left to us is that of Plato, who in his *Timaeus* and *Critias* reports what his teacher Socrates learned from the Greek sage Solon - and the latter from some Egyptian priest.

Summarizing Plato's account, we can highlight the following: the mythical Atlanteans were the bearers of a spiritual, superior civilization. Sailors arrived from an island in the West, where they lived in incomparable prosperity, and they were the first colonizers of Europe. The cataclysm that befell them - due to "God's wrath" - was in fact a consequence of

---
34   Plato, *Timaeus*, 25a in Plato, *Complete Works*.

spiritual catastrophe: "Zeus, god of the gods," Plato laconically concludes, "resolved to punish them."[35]

Out of all the numerous, later swathes of literature dedicated to Atlantis, which today encompass tens of thousands of bibliographic items, let us mention the already classic work of Otto Muck, who imparted a certain scientific argumentation to this myth. This author (and not only him) identified the mythical Atlanteans with Cro-Magnon man, the bearer of seafaring and agriculture, whose colonization also proceeded in a northwest-southeast direction.

Plato's work is the oldest and most complete report about this lost civilization. Plato's account is rich, meticulous and filled with incredibly precise details of the life of the Atlanteans. In relation to it, all later reports are inferior and have only secondary significance. They are often reducible to mere repetition of Plato or are simply evidence of the fertile imaginations of their authors.

America - The Bearer of Atlantean Prosperity

The literal truth of the Atlantean myth is of little interest to us here. In principle, myths are ambiguous and can be interpreted in various ways, from the highest level related to the spiritual reality down to the lowest, "naturalistic" level. Here we are primarily interested in the truth at the level of the collective unconscious and its archetypes. In general, it seems that this myth is very deeply rooted in the structure of the unconscious of many peoples. Myths about Atlantis continually arise, even when they seem to be completely forgotten, to the point that

---

35 Plato, *Critias* 121b-c in Plato, *Complete Works*.

in certain historical periods, such as the past few decades, it has become quite justifiable to speak of a real "Atlantomania."

The parallels between America and Atlantis impose themselves. America is the bearer of Atlantean prosperity, a point which is highlighted in the myth described by Plato (although in this legend it is emphasized that this is primarily a matter of spiritual well-being). America is also the bearer of a "superior" civilization, and Americans are also sailors and colonizers of Europe who arrived from an "island" in the West, and so on. Through America, therefore, in the end, a long-dead world that disappeared beneath the ocean waves was resurrected, bringing to mind the apocalyptic motif of the "resurrection of the dead." There is also the symbolism of water (sea and ocean): in its negative aspect, this is the symbol of death, chaos, and Non-Being, while in its positive sense this is regeneration and "cleansing from sin." This, in the end, fits well with the symbolism of the West which is in many diverse traditions not only the "cursed corner of the world" but also the "land of the dead", the "kingdom of shadows" in the West towards which souls set off after death.

However, America is a false and parodical embodiment of the Atlantean myth, in which higher, spiritual values are systematically reinterpreted and substituted with lower, material ones: the heavenly prosperity of Atlantis, the true Golden Age, is replaced by America's material wealth and by its presumed superiority over the "rest of the world" manifested in consumer goods and technological civilization. Thus, the superior Atlantean colonizers who brought the light of a spiritual civilization are turned into colonists-captors, envoys of an extremely materialistic civilization, who appear under the grotesque symbols of Mickey Mouse, Coca-Cola, and McDonald's.

From Eschatology to Utopia

The New Jerusalem and New Atlantis are both archetypes of paradisal prosperity. But this, however, can come only after the end of the world. Paradise, the new Golden Age, lies beyond history and belongs to the beginning of a new cycle of time or, in Christian eschatology, after the Second Coming of Christ. Both are also, in the late age of Europe, the favorite spaces of utopian projections, imaginary spaces such as Francis Bacon's New Atlantis. America became such in a concrete way soon after the discovery of the continent. America, therefore, quickly turned into a space for the realization of utopias. Eschatology is reduced to the modest measure of utopia as a consequence of the secularization (and in fact parody) of what was, at its core, one religious idea.

Thus, the first attempt to establish utopia on American soil (the "City of God" on Earth) was undertaken by the Puritan and Masonic "founding fathers." American soil gave rise to the first communist colonies, such as Icaria, built in 1848 in the wetlands of Missouri. Since the earliest times of its history, it has been that the "history of America is truly the history of a dream of utopia" (Dragoš Kalajić, *Map of (Anti-)Utopia*). Utopia, however, is a parody of eschatology that is natural whenever the superior is explained in terms of the inferior, when the "beyond" is made into the earthly here and now.

America - The "New Earth" of the Apocalypse

False Atlantis and false Jerusalem are connected in a particularly "happy" way by American syncretic superstition, the pseudo-religion of the New Age whose messiahs and prophets sent us the following message: the New Age, the Golden Age, the Age of Aquarius, has already begun - on American soil, of course. America has not only saved the world from history (which Americans otherwise deny any value) and its hopelessness and ended it, since America is in possession of its meaning, but America itself is, as its "founding fathers" believed, the "New Earth" of the Revelation of St. John the Theologian. Just as Christians participate in the mystery of Christ's sacrifice by taking communion with bread and wine, so does participation in the mysteries of America involve drinking Coca-Cola and eating McDonald's.

It is interesting that this idea was expressed by Christopher Columbus himself, the first truly mythical figure of the "New World", its mythical discoverer, when he proclaimed: "God made me the messenger of the new heaven and the new earth of which he spoke in the Apocalypse of St. John...and he showed me the place where to find it."

America – The Kingdom of the Antichrist

By way of regressing to the Old Testament mentality (according to which the Americans are, like ancient Israel, the "chosen people" and America is, in the consciousness of the first settlers and voluntary exiles from the "Egypt" of Europe, the "Promised Land" and "New Canaan") and then transposing this religion mentality into lay terms and such eschatological terms into spatial, utopian ones, America has not given up its messianic pretensions. In fact, it seems that the messianic ambitions of this happy "island of Utopia" are growing in step with the secularization and de-Christianization of the "New World" that is reaching grotesque extents today.

The process of secularization and de-Christianization which in America seems to be taking place faster and more radically than in any other part of the world, on the one hand, and on the other the fact that America is still a utopian space, perhaps even more so than ever before, has led to a paradoxical outcome. The long line of utopias concludes with the "New World Order" (which, in the mouth of Fukuyama, also foresees the "End of History") - an "order" that is, in many aspects, not only radically anti-Christian but anti-traditional in general. This gives credence to those who recognize in today's America the "kingdom of the Antichrist" or, in the very least, a creation that, among all those known to human history, has come closest to such. On this motif, which is gaining ground not only in the consciousness of non-Americans but also Christian America itself - and which, in our opinion, will rapidly gain in significance in the near future - we shall end this brief excursion through the spaces of mythical, "otherworldly" America.

***

THE IDEA OF THE CENTER

The Idea of the Center can be found in many diverse traditions. All studies confirm its exceptional prevalence and antiquity to the point that we cannot dismiss the supposition that this idea is universal. Even attempting to list all the different symbols and ways of representing this center would take us too far. However, properly speaking, the Idea of the Center attains its highest and fullest meaning in the Indo-European traditions.

Ideally, such a center precedes any space: it defines and determines space, chronologically, qualitatively, and hierarchically. Although invisible in the material world, it exists objectively, not subjectively. It even precedes the subject that cognizes it. Yet the subject is identical to it, just as he is overall identical to the very sacred principle of the cosmos. To the question "Who are you?", a famous Vedic formula replies: "Thou art That" (*Tat tvam asi*). Without the existence of such a center, moreover, the existence of any structure, of any order itself ("cosmos" etymologically means ordered whole), any kind of hierarchy, is unimaginable.

"At the Center of the Light of Heaven"

In Indo-European traditions, the idea of the center is represented and symbolized in very different ways: from the symbol of the "polar cross" to the "axis" or "World Tree" to the Holy Grail (the quest for the Grail is in truth a quest for the lost Center). One of the most memorable representations of the center was left to us by Plato in his *Republic*. Plato speaks of a place where one sees "light that stretched over the whole heaven and earth, more like a rainbow than anything else, but brighter and more pure." There, "in the middle of the light", Plato's people "saw the extremities of its bonds stretching from the heavens, for the light binds the heavens like the cables girding a trireme and holds its entire revolution together. From the extremities hands the spindle of Necessity, by means of which all the revolutions are turned."[36]

This light is the axis of the world connecting heaven and earth, the human and the divine. This axis is intangible and supra-temporal. Human history is a departure from this center, and thus a departure from the primordial. It is no coincidence that modern culture has been lucidly defined as a culture of men afflicted by "loss of center" (*à la* Hans Sedlmayr) - this is one of the keenest and most astute definitions of the modern era and of modern man in general. Modern man is he who has lost his center, or the man of an era which has lost its center. In the age of this "loss of the center", the very idea of the center takes on negative connotations and meanings in critiques of all kinds and forms of "centrism." Conversely, a positive sense is imparted to "de-centralization": the loss of the Center and displacement from the Center means liberation from the "dictatorship" of the Center.

In other words, the modern age is an age in which the spirit turns away from its own center of being, in which the spirit detaches from being, and the psyche detaches from the spiritual. The consequence is the "free spirit" - the spirit free from Being - which revolves around its own speculations, finally eroding its being with its own dilemmas and doubts. Modern philosophy is, with rare exceptions, the product of this so-called "liberated", autonomous spirit.

---

36   Plato, *Republic* 616 in *Complete Works*.

By analogy, "free and autonomous art" is art that is separated from all higher norms and demands, and it is not by chance that such often becomes a mere instrument of self-expression for the psychological states of artists. Ultimately, only the lowest, spatial conception of the center remains, where the center is thought of only as a mere focal point of perception and the spatial center itself becomes extremely relativized and mutable.

The One Who Turns the Wheel

But the age of the "loss of the center" has another, hidden meaning, represented by the myth of the quest for the Grail. The Grail (*Graal*) is, as already mentioned, a metaphysical center that has been lost, and this has the meaning of a real (first spiritual and then physical) catastrophe. In the attempt to forestall or at least restrain such catastrophe, the Knights of the Round Table set out in search of the vanished center.

Another symbol of this Center is the mythical Hyperborea: the lost Northern homeland to which, like the mythical heroes Perseus or Heracles, the lonely people of the "age of loss" seek to return. By conquering the lost Center, they regain "immortality", thus reaching the fullness of the primordial state. The center is that distant point which, itself motionless, enables the movement of the world, hence why the Hindu tradition describes the perfect man as the *Chakravartin*, "the one who turns the wheel." The mythical image of this is the Vedic Indra who, standing at the axis of the world, turns the heavens himself. Conquering the Center is conquering the very state of the fullness of Being itself.

The topic of the loss of the Center, separation from it, and the search for the lost Center have become an important matter in contemporary art. It is also a great divide, which, on the one hand, separates all those who, like the hero of the novel Among the Hyperboreans by Miloš Crnjanski, venture on such a quest, and, on the other hand, those who distance themselves from the center, destroying and denying its very existence. It should be said that such considerations go far beyond the purely aesthetic field conceived in the bent and narrow framework of modern notions; they venture into the field of the metaphysical in the sense of the realization of the ultimate possibilities that are generally given to the human being. But they are also closely related to the idea of beauty. The idea of beauty is intrinsic to the idea of the Center, for beauty is a matter of measurements, symmetry, and order, whereas separation from and loss of the center inevitably leads to anarchy and entropy, i.e. towards the "aesthetics of ugliness."

Thus, on the one hand, there are works of art whose structure faithfully reflects the order of eternity, and on the other there are works that have no structure, or whose structure is incidental, chaotic, random and arbitrary. On one end there are works whose authors follow the ideals of artistic traditions, of eras in which the center was obvious and accessible to all, and on the other there are works which are the results of "experimentation", destruction, and degradation.

On the opposite side of the light of the center is darkness, chaos and emptiness, which ultimately end in oblivion and escape from being.

Prehistoric Roots

Those works of art in the modern age which embody the idea of the center are the fruit of intuition and the great metaphysical awakenings and endeavors of their authors. Their lasting significance is truly metaphysical, as such goes beyond mere representation. The novel *Among the Hyperboreans* by Miloš Crnjanski very faithfully and accurately conveys the Idea of the Center as meaning the idea of the central position of man in the world, the centrality of the world and the centrality of its structure. These works are, in the end, also the externalization of the inner content of their creators. However, such contents are not the peculiarities of the authors themselves, or their individual psychologies, but only particular expressions of what is common, of expressions of tradition, ideas, and values. Of course, the same applies to authors whose works deny this very tradition and idea. By transmitting suggestive experiences of chaos, darkness, and the chthonic, as opposed to luminous and heavenly order, they are continuing an opposing tradition of values and ideas. Ultimately, these are two different opposing psychoideologies, and thus two different, mutually exclusive, irreconcilable human types.

As has already been said more than once, the origin must be sought in the deep darkness of prehistory. The oldest spiritual monuments and symbols of humankind exhibit the same basic dichotomy of worldviews and fundamental ideas, a dichotomy that can be essentially reduced to the matriarchal and the patriarchal (J.J. Bachofen), or, in the terminology of Dragoš Kalajić, the Chthonic and the Uranic. Paradoxically, many works of modern art, texts, and manifestos faithfully convey the basic content and ideas of ancient chthonic psychology and its *forma mentis* to the extent that we can say that modern art only repeats or reformulates ancient archetypal and chthonic patterns of thinking. For example, as pointed out by Kalajić in his work, certain works of contemporary body art (and many other avant-garde art practices) can be interpreted as renewals of the ancient Dionysian ritual of the "dismemberment of the dismembered"; these are, admittedly, extreme expressions of contemporary art, but here the general rule is that extreme forms of a phenomenon reveal its true, albeit often hidden content.

The origins of these two worldviews are to be found in remote prehistory. The most complete and purest expressions of the Uranic, "heavenly" tradition are to be found in such ancient spiritual monuments as, for example, the Rig-Vedic hymns or the Upanishads, and in various other epic and myths throughout the Indo-European or Aryan continent of spirituality. What is essential is that this ancient tradition conveys patriarchal ethics which cannot be reduced to any morality, for every ethics, as has already been said, is an imperative, a commandment of Being, whereas morality is the product of mere speculations on the spirit. Besides, ethics is always affirmative, dictating what a person must or should be, whereas morality is based on prohibition, on stating what a person must not do.

All other cultures and traditions, with the exception of the Indo-Europeans, are derived from telluric, chthonic cults and forms of religiosity. When Uranic contents appear in different cultures, we ought to think of either direct or indirect influence from Indo-European traditions.

If the true bearer of Uranic spirituality and tradition is Indo-European man, then it remains an open question as to who is the bearer of the opposite, chthonic tradition. It is indisputable that the basic values and ideas which sprung from the chthonic religions and cults encompass the great Southern belt of the Eurasian continent, just as the source of Uranic tradition is undoubtedly in the Far North of the continent.

Staying in Hell

The fact that a given literary and artistic work of the twentieth century affirms Uranic ethics (as opposed to the variable and relative morality of chthonic man) is of extraordinary significance, evidencing the vitality of patriarchal ethics and traditions. In fact, such is one of the few remaining and lonely expressions of this historically defeated tradition. This tradition lives on only through the personal ethics, heroic works, absolute acts, and rare works of art that represent its more or less pure manifestations.

The time in which this tradition educated and inspired the entire human community – the "community of noble people" – belongs to the past. Today's Uranic individual is alone, "lost" amidst the hostility of the "chthonic" masses. Novels such as *A Novel of London* and *Among the Hyperboreans* by Miloš Crnjanski, *The Expulsion* by Momčilo Selić and *On the Marble Cliffs* by Ernst Jünger can be read as testimonies to the passage of such heroes through the hell of the modern world, through the very center of the vortex of modern nihilism in its most extreme and destructive form. Their stay here in a world that has become truly monstrous and the exact opposite of the celestial order is akin to staying in hell. Such a hero endures life as if it were war. He lives in constant war, in the midst of a hostile environment, under siege. This is his ordinary, everyday experience. But the experience of nihilism is necessary. At the end of that road the light must be found; the light of order, the light of the sacred principle of the cosmos.

In truth, this is the same light that such a man already possesses within himself, for he already has his own center, since he is the true embodiment or incarnation of the principle of order. The fight which such a hero wages is a fight for the manifestation of order in the surrounding world. In principle, he is indifferent to its outcome in terms of victory or defeat, because such cannot change his position or his being. The only reason why he persists in this struggle is because it is that very struggle between the principles of order and chaos, light and darkness, order and anarchy. It is clear, indeed, that the complete victory of any one principle is not possible or even desirable, for such would mark the end of the cosmic drama, and thus the end of the created world founded on dualism.

The monstrosities of this world, i.e. the chimeras of modern times, are utopias, from the liberal to the technocratic, from the communist to the androgynous. Utopias are eminent expressions of the chthonic mentality; dissatisfied with what he is (or more precisely, what he is not, as such a person seeks to be something different from what he actually is), he is forced to constantly seek a replacement, a substitute for the lost or missing fullness of Being. His principle is therefore not permanence and immutability, but continuous and aimless change for conforming to the forces of nature or history which determine such. His space is utopia (whose destination is "nowhere"), whose space is that of escape from the truth of Being. He exists, and therefore he does not exist, that is he exists outside Being, far away from the Center. His existence is, in a word, a panicked escape from Being. Uranic man and Uranic tradition are his true enemy, because in the Uranic, like a mirror that shows the truth of being, he is revealed his halfness, his inadequacy. We do not know, nor can we know what motives really drive him, nor can we describe his actual position, because we do not possess any experience of the sort, but if the position of the man in possession of the Center is "in the middle of the light of heaven" (Plato), then the place of the former can only be described as the very heart of hell.

The Judgement of the Court of the Dead

At the end of the path the light must be found. The legacy which is in question here does not confirm - nor can it confirm - victory in apparent history. On a personal level, for the man of Uranic tradition this battle has already been won in advance through the conquest of the Center, through mastering the state of the fullness of Being. In the historical world, victory or defeat are merely ephemeral or possible outcomes that cannot influence him. He is, therefore, truly indifferent. For him is ture the ancient motto expressed by Giordano Bruno: "I fought, and that is enough."

Of course, the outcome of his struggle is by no means accidental, for in the end it does not depend on "historical circumstances", but on predestination and the sacred truth of history. For Uranic man, unlike chthonic man, the imperative is not victory but being true to Being. The fact that the historical circumstances are unfavorable for him and the tradition which he represents does not pose a problem for him. For, as one of the heroes of Jünger's *Heliopolis* would say: "We do not know nor do we have the right to know what history is in essence, in the Absolute, beyond time. We can guess, but we do not know the verdict of the Court of the Dead."

The true course of history, then, is not evolution but involution, gradually and rapidly falling away from the sacred principle. This inevitable decay affects all that has been created and represents for the man of the Uranic tradition an extraordinary test of integrity. The strength of his integrity, as opposed to the man of the chthonic tradition who voluntarily complies with the whims and changes of historical transformation, wages his own struggle "against history", against its randomness and contingency. It should be said, however, that such a position is only seemingly and superficially conservative. Although he resists historical change in principle, knowing that each change has the effect of worsening the already desperate situation, his real goal is not and cannot be the preservation of one necessarily imperfect state, but the revolutionary return to the primordial, best, ideal state, the state preceding history itself.

In principle, this cannot be achieved within this temporal and historical cycle. What can possibly be achieved is not some political and social program that would lead to renewal, but only the expression and manifestation of the tradition which he himself, in his integrity and deeds, represents. In other words, he cannot hope to win. The meaning of his struggle is only the preservation of his own integrity, the values which he himself represents so that they may, outside of the framework of this historical and temporal cycle, be laid as the foundation for a new crystallization of order.

In this struggle, therefore, he does not expect vindication from the "court of history." Rather, he expects only the "court of the dead" - the dead whom he, being true to himself, rightfully confirms and represents.

The Tradition that Transmits Itself Through Time

From the highest point of view, however, he is "right" only inasmuch as he represents the opposite of the tradition which we have designated with the borrowed terms "chthonic" or "matriarchal." Within history and in his personal existence, man has the freedom to decide between the great and irreconcilably opposed principles of Heaven and Earth. Every person, after all, is a field, an arena of the great spiritual drama which has repeated itself in different conditions over the ages, throughout history. In the language of great spiritual symbols, this is the choice between the light of Paradise and the darkness of Hell, between the fullness and duality of beings, between that which is Hell for one and Paradise for the other, and vice versa.

Having opted for the Earth instead of Heaven, Chthonic man attempts to create an earthly paradise through a series of utopian endeavors, all of which lead to Hell. Only in this aspect is it possible to speak of the failure of utopian attempts. As Emil Cioran observed, utopias are achievable, but only in a spirit opposite to the one in which they were imagined. Wherever the spirit fantasizes about freedom, it will face tyranny. Wherever it dreams of peace, it will encounter terror.

But the utopian energy and tension of the chthonic substrate cannot be exhausted or spent. The apparent "failure" of one utopian project only frees up space and energy to achieve a new one, which results in the progressive deterioration of historical conditions. The failure of the "communist utopia", for example, only releases energy for the realization of another utopia, such as the liberal one or any other, but each of these attempts has consequences which are, in a historical sense, irreversible. From the Uranic standpoint, the only significant result of all such endeavors is the destruction of the last remnants of the old patriarchal institutions and values. From the chthonic standpoint, however, this is a revanche against the former historical victors, a belated historical confirmation of chthonic values over Uranic values.

The "destruction of the last remnants of the old patriarchal institutions and values" nevertheless creates a completely new historical situation for the bearers of the Uranic tradition. The absence of external backing and support from patriarchal institutions, all of which have been destroyed, compels the last people of the Uranic tradition to seek support exclusively within themselves.

Such sudden insights and manifestations "against history" clearly testify to this tradition's extraordinary strength and vitality. This tradition's manifestations, in their pure state beyond the "trajectory of history", without the support of institutions, and through lonely efforts, existential fractures, and sudden fruits of individual knowledge, confirm that this tradition truly has the power to transmit itself over time.

***

Symbols of Hyperborea

ITHACA

We are sailing to Ithaca. From one coast to another, from one star to another. From one time to another, from one inhospitable country to another, towards lost kingdoms.

Through the chaos and anarchy amidst which there is no longer above or below. Through sickness and eclipse. Through the meantime, in which nothing is close or far away anymore.

Through confusion and through error. Through the long night and short day. Through war that is no longer freedom and through peace that is not peaceful. From the Golden Age to the Iron Age, from Christ to the Antichrist. From the beginning to the very end. Some call it progress, advancement, but this is progression in death, because we are dying every day, going from the dawn of the Golden Age to the full eclipse, into the deep night of the Iron Age.

We are sailing into the wilderness. Through the ruins of cities and civilizations. Through dejection and through fear. Through the dream and promise of another beginning. Through joy and through muffled pain. Through life that holds us back and through death that liberates. Through ice and through night. Towards stellar fires, from the Iron Age to the Golden Age, from the Antichrist to the Second Coming.

Our language is the ruins of Knowledge, our words are hollow echoes. Our thoughts are a blurry memory. They are powerless to express the truth. They are powerless to express who we are and where we are going – we humans of the iron race are imprisoned in the Iron Age. They are powerless to express the inexpressible.

**

THE LIONS OF KALEMEGDAN

In the already historical age, just a little more than two thousand years ago, lions still lived in Macedonia. Information on this can be found in the writings of Herodotus. During his lifetime, lions lived in Crestonia, which is roughly the area between present-day Vardar and Struma in northern Macedonia. "No lions are found anywhere in eastern Europe east of the Nestus or in the rest of the continent west of the Achelous; they only ever occur in the region between these two rivers."[37] Alexander of Macedon would hunt these amazing and beautiful animals in his youth.

This feat was more worthy of kings and heroes than any other. The task which Eurystheus demanded of Heracles was defeating the Nemean lion. The beast that ravaged the area of Nemea had a pelt that could not be pierced by a spear nor cut by a sword. It was the offspring of the monstrous Typhon, or Selene, or Chimera, or the dog Orthrus. To overcome the Nemean lion, Heracles had to strangle him with his bare hands and then only with the lion's own sharp claw could he pierce its skin. From then on, Heracles wore the skin as impenetrable armor, as a symbol of immortality and invulnerability, and donned the heavy lion head as a helmet.

The lion also symbolizes the kingdom or empire. It was lions tied with iron chains that guarded the entrance to the Celtic "Spinning Castle", the abode of the Fisher King and the secret hiding place of the Grail in the cycles of the Grail legends.

The lion is an archetype. What Borges said of the tiger is also true of the lion: one tiger represents all tigers that have

---

37 Herodotus, *The Histories* VII:126, p. 1169.

been and all tigers that will be, because "the individual, in each case, is the entire species."

The connection between kings and lions is, without a doubt, both ritual and essential. In later history, when the custom of hunting had disappeared along with the lions, only kings remained the collectors of these rare and exotic beasts. There was no worthier gift for a ruler than a lion imprisoned in a cage delivered to him by boat from a distant and fabulous country thousands of miles away. Subsequently, the lion moved into the field of heraldry, becoming an almost mandatory addition to royal and noble coats of arms. Sculpted from stone, cast in bronze or forged of iron, we find them even nowadays at the gates of old castles and magnificent palaces, being not so much a symbolic threat as more of a memory of the age when the lion and royal dignity were equivalent.

I do not know if the following experience belongs to the realm of reality or to the images we only see in dreams. It was a late summer afternoon, almost evening, when, climbing up the Kalemegdan fortress, I wished to get up to that high plateau from which the confluence of the Sava and the Danube, and the War Island itself, can be seen. Before that, I remember I was wandering for a long time through the underground rooms of the fortress. In one of them, next to a pile of waste, garbage and other rubble, a stack of neatly laid stone cannonballs were still laid out. After those stuffy underground rooms, narrow passages and dark hallways, which can be found in any old fort, reminiscent of tombs, I wanted to set foot in a place that would afford me a breadth of sight and freshness of water. The murmurs of many passers-by, the screams and squeals of children in the summer night did not bother me; this was something completely different from the musty and assumptive dust of ages.

It was the last hour before sunset, when the sun is at its strongest. Kalemegdan's fortifications turned brown and golden in color. Beneath one of them, not very high above our heads, I suddenly spotted two lions, gallant and lazy, marching under the sun.

These were the lions from the nearby zoo, but no visible fence divided us from them. It seemed as though they were completely free to move around, and that the ancient fortress was their natural environment, that they were an integral part of it. This vision might have been born of a dream and belonged to some other, almost mythical era quite different from ours.

The earliest recorded name of present-day Belgrade is the Celtic "*Singidunum*", a compound in which "*dunum*" means fortress or castle. The meaning of the word "*singi*" is still unclear and is the subject of much speculation and conjecture. According to some interpretations, "*singi*" means lion, and, therefore, the meaning of the name is "Lion Fortress." The etymology is doubtlessly fictitious, like so many others, and yet it is the key to this dream.

***

ONE DREAM

A dream. in which I am climbing up a very high tower for a long time. Like a cliff, it rises high above the landscape and a town surrounded by two rivers. Around it, like bunches of grains, are clustered many other things – shops, stores, and autumnal gardens. The variegation of the new buildings conceals a colossus: only in some places is the massive wall of stone and brick visible, with cracked stone beams protruding between them. The view from the top over the jagged rampart causes dizziness. The air here is sharp and fresh, as if I had suddenly dived into clear, cold water.

Quite a while afterwards, I was passing through countless chambers, now dim, later bright, some of which were decorated like residential rooms and others like museums. The tower is simultaneously an apartment and a treasury. The corridors intersect like a maze. Salons and libraries continue throughout them. Then, in the dining room, which seems to be built for giants, I attend a sumptuous meal, a real feast at which I am the guest of the ancient family residing here. The act is more reminiscent of a very complicated ritual than eating. During this meal, interesting conversations are being kept. But these are conversations with the dead. Apparently, every action also opens one's eyes to the invisible: the rooms are filled with shadows. Finally, at the end, I became aware of the presence of the forefather, the patriarch of this old family, a presence which is more felt than it can be seen by the eyes. He is like a very long shadow that stretches across the table.

Unlike him, the characters of the two sisters are quite real. They showed me two objects: the first has faded from my memory (it was some kind of very old piece of weaponry), and the second was made of animal bone. The material is prehistoric. Carved into the bone are two stylized falcons with their heads facing each other. All of this was accompanied by detailed interpretations that cannot be translated into the language of the awake. The last picture I see before waking up is the hair of one of the sisters, hair that is the color of old gold against the backdrop of a garden intersected by low stone walls.

The images disappear, but the sense of discovery, surprisingly, follows me for a long time in reality.

***

HYPERBOREANS

Somewhere in the darkness of the North, among other lands and peoples, lay Hyperborea - an invisible, other homeland. All have striven towards it - not only polar travelers and explorers but also entire peoples. Wherever all possibilities are exhausted, we return to the origin, to the source, to the beginning. Hence, reaching the Pole or rediscovering Hyperborea - the land beyond the North Wind - could be equated with discovering the lost meaning of life. Perhaps, after all, we have already trod its sacred ground without knowing it. An island lost in the wasteland of the North Sea could have been the peak of the mythical Mount Meru. Shrines such as those seen in distant Lapland, on the Kola Peninsula – stone burials crowned with deer horns – were signposts or memories of it. Now, however, people have left the North, defeated, with sickly eyes and wounded bodies, rejoicing in their country like children...

***

Here, in the wastelands of the North, meeting people meant the greatest joy. There were no more French, Germans or Russians – just people who want to engage in danger, adventure, and who are willing to help each other. This gave them value and determined their place. Vanity was unknown to them. Scarcity did not humiliate anyone. The icy wasteland of the North was the place of their beauty...

***

All of them, from the first to the last man, were well aware that they did not put themselves in danger for the sake of trade routes or scientific research whose results, at the cost of life, came through all adversity. Some of the strangest human tales are those written through feats and suffering by polar travelers, conquerors of the Pole. They were not driven by greed or avarice. Here, in the polar circle, only for glory did people live and die.

At this Pole was the center, the invisible center towards which one goes without asking the price. For them, the Pole radiated an invisible light similar to that spread around them by the polar dawn. The harshness of the polar circle did not suffer anything vague, half, or weak. Upon entering it, all of them, in some incomprehensible way, quickly became aware that this distant point, beyond the horizon, was also their invisible center. Hence, all those who returned from the North returned transformed - not different, but consolidated in what they are. The North tied together everything with invisible threads - individuals, peoples, and continents…

***

Throughout history, peoples have moved from North to South, to warm regions and seas. This movement composes the tale of civilizations, peoples, and races, wars between people of the North and people of the South. But, despite conquering everything there was to conquer, they still could not survive in warm climates. The path of history is the path of degeneration – whether faster or slower, still equally inevitable. And they all quickly perished, dissolving into a sea of foreignness.

Polar travelers and explorers are a phenomenon of our times. They appeared only after all the other points of the planet had been reached by overseas travels and conquests, once not only the peaks but also the valleys had all been mastered. There was nothing on Earth worth having anymore. Their direction is no longer South, but North.

These are the Hyperboreans of our time, those who leave the warmth of their homes and the seeming security of their homelands in order to set off again. For the primordial…

***

IRAN[38]

Black emblems, black scarves.

Cohorts of warriors in black robes.

Flash of steel, a knight riding through a field, enduring the sparrow's mock.

Shepherds and their flocks scattered across the plateau. Their children will gain glory in battle. They will rush towards deserts and unknown lands, over high mountains like the flock of thirty birds of Simurgh flying non-stop until the end of the world.

The angry king was whipping the sea, the army followed his cue, but by then it was already too late; the empire was bursting into the air. Under the day's events, a clearly discernible chaos was emerging. Intrigue and adultery reigned in the courts. Concubines, princes' whores, were ruling famous cities and provinces. They ruled with cruelty in debauchery and blood.

They forgot Zoroaster and the priests who worshiped fire.

They forgot the eagle and the snake and the sacred books in which Ormuzd and Ahriman fought as light and darkness.

They forgot the words of Ahura Mazda, sharp as arrows and woven out of flame.

This lasted a thousand years. Until one day, out of the desert emerged followers of another prophet under the crescent moon and green banners. Iran embraced faith in a single, omnipotent, invisible God.

---

38 Featured in the first English edition of *Return of Myth* (Melbourne: Manticore Press, 2016), previously unpublished in Serbian.

O, extinct glory of the ancient race! Walls and beggars, darkness of ages. Walls and empires, lonely fortresses destroyed by wind, sharpened swords, and the yellow dust of years.

You shall rise in new light.

***

CITY OF THE GODS

Somewhere in a vague and distant region (which some place in the North and others in the East) is a city that exceeds everything that humans have ever created. Above the city is a tower from which one can see each and every populated country and even the dark and inhuman fields marking the end of the world. In its center is a field used by the Gods for play. But above it is a hall with twelve thrones, of which the highest one belongs to the most powerful among the Gods. His name means "One" and he is the father of Gods and men. As he sits, two ravens rest on his shoulders and tell him of everything going on in the world.

Surrounding this hall are numerous castles. Waves of ice roar up against some, others are raised into the sky, while some rest on seacoast. There is also a huge gate under which is a grove with leaves of red and gold. It leads to another, even more spacious hall where feasts are held all day long, where brave warriors are welcomed as guests. These warriors were killed in battle. The most powerful among the Gods is the Father of Fallen Warriors. They ever eagerly feast on boar meat cooked in a magic cauldron. The father of the Gods does not eat wild boar, instead he only drinks wine; he feeds his own flesh to two voracious wolves which follow him always and everywhere.

This is Asgard, City of the Gods, a city built by the giants and the Gods. It is impossible to describe all the wonders and treasures it contains. Right next to Odin stands invincible, powerful Thor, who defends the abode of the Gods with his iron gloves and deadly *Mjölnir*, the mallet or hammer that always comes back into the hands of he who throws it. His estate is called *Thrudvangr* or *Thrudheim*, which means "fields of power." The Goddess Idunn keeps the golden apples in her shrine, thanks to which the Gods do not age. At the southern end of the sky is the castle Gimlé, "brighter than the sun", which will remain in place even when the whole world collapses. There is also a deer that every day nibbles the leaves of the Sacred Ash, the World Tree, whose roots reach into the dark underground and from which flows the dew that is the source of all the rivers of Valhalla. At the very end of the sky, by Bifröst bridge, sits Heimdall, the lookout of the Gods who will sound his miraculous horn when the battle for the end of the world begins.

We owe this description of Asgard, with all of these fantastic details, to Snorri Sturluson, an Icelander who between 1222 and 1225 wrote the *Edda*, a complex compilation of the myths and beliefs of the peoples of old Scandinavia. In fact, these beliefs were common to all the tribes and peoples of the entire Germanic-speaking area, or perhaps even wider. It should be said that the scientific world long rejected the Edda as the fruit of its author's imagination - that is, until an even older manuscript was discovered in Iceland four centuries after Sturluson's death, in 1643, by Bishop Sveinsson. This book is called the *Elder Edda*, as opposed to Sturluson's *Younger Edda*, and was immediately included in the Eddic cycle that would eventually become the subject of serious scholarship.

The *Edda* contains the story of the Aesir, a kind of genealogy of the Gods, as well as an account of their migrations and the countries through which they passed. Sturluson's story begins in a region located north of the Black Sea. This sea divides the world into three parts: to its East is what is called Asia, to its West is called Europe or Énéa, and to the North of the Black Sea is Great or Icy Sweden ("Great Sweden", *Svíþjóð*, or *Svetja*, which means Sacred or Bright Land - as distinct from Sweden in Scandinavia). This sets the stage for future great events. Through this Sweden, we read in Sturluson's work *Heimskringla* ("The Circle of the World"), runs the River Tanais, which was earlier called Tanaquisl or Vanaquisl (and is the Don River which flows into the Black Sea).

The author claims that the region around the confluence of the Don was called the Land of the Vanir or Settlement of Vanir, the first rivals and later allies of the Aesir Gods. The first war in the world was waged between them. The Aesir learned magical skills from the Vanir, who are older and wiser than the Aesir. And further: "The country east of the Tanaquisl in Asia was called Asaland, or Asaheim, and the chief city in that land was called Asgard. In that city was a chief called Odin, and it was a great place for sacrifice" (*Ynglinga Saga 2*).

The story contained in the *Younger Edda* is extremely accurate, not only geographically but chronologically. Odin left his land because he knew that, according to prophecy, his descendants would inhabit the Northern part of the world. He leaves his two brothers in Asgard. His son was called Skjöld and he ruled Denmark, Skjold's grandson was named Fróði and ruled in the time of Emperor Augustus – "when Christ was born." These events fall in the first century of the common era.

Odin's path, an old chronicle claims, passed through the land of the Saxons. He appointed his son Beldr or Baldr as ruler of Westphalia. He came via Denmark to Sweden (the one in Scandinavia), which was then ruled by Gylfi. But Gylfi, defeated by the God's wisdom and beauty, handed over royal power to Odin and set out for Asgard. He set off on this journey "secretly, disguised as an old man." Finally, after an exhausting journey, he discovered the "high castle with a roof covered in gilded shields." Inside, he saw many great people who, just like those in mythical Valhalla, feasted as guests at the table or fought with arms.

Odin's glorious and long reign ends in the following way: in his new land he died of disease. Before his death, he told his subjects that he was returning to the abode of the Gods (we read this in the *Ynglinga Saga*) and promised that he would receive his friends there in the future. After his death, he appeared to Swedes before great battles, "to some giving victory, others inviting to join him." His body was burned in a pyre, which gave off a "brilliant light." He left his throne to Njörðr of the Vanir from Nóatún. One of Njörðr's descendants, Sveigðir, will repeat Gylfi's feat and will go straight to the land of the Turks and Great Sweden to find the old residence of Odin. The journey takes five whole years. In Svíþjóð, in Great Sweden, he found plenty of tribesmen and married a woman named Vana (whose name tells us that she was of the divine race of the Vanir, or the Vyatichi as they were known to Slavs).

Are the Gods the fathers of humans or are humans the fathers of the Gods? Do people create Gods or, on the contrary, did the Gods create humans as their companions, helpers, and comrades? The story of Odin and his kin we have just introduced is undoubtedly correct. It could be a memory of deified rulers and ancestors, but this does not call into question the cult and belief in the divine Father of the Gods and men.

Following the narration of this ancient chronicle, the Russian explorer Vladimir Shcherbakov believed he had found the mythical Asgard. He found it right in the place to which the chronicle of Aesir pointed: Nisa, the ancient capital of Parthia, the rival of Rome in the East and, alongside Rome, the largest and most extensive empire of that age.

As noted by Shcherbakov, the poverty of historical sources for Parthian beliefs is devastating. But archaeological reconstruction of the Parthian capital and its cult places comes to the rescue. Without dwelling on all the architectural correspondences between mythical Asgard and ancient Nisa (that is Old Nisa, but the situation with cult places in New Nisa is almost identical), let us mention that this is a veritable "copy" of Valhalla. There is a mysterious Round Temple. The contours of the walls are square but within them there is a circular room twelve meters high. On the second level of this hall were pillars and colored clay statues. These were statues of the Gods or deified ancestors. The Old Parthians nurtured the cult of the ancestors: "The deified ancestors, the Aesir, received guardians and other warriors here. These were statues that would have, as in other temples, created the effect of their presence here."

This explorer noticed one seemingly incidental detail: Odin, as is written in the *Edda*, participated in feasts alongside his warriors. But he never ate there, wine was enough for him. In other words, his presence was symbolic, not "real."

A series of highly complex and obvious coincidences may not yet prove that memory of the actual Asgard - the abode of the Gods in Old Nisa, the capital of Parthia - is factually preserved in the descriptions of Asgard from Scandinavian myths. But they confirm the oneness of the beliefs of so many spatially remote peoples, beliefs which, as the *Edda* points out, originated in the region above the Black Sea, the actual environ of the Aesir and the Vanir. The Chinese chronicles of the Tang dynasty called the Parthian state *Ansi*.

∗∗∗

SYMBOLS OF HYPERBOREA

The Eagle

According to Greek legend, eagles are the guardians of the Golden Age. "There is the land of the gold-guarding griffins," Herodotus quoted ancient legend, "and beyond them the Hyperboreans..."[39] This gold is of the first and best age, the Golden Age; in this cheerful legend, originality and freedom are attained. He who has never seen the flight of eagles, at heights which other birds cannot reach, or he who has never heard eagles' cries of joy in the wild, does not know that this is an omen of a very different and free life, one released from the bondage of the material world, in the aether. More so than any other animal, whether bird or beast, the eagle is associated with the beyond, the otherworldly.

Hence why the eagle has, ever since Rome, been a symbol of eternal empires, timeless kingdoms that rise above earthly chaos to realize the heavenly order within the transient world of death, randomness, and the ephemeral. The imperial eagle, from Rome to Byzantium and from Byzantium to the Russian or Serbian imperial eagles, not only symbolizes this idea, but the great conquerors and founders of empires generally bore eagle-like traits. Since ancient times the "eagle nose" was taken to be a physiognomic sign, an external trait of nobleness. The "eagle eye" is fearless, for it has the power to dispel all the phantasms of the inferior part of the human psyche.

Later, when empires no longer needed such people, the "eagle profile" would appear only in exceptional cases.

---

39 Herodotus, *Histories* IV:13, p. 680

The cities overflowed with plebs. Estates and castles were penetrated by masses whose traits can no longer be described. They resemble everything except the time when man was called upon to be something more than merely brave. The temples are occupied by merchants and money changes. Scum infiltrates the palace. The facial features of the distinguished become softer, more sensual, almost effeminate. The "eagles" retreat to their hidden nests, to their distant mountainous habitats - a reliable sign that the age of the hero has rung out and the empire has followed the path of decadence and disintegration.

It seems to us that the capacities of animal species are potentialities given to every man; they are "masks that fall off the human face" (Ernst Jünger). Each species contains a trait which is in the very least latent, present within man. In other words, man (any person) can become like a wolf, a lion, or an eagle, but also like a rodent, a hyena, or a pig. A significant part of this pertains to heritage but, as it is said, after the age of thirty everyone is responsible for their own features…

To become like an eagle, to become an eagle, the only animal that can stare into the sun, represents one of the, dare we say, highest possibilities ever given to the human being.

The Deer

The deer is one of the great and timeless symbols of the North - of Hyperborea. Valery Demin quotes Pausanias, the ancient writer of the second century, who in his work *Description of Hellas* (X, V) states that the first priest-prophet of the Temple of Apollo at Delphi was called Olen – *Olenj, Jelen* – i.e. "Deer." Above all, the deer is a symbol of the sun, which in Hyperborea never sets. On the Kola Peninsula in Russian Lapland, in the Far North of the continent, according to the same author, there are shrines of the Sami people, so-called *sedie*, piles of stones on top of which are mounted stag skulls with horns. The deer is one of the oldest art motifs, which, with astonishing frequency, we find on the walls of caves and ancient weaponry.

There is a picture taken in 1942 during the German bombing of Murmansk, in which a stag is seen in the foreground, with a slightly tilted head, startled by the explosions, while in the gray sky above him fly German bombers. War photography rises to the level of symbols which, like all others, eludes interpretations and explanations. Sir Edwin Landseer attained worldly fame for painting deer motifs in the Scottish hills in a way that goes beyond mere realism.

The stag, like the lion, wolf, or eagle, reveals an archetype and an ancient memory. More than any others, the deer is most directly related to the Northern ancestral homeland, Hyperborea. In fact, the deer - the solar deer, the deer of the forests and steppes of the North - is but a memory of Hyperborea, lost along with man. Herman Wirth argued that the deer was the subject of a most ancient Hyperborean cult and that its raised horns symbolize the solar divinity, the Son of God, at the moment when, with hands raised high, he rises above the chaos and darkness of the Earth. Perhaps that is why this noble and distinct animal, in any environment and any country, looks like such a complete stranger to us.

The Raven

Every winter, when he goes to Hyperborea, Apollo is accompanied by ravens and song. Aristeas of Metapontum, who accompanied Apollo to Hyperborea, reappeared at his native place after death in the form of a raven. Whenever Odin climbs his tower to watch the earth beneath the morning sun, two ravens land on Odin's outstretched arms. The name of the first is Thought, and the name of the second is Memory. Hyperborean Apollo is generally associated with birds. Like the raven, the swan is a bird of Hyperborea. A statuette found in Dupljaja, near Vršac in the Banat region, depicts an enigmatic deity, a man with a bird's head. His chariot is pulled through the air by swans. On this "birdlike idol on a cart drawn by pond birds", Živojin Andrejić says: "This depiction is undoubtedly linked to the myth of the Delphic Apollo who spends six months in the land of the Hyperboreans, a distant and fog-covered region…and then spends the next six months in sunny Greece. It could be said that this is the forerunner of Apollo-Belenus, who is in our region worshipped as the god of the Sun."

The ancient Germanic epic tradition calls the raven the "swan of red beak." In a happier time, the raven was considered an auspicious omen: if he followed the hero, it meant that his sword would be saturated with blood that day, that the outcome of his endeavor would be favorable. The mysterious connection between heroes and the raven is highlighted in myth. In the Ossetian myth of the Nart people - the strongest people in the world - we find this motif: after the battle fought for the Heavenly Kingdom, a son's severed hand is dropped into his mother's lap by a raven, and she thus learns of his evil destiny.

We find an identical motif in the songs of the Kosovo cycle, where the same happens to Jugović's mother: the raven lowers the bloodied hand of her son Damjan into her lap.

Symbols are ambiguous. As a general rule, they have both "positive", luminous and "negative", dark aspects. Hence, the lost Northern homeland can be symbolized not only by the "white bird", the swan, but also an ominous black raven. One testifies to joy, the other reminds of loss.

The French poet Arthur Rimbaud sensed this strange, dark joy carried by the raven in his poem "The Ravens":

> *Lord, when the meadow freezes…*
> *Upon deflowered nature*
> *Let fall from great skies*
> *The dear, delicious crows.*

The Wolf[40]

A silent shadow, stooped and gray, the wolf runs in the last twilight, his eyes glowing in the dark.

This is the wolf of the Northern forests and the old Icelandic Eddas.

This is Geri and Freki, Odin's divine wolves. An angry pack of wolves also follows Saint Sava. This is Borges' last wolf of England, who knows that the iron of his death has already been forged.

This is the wolf that walks in a cage, bound, confused, knowing that the hour of his death is near.

---

40 Featured in the first English edition of *Return of Myth*, first published in Serbian in Boris Nad, *Nemi bogovi [Silent Gods]* (Belgrade: Žagor, 2008).

This twilight is known as the Twilight of the Gods, the irrevocable and final end of the world.

This is his time, the age of the Wolf, the "era of winds and wolves, when shields are broken." And when wolves devour the Moon and the Sun, their race shall be extinct. In battle, in storm, and in the heavenly fire, the world shall end.

Until that happens, it shall stroll alone, confused by the darkness of the cage or forest but with no way out.

The wolf trembles, no water and no blood of man can quench his thirst. The chase concludes his winding run. Odin's eye is watching him. In vain, wolf, you shall die, too. Your fate is written in the stars and on ancient stone. Neither Odin or Thor, nor any other Gods, can change this.

***

Stories and Chronicles

ODIN

One day, a cursed ship made from the nails of the dead shall darken the world. It shall be preceded by a three-year-long winter, the howling of a wolf, the crowing of three red roosters, and many other equally ominous signs. As he ascends on his aerial throne – an immensely tall tower that rises above all that was ever built by either Gods or men – Odin watches it grow every night.

Until that time comes, until that hour strikes, Odin will each morning look at the world with joy. From the top of his tower, he will look down at the vast lands of giants and people, seeing the earth shine under the first glimmers of the morning sun.

And then, on Odin's outstretched hand two ravens will land; Thought is the name of the first and the name of the other is Memory.

The earth is green and fertile now, but it was not always so. In order for this earth to become a homeland for people, many hard battles with rocky giants had to be won. The beauty of the world is perishable. There will be a time when all this will perish in fire. Heimdall, the guardian of the bridge that connects heaven and earth, will announce it with a single powerful blow of his horn.

This will be the moment when the giant serpent of Midgard, green as the sea, awakens. From its powerful movement the world will shake. This will be the day when the bridge Bifröst, with a terrible roar, will collapse under the weight of the celestial armies. The day when the celestial wolves will devour the moon and the sun, when a dense eclipse shall cover the world, and Odin and Thor, and many other Gods, will fall in an unequal fight.

The battle will be fierce but short. The outcome of the battle at the end of the world is already predetermined. The Gods and all those people who will fight by their side – all those who have ever fought bravely on this earth - cannot change it. And no matter how bravely they fight this time, black Surtr, who will ride into the battle before the children of Muspel, will eventually set the ground on fire with his sword brighter than the sun, whose flames will flare up in all four corners of the world. One by one, the stars will extinguish. The earth will eventually sink into the ocean. Non-Being shall prevail over Being. This will be the most famous and most difficult battle ever fought since the beginning of time, a battle in which the Gods and men are not required to win, but only to fulfill their duty, irrespective of the outcome, to carry it out until the very end.

Odin knows this. He knows the secret of the runes. And he knows that, unable to endure insult, he will one day cast his spear, which will bring death to many, including his own son, and will thus initiate the fatal chain of events that we know as the "Twilight of the Gods." Odin knows that he will die in the first battle, swallowed, devoured by the monstrous wolf Fenrir. He knows this because he spent nine days and nine nights hanging upside down over the face of the abyss, hanging on to the roots of the great ash tree, and he knows this because he sacrificed his own eye to drink from Mimir's spring, the spring of memories.

Odin is prepared for all of this. When the hour strikes, he will not, like reckless Freyr, mourn his lost sword. At dusk on the day of the unspeakable eclipse, he will bravely step onto the battlefield, leading the Einherjar (even their quarrels will be dear to him). Finally showing his face underneath his golden helmet, he will not hesitate to look death straight in the eye.

When, after all this, the first people will emerge out of the forest of memories onto the earth, resurrected like spring, the surviving Aesir will remember Odin's deeds and will remember his magical runes.

It should be noted that, from the vantage point of myth, the fact that we now no longer possess the right key to the mystery of the runes is not only to be expected, but is also quite logical. Knowledge is memory. The memory of Fimbultyr's golden runes, knowledge of the Golden Age, will be renewed through the fire of ruin and the resurrection of divine and human powers, and in this fire will be renewed the entire cosmos.

***

ACHILLES

I will die before the city is conquered. Before the fire cleanses the streets of the Troy I hate, before the blood washes away all the insults inflicted upon the Danaans. It is my destiny, until that time comes, to each and every day stand silently in front of an enraged and furious crowd. One of those dark-skinned people is my killer.

I do not feel fear while rushing in my chariot through the tumult of war, approaching the walls and gates of Troy (through which I will never pass). Their hatred, spears, and arrows cannot hurt me – not before the onset of the appointed time. As Xanthus, the horse that understands the secret signs of the Gods, warns me every morning, I do not have much time left.

I am the son of Peleus who sailed with the Argonauts, my mother is a Goddess, not a mortal woman. As a boy I was bathed in the River Styx. Since that time my body has hardened like iron in the furnace.

I do not feel envy toward the other heroes with whom we share this vast battlefield, for I know that I am the best of both armies. There is loot that I could win, but it is of no significance to me, because I will not, like Agamemnon, return home. I do not yearn for wealth; to have kings honor me daily is enough. Who else among the Greek heroes can take pride in how he has destroyed as many towns as I? My sword has brought death to many, and it will bring death to many more. I remember Hector, the greatest among the children of Ilion - by his death I avenged the unfortunate Patroclus. I remember the Amazon Penthesilea who died in my arms. I also remember Thersites, whom I killed because he mocked my tears as I mourned her death. Everything I have done, I have done for glory. I despise long, tranquil life and death in bed. I instead choose the happiness of the warrior. I know that one day they shall raise shrines and temples to me, and the Greeks shall say my name alongside the names of the Gods and other brave men in battle. I know that one day there will be a king and conqueror of the world who will want to be like me. My mother does not need to be ashamed that she gave birth to a mere mortal and not a god.

All of this is not enough for victory. The Trojans will be defeated not by the insane courage of Achilles, but by the treacherous cunning of Odysseus.

***

ATLANTIS: THE KINGDOM OF SHADOWS

A vast island, or even a continent, suddenly rose out of the emerald sea, out of the giant world ocean beyond the Pillars of Hercules, only to just as unexpectedly sink again. This happened in some indeterminate, distant time. According to Plato, this calamity took place in 9600 BC.

This collapse was the consequence of the wrath of the gods, of Zeus himself in fact. It will disappear in fire, a heavenly fire that will rain down upon the island. The waves will then merge into one to overwhelm this essentially already stagnant, petrified world. According to Plato's account (based on Egyptian legend), this catastrophe will take place over a single day and night. In its place, according to sailors, the sea will remain barren for millennia: one of Plato's contemporaries speaks of "12 days of sailing beyond the Pillars of Hercules" (the Strait of Gibraltar) hampered by sandbars, silt, seaweed, and pumice (from a volcanic eruption) reminiscent of the Sargasso Sea. The Carthaginian sailor Himilco reported that "thick seaweed rises above the gulf", "abundant sea creatures swim amongst all the sea, and great terror, because of these creatures, abides in the deep" of this water where "no breezes drive the ship."[41]

Memory of this island, nevertheless, would live on longer, for thousands and thousands of years, in dark and misty legends of a "land of the dead" or "green land" lying somewhere in the West in the infinite Ocean (hence Greenland's name). This is the forbidden world of the dead. Sailing beyond the Pillars of Hercules would remain forbidden for a long time, and not only because of the

---

41 Avenius, *Ora Maritima* (trans. by Ralph Morley, *ToposText*, 2018).

Phoenician monopoly over the sea. An English map from 1500 shows Atlantis connected to Labrador and Greenland as if it still existed.

Dwarves and Giants

Its inhabitants, according to René Guénon, came from the North at the dawn of human history, from a country that was suddenly destroyed by cataclysmic cold.

Here, on this paradisal island-continent, refugees from Hyperborea, true man-gods, spawned a new human race: the Cro-Magnons of perfect features, a race which knew seamanship, agriculture, magic, and the art of metalworking. These skills were taught to them by the Titan Atlas, who, ancient tradition says, carried the world on his shoulders. Diodorus Siculus says that this is a mythical expression of the fact that Atlas was a connoisseur of astronomy and the inventor of the sphere.

Named after the Titan Atlas, this civilization, according to Plato, cherished the custom of sacrificing bulls (the cult animal of Atlantis) and, according to other authors, they practiced a ritual of eating fresh bull meat and drinking bull blood - a custom that would be preserved for a long time in the Mediterranean region, mostly in its Western part. Spanish bullfighting is a remnant of their ancient, sacred games with bulls, and archaeological evidence finds the very same cult on Crete. A trace of this comes down to us in the form of the vague legend of the Minotaur to which girls and boys were scarified in the labyrinth in which he was allegedly imprisoned. Today, both the ocean and a mountain in Africa owe their name to Atlas.

The Atlanteans possessed metal - the mysterious *orichalcum* - astronomy, navigation, shipbuilding, and writing skills. On the island they had coconuts, elephants, and according to some researchers, corn and bananas. If we believe Plato and his Egyptian source, their military strength was without equal in the world for quite a long time. Hence why their colonies spread throughout the Old and even the New World - in America. This colonization generally proceeded in the northwest-southeast direction across the globe from the Northwest Atlantic down to the Pacific, leaving behind many traces, one of the most striking coming down to us in the names of the African Moors, the Biblical Amorites, and the Pacific Maori, names which all mean "people who came from the West." Archeology provides us with unexpected confirmation of this myth in the form of the so-called Cro-Magnon enigma. Cro-Magnon man appeared suddenly and without transitional forms, appearing in North-West Europe and pushing the Neanderthals, dwarves just over one meter tall, into the mountain hills which would, as in later times, become the refuge of archaic races.

It should be kept in mind that this scheme fits ancient legends and fables, such as those of dwarves who inhabit caves and live in the bowels of the earth and those of giants who live on islands or descended from them (the Cro-Magnon had an average height of over two meters). There are also the struggles of the Gods against the Titans who all come from the West (and the legend of the dragon fits another mystery of the Earth's past, that is the disappearance of giant lizards from the Jurassic period).

Flying Cities and Flaming Arrows

Other admirers of the myths of Atlantis have added just as miraculous details to this story. Diodorus Siculus, in the third book of his *Bibliotheca historica* which describes the geography of the East Atlantic region, recounts a complex story of wars which the Amazons, and then another people of "women-warriors", the Gorgons, fought against Atlantic colonists in Northwest Africa. This history is full of incredible details and miraculous twists. The great Greek geographer Strabo as well as Pomponius Mela believed Plato, and wrote of Atlantis as a completely real country. In his book *The Atlanteans*, Vladimir Shcherbakov speaks of a race of giants, of man-gods who:

> possessed technology and aircraft of various constructions which flew at an altitude of several kilometers. Their science was supposedly close to art and resembled magic...They had rockets, jets and railways...There was no computational technology, but anyone from Atlantis could successfully rival a computer in their complex calculations [due to thinking powers incomparably greater than those of today's man, but also due to long lives, which numbered in the hundreds of years - B.N]. Instead of computer games, there were live games...There were also industrial centers with underground factories and scientific research complexes...as well as flying and underwater cities protected by transparent domes.

And furthermore: "Extremely tall - up to three meters - the Atlanteans could affect all living things...Their proto-civilization existed. But so did they have wars - magical ones, since we cannot even call them anything else because of our narrow horizons." These wars led to the destruction of this island's technocratic civilization, to the scattering of its colonies throughout the world, and to a cataclysm that affected the whole Earth and all of mankind, leading to geological, climatic, and other changes, including the extermination of some human races and many animal species (such as mammoths). Were these not the wars fought with fantastic weapons described in the ancient Indian epic, the *Mahabharata?* The third book of the epic, for example, mentions the "flying city" of Saubha: Salva rushed to Dvaraka with the flying city of Saubha and attacked without mercy the young prince of Vrishni, after which he flew back into the sky on Saubha. One of the weapons used in the battle was called "the weapon of wisdom", *Prajnastra*. The battle of the Gods takes place in the air, above a sea, and includes weapons which "penetrate all" - thunder and flaming arrows which destroy the flying city, plunging it into the sea. *Vimana* are the aircraft described in the *Ramayana*. Some of them, the so-called *Jalayan*, were able to move through air and water, while others, called *Trichakra-rama*, were "three-wheeled vehicles designed specifically for aerial operations."

It is difficult, if not impossible, to determine the time and place of such epic battles. But it is almost certain that they are not the product of mere imagination, that they hold memory of something ancient and very significant, something presently beyond our capacity for understanding.

The Earthquake that Marked the End of a World

According to Shcherbakov (as well as other authors), traces of the proto-civilization of Atlantis are scattered all over the globe - from the Atlantic to America and from the Himalayas to the Pacific – in the form of burial remains of long-lived giants, and in archaeological remains and traces of a highly technologically developed civilization surpassing all others seen in history. One of these necropoles was found near the Khalkhyn Gol in Inner Mongolia in the 1940s by an excavation led by I.A. Efremov. Beneath slabs of stone were found the remains of a giant whose height was two-and-a-half meters.

The Tibetan Lama Lobsang P. Rampa (who attained the highest level of spiritual initiation in Tibet) describes in great details what he called the key event of his life: he visited a cave in Tibet where he saw, among other things, flying devices, holographic projections, and human bodies preserved inside a sarcophagus of black stone, the largest male of which was of a staggering height of five meters.

Similar places, according to Lama Lobsang P. Rampa, can be found all over the world. Yet most amazing of all is that this Lama's visit to one such secret place enabled him to experience reality as it was thousands of years ago: "The sphere showed the world of the distant past...Different people walked the Earth...Mysterious machines flew just above the ground, machines which could then soar miles upwards." What follows is a description of destruction, in which the whole of Earth is covered in ash and scarlet-red clouds. But hidden places of this sort have remained to testify to the existence of an "ancient maritime civilization of the age of Atlantis" and its superior achievements.

In 1869, in the town of Leeuwarden in the North of the Netherlands, the remains of an ancient book were discovered which provided belated and unexpected confirmation to Plato and the classical geographers' acceptance of the existence of Atlantis. It was named the *Oera Linda Book* after the family that owned it, and it contained an altogether exhaustive history of the Frisians, an exceptionally old people who are mostly Germanized today. Among other things, it speaks of the submerged land of Atland (another variation of which name is given as "Aldland"), and the book itself, according to its authors, was first written down 3,449 years after the destruction of Atland (the copy kept in the Leeuwarden library is, of course, only a later transcript from the year 1256). The disaster that befell Atland is described as follows:

> During the whole summer the sun had been hidden behind the clouds, as if unwilling to look upon the earth. There was perpetual calm, and the damp mist hung like a wet sail over the houses and the marshes. The air was heavy and oppressive, and in men's hearts was neither joy nor cheerfulness. In the midst of this stillness the earth began to tremble as if she was dying. The mountains opened to vomit forth fire and flames. Some sank into the bosom of the earth, and in other places mountains rose out of the plain. Aldland, called by the seafaring people Atland, disappeared, and the wild waves rose so high over hill and dale that everything was buried in the sea. Many people were swallowed up by the earth, and others who had escaped the fire perished in the water. It was not only in Finda's land that the earth vomited fire, but also in Twiskland (Germany). Whole forests were burned one after the other, and when the wind blew from that quarter our land was covered with ashes. Rivers changed their course, and at their mouths new islands were formed of sand and drift. During three years this continued, but at length it ceased, and forests became visible…[42]

---

42 *The Oera Linda Book* (trans. by William R. Sandbach; London: Trübner & Co., Ludgate Hill, 1876).

The Atlantean Legacy

Perhaps the blonde Guanches, the indigenous inhabitants encountered by Spanish conquistadors in the Canary Islands (who were completely exterminated around 1500), were the last descendants of the unfortunate Atlanteans? Spanish monks recorded the myths of these ancient peoples as believing that God forgot them and left them to live on this remote island. Perhaps the Basques are also descendants of the mythical Atlanteans (as Otto Muck claims in his book *All about Atlantis* there are certain linguistic similarities and various customs which correspond between the Basques and certain Amerindian tribes on the opposite side of the ocean)? The Mayan and Aztec civilizations and ancient Egypt and Carthage exhibited certain traits which quite easily and naturally link them together. The so-called cyclopean buildings scattered throughout the Old and New Worlds might be the remains of the Atlanteans' building skills. Perhaps the Azores are the last trace of the vanished continent, the snow-covered peaks of Atlantis' mountains, as Plato described them?

Cro-Magnon man appeared around 40,000 years ago, bringing with him the advent of agriculture, sailing, and art. The Cro-Magnons also brought a characteristic obsession with death (which may be the source of the custom of mummification that is characteristic of many civilizations of the Atlantic region), the cult of the bull, the color red (with which they "coated" their dead), and the sacrality of bone and stone (which is the "bone of the land"). This is what has been described as the "Atlantean cultural complex." Moreover, it is not excluded that the Atlantean heritage included witchcraft, ritual cannibalism, and the cruel custom of child sacrifice recorded on both sides of the Atlantic, for instance among the Aztecs and the Carthaginians - might this be another instance of the degeneration and perversion of the late Atlantean tradition? Plato alludes to various perversions attributed to late Atlantean civilization, but this list of "sins" is neither defined nor explicit in his work.

Cro-Magnon man, as has already been said, appeared suddenly "out of archaeological nowhere." There are no transitional forms between him and the autochthonous Neanderthal, whom he suppressed in a relatively short span of time. Aurignacian man and his related forms were not the result of the evolution of Neanderthal man into Cro-Magnon, but rather of degenerate forms, sub variants of Cro-Magnon, or the fruit of his crossings with the native population. This invasion gradually created the Old Europe of Iberia, the Iberian race. Only later in the Neolithic will the Aryans invade from some mysterious center in the Far North of Eurasia, which some Irish myths remember as the coming of the Tuatha Dé Danann, a truly divine race whom they record as at war with the Fomorians, a people of sailors from the West (the descendants of the Atlanteans?), encountered on the island.

All of these events in question do not belong to history, but rather to the mythical, legendary past of the Earth. Their remembering does not make them any less true; on the contrary, it is the legend that is important and worth remembering and knowing.

***

BAGHDAD

> "He remembered that the dreams of men belong to God, and that Maimonides wrote that the words of a dream are divine, when they are all separate and clear and are spoken by someone invisible."
> - J. L. Borges, The Secret Miracle

I dreamed that I found myself in Baghdad.

The mighty ivory walls towered over the red-hot sand; above the desert there were horrific images quivering in a swelter, in unbearable ardor.

The city had a hundred golden gates that glowed in the morning sun. A stream of travelers collided in front of the city gates. The movement of armies, vast troops on camels and horses at gallop were raising a cloud of yellow dust that shrouded the view of the minarets and gilded cupolas of mosques. This must be, after all, the time of prayer, because the protracted muezzin chanting permeated through the sound of the horses and the shouts of the horsemen.

I passed through it all and slipped through the Caliph's guards holding spears and curved sabers, whereafter I found myself in a tight street flooded by streams of dirty water. From the dried mud hovel, dark-skinned women with big, dark, warm eyes were curiously peeping out; a pack of poor, barefoot urchins ran past me screaming at the top of their lungs. I did not understand the language spoken by the city's inhabitants. However, I understood that invaders were approaching the city: hordes of slant-eyed warriors, of forty, fifty, or even a hundred thousand horsemen pouring in like an avalanche from the Mongolian steppes...

Baghdad had hundreds or thousands of these same streets, and countless squares where fairs and colorful bazaars were held throughout the day. Merchants from Cathay with slanted eyes, blue-eyed Muscovites, Genoese and Tatars, caravans from Abyssinia, Cairo, Libya - all of them barely speaking a word of Arabic. At the mosque entrances sat scribes with red turbans, thoughtfully inscribing calligraphic characters on camel skins. Under the stands on the squares were money changers counting copper, silver, and gold coins. In front of a fabulous palace I heard drums and *zurna* and saw a golden palanquin with a cortege following it, and in it the Caliph of Baghdad himself; he was dressed in silk with golden threads, black and white pearls. Some mighty prince from the lands of the evening light rushed to meet him. A hundred knights with silver armor and colorful banners were surrounding the sovereign with proudly raised heads.

But what is earthly power, when downfall is already written in the stars? One court astrologer misinterpreted the signs of the disaster; others spoke of a comet visible in the night sky foretelling plague. And indeed the plague appeared in Basra.

I was a stranger in Baghdad, but I still knew that in some dark alley dwelled an old man with a beard white as snow. When I finally found him, he was on his deathbed. He was lying on a bed dressed in tattered rags as expiring, painful cramps quivered his emaciated body; he certainly was more than a hundred years old. He was the most miserable old man in the whole city. Poor old man! I leaned over him, under squinting candle light, but did not manage to hear the words that were coming out of his dry mouth in agony. I realized that he was dying, and that with his death the hordes of wild

Tatars would break through the walls, causing the whole of Baghdad to perish in flames. The Caliph would be murdered in his palace, its citizens would be slaughtered or taken as slaves. Blood will flow in the streets...

In God's eyes, the lives of these hundreds of thousands of people depended not on the mighty Caliph, but on this miserable old man exhaling for his last time in front of my eyes.

I realized that even I could not avoid the slaughter, for I failed to understand the words he whispered to me on his deathbed.

***

TWO DREAMS

I had a dream in which I was walking along a dimly lit corridor, thinking of already lived experience: the moment in which the spirit leaves the body. The thought of it is enough to repeat the experience. A sort of spasm or loss of consciousness overtakes me, after which I am left lying on the cold floor, staring for a long time at a half-open door leading into a very dark room. Then I watched my own body, observing it as I floated invisibly in the surrounding air. People unknown to me gathered around the lifeless body. At that moment, I woke up.

Although sleep has its eerie moments – the moment of losing consciousness, for example – on the whole it is not unpleasant. I think about it while I lie awake in bed. Liberation from the body at first brings chills to me and then an extraordinary sense of freedom. Unpleasant is also the view of the darkened room – the entrance to the second mode, the world beyond death and bodily existence. Darkness is opaque only because the spirit cannot be easily separated from the body.

Immediately afterwards, I had another dream in which I was able to take on different forms, whether that of a rock lying in the desert, red and blue pebbles scattered on the bottom of a dried stream, or even become a colorful part of earthly crust - but not part of the Earth, but rather a landscape from another planet.

In that state I was exposed to the blows of unknown forces. They caused painful and deafening shock, leaving behind traces of sinuous marks and scars resembling those left by a lightning strike – ones that, therefore, can also give me structure. This observation in no way changes my position: their impact is no less painful because of that. Moreover, the electrical discharges are being amplified – the moment in which it reached the highest intensity, blinding me, was also the moment of awakening.

Awake, I realize that sleep can lead to a logical connection: these are dreams of death, or what follows it. This was, however, preceded by a strange feeling with which I emerged from the second dream: I have already died once in another world so that, after a long wandering, I would wake up in this hour on Earth.

***

PANNONIA[43]

Once upon a time, fearless Sarmatians, in an extraordinarily beautiful image, fought and lost a battle with Roman legions on the frozen Danube, because they rushed on horseback into the impenetrable battle formation of legionnaires who had been hardened in countless battles around the world, from Britain to Libya. This battle of mythical beauty took place not far from today's Belgrade.

Just like their Scythian cousins, whose barbaric customs were described by Herodotus, the Sarmatians worshipped an unknown god in the form of a sword plunged into the ground, a god to whom neither idols nor temples were erected. The Scythians, if Herodotus is to be believed, offered this god human sacrifices on a kind of raised platform made of reeds, under which the "sacred sword" was ritually sprinkled with the blood of the sacrificed captives.

Somewhere around the time when the Sarmatian name ceased to be mentioned in annals and chronicles, the Scytho-Sarmatian motif of the "sacred sword" appeared on the other side of the continent, in the British Isles. It was the "sword in the stone" from the cycle of Celtic legends of King Arthur. This appearance is perhaps less mysterious if we bear in mind that the Roman legions in Britain were largely composed of Sarmatian warriors who remained there even after the collapse of the empire. Even more significantly, however, is the legend preserved by the Celtic peoples of Britain that their own ancestral homeland was in the East, somewhere in "barbaric" Scythia.

---

43 Featured in the first English edition of *Return of Myth*, first published in Serbian in Boris Nad, *Nemi bogovi [Silent Gods]* (Belgrade: Žagor, 2008).

The Sacrality of the Plains

We do not know whether it is justified to speak of the "sacrality of the plains" any more than the sacrality of mountains, forests, or any other earthly environment. However, one thing remains beyond discussion: that incomparable sense of space possessed by the nomadic inhabitants of the plains (unlike the sedentary, agricultural, or maritime populations). Does this feeling not lie at the root of those miraculous endeavors dared by the nomads of the steppes, who ventured to create vast empires and kingdoms comparable in size to that created by Caesar?

The custom of modern historians to refer to the Greek *poleis* as states, while denying this right to the gigantic political creations of the Eastern nomads, such as the Scythians or the Huns, is mere arbitrariness. These were not just "loose tribal alliances' (the momentum of their conquests already precludes this assumption), but evidently well-organized states and empires - states that rested on tribal alliances. Like the Gothic kingdom that once (in the third to fourth century) stretched in a wide belt from the Don to the Thames. Or the short-lived empire of Atilla, leader of the Huns, whose power extended as far as Italy and Cyprus, who minted his own money and whose funeral, accompanied by rituals of unsurpassed brutality described by Priscus, took place on the River Nedao, which might very well be the River Nadel in the immediate vicinity of today's Pančevo.

Both the Huns and the Goths were not ethnically compact communities but in all probability motley alliances of various tribes, peoples, and ethnicities. The same was basically true for Russia, an enormous Slavic empire whose first historical center was located on the plains, on the South Russian steppes.

Nestor the Chronicler, in his *Primary Chronicle* (the oldest preserved chronicle about East Slavic people), preserved a Slavic saga about an ancestral homeland which, according to the chronicles, is located somewhere near the River Danube in Pannonia.

Since ancient times, nomads have followed the same or very similar paths of migration. In later periods as well, they moved to the plain lands, to the Pannonian plain. The remains of Neolithic houses (found not far from Vršac), with their triangular gables and bright painted colors, are strikingly reminiscent of the rural houses still built in Pannonian villages at the beginning of the last century, which suggests that the way of life of the sedentary population of the past was much more similar to today's than is usually thought.

The Mystery of Pannonia

Without a doubt, Pannonia harbors mysteries that are still waiting to be solved. They begin with the oldest: the Paleolithic hunters who lived in tents made from mammoth tusks raised under the open sky and built with their enigmatic weapons and tools made of bone and stone, and with their even more enigmatic deities. In addition to the cave wall paintings, those hunters always left the same enigmatic sign: the handprint. Another of these mysteries is that the cultures of the Neolithic progenitors of Europe flourished on its edges, in the lower Danube, for long periods of time.

Indo-Europeanization was a long process that went through several successive waves of migrations, gradually changing the look of the continent, the composition of its races, peoples, and ethnoi all the way up to the Europe which we know. This was a "process" whose key ploys and plots we do not know, because in modern science there is no consensus on the issue of where the Aryan homeland was. However, it is certain that some of the major routes of Aryan migrations in Europe led through Pannonia.

Gold of the North

In his book *Hyperborean Dacia* the Romanian author Geticus issued a fantastic supposition that is corroborated by toponymy and Romanian folklore. His idea was that Dacia was an ancient center of Hyperborean traditions between two circles of civilization, the Mediterranean and Northern. The center of the cult of Apollo, according to this author, was precisely in the Danube Delta, and that center radiated its influence from the Danube to the Mediterranean, to the peoples of the South. The "Gold of the North" is golden because it represents the spiritual heritage of Hyperborea. Some artifacts, such as Apollo's sun-chariot found in Dupljaja near Vršac, are more astounding than Geticus' hypotheses, which themselves offer more elegant explanations than those provided by archeology, which claims that influence ran from the South to the North, from centers in the zone of Mycenaean culture.

***

BARBARIC SCYTHIA

It was only the beginning of July, but a long drought had turned the fields into yellow, hot deserts. The monotonous plains resembled a motionless sea. Vršac Hill, the last slope of the Carpathian Mountains, rests in a blue shadow. A half-empty bus moved quickly along the old road that stretches from Timişoara to Pančevo and then further on to Belgrade. It stopped at one of the intermediate stations, one of the many villages in the Banat region which all resemble each other like peas in a pod. The houses are much nicer and more spacious than elsewhere, although their facades have been ruined, particularly those inhabited by the Germans who arrived during the Austro-Turkish Wars. Just a few kilometers away was a place named after a Turkish *pasha* who was stationed there with his army during one of the many war campaigns.

As rare travelers exited or got onto the bus, the others had the opportunity to enjoy the somewhat atypical Banat landscape. On the right-hand side, under terraces of forest once lay a marsh, now dried up and transformed into fertile fields swaying in the summer heat. Yet it is too rarely mentioned that that this soil is also still full of traces of ancient life and graves dating back as far as the Eneolithic. Numerous archaeological finds, for instance weapons and bronze-caste tools, are scattered across these rural estates. At the mine of the nearby brickyard, excavations have, at times, unearthed human bones alongside pieces of black pottery. This rare information can only be found in specialist publications.

The bus started up again slowly, coming back to the main road only to stop after another few hundred meters. A funeral procession slowly passed by on its way to the cemetery.

Walking in front of everyone was a young priest with a long beard, and in front of him a car slowly towing the coffin of the deceased. The second highway lane was free, but the driver had no intent of passing them. Not responding to a few protests from passengers, he calmly lined up at the back of the procession. Minutes passed as the bus, followed by a growing column of vehicles behind it, neared the village cemetery at a snail's pace. Not much further, we saw a collapsed brick wall and the walls of a chapel that had turned gray with age, behind which the procession raised the cross.

Thus, all of us - willingly or unwillingly - participated in some kind of ritual. The scene obviously took place outside of time, in an elegant negligence towards time and timetable. The fact that the driver so stubbornly adhered to custom obviously had deeper reasons - the custom must have been very old, many aspects testifying to its great antiquity.

Indeed, in his book *Migrations* Miloš Crnjanski described the Serbs' custom of seeing off their dead to the cemetery. Back then, they were still carried in an open coffin, and in the mid-18th century this custom astonished foreigners, but Serbs persistently adhered to it, even despite the Germans' efforts to eradicate it. Even in the mid-20th century, a similar custom still existed among Russians. It has been described by, among others, the German writer Ernst Jünger in his writings from the Caucasus. Jünger found the custom pleasant, as if the deceased were thus exposed to the sun, to daylight for the last time, "bidding farewell forever before he descends."

We suspect, however, that no one among this trip's passengers then thought about Herodotus, who spoke of the funeral customs of the Scythians. Verily, we were in one of the outskirts of ancient Scythia, which once stretched from the Black Sea and the Don all the way to Pannonia. The nearby mounds rising over the plains, undoubtedly the work of human hands, could very well have been Scythian.

The available information on the Scythians - a people who inhabited the steppes and plains of Eastern Europe for a long span of time only to then disappear - is one of the many illogicalities that abound in modern historical science, whose accounts of the Scythians are extremely scarce and sometimes indisputably, extremely malicious. Perhaps it is the malice of the Greeks towards this numerous and free people of the East that explains the infamy which the "Scythian barbarians" have enjoyed in later centuries - a glory equal only to that which to this day accompanies the Huns and the Goths, Genghis Khan's warriors as well as Stalin's millions-strong armies. This ancient archetype of Hellenic historians was repeated by the modern English geographer Halford Mackinder in his famous lecture which, although a stunning mixture of lucidity and extreme blindness, nevertheless added a new dimension to this perception, an almost perfect expression. For this famous English scholar, the Scythians of Homer and Herodotus' stories, the Scythians who "drink mares milk" were nothing more than one among many "slant-eyed" conquerors. They were the true archetype of barbarism, the prototype of all later "ruthless Asiatic horsemen without ideals." Civilization, the invention of the maritime peoples of the West, was the "fruit of a centuries-long struggle" against the nomads from the East, the "Scythians." This concept has racial connotations: the slant-eyed Scythians, Huns, Turks, Mongols, etc. are contrasted to the white dolichocephalics of the North, West, and South of Europe.

Mackinder, however, was wrong: the Scythians were pure Indo-Europeans, while the Huns and Goths did not represent a homogenous whole in racial terms, but rather were in all likelihood more of a motley alliance of diverse tribes, peoples, *ethnoi*, and races.

What were those gruesome barbarities that earned the Scythians such malice for thousands of years? Was it the human sacrifices - every hundredth prisoner was sacrificed - and the custom of cutting off the victim corpse's right hand, throwing it into the air, and leaving it lying where it fell? Or was it the custom of ritually drenching the "holy sword" with blood, a funeral ritual which entailed the killing of dozens or even hundreds of the king's wives and servants? More or less the same things are attributed to many other "barbarians." For instance, Orosius wrote that the Celts cut off their captives' heads to drink from their skulls whenever they need a cup, and Strabo accused the Celts of cannibalism. We can only wonder whether these were really impartial eyewitness reports, or merely some kind of political propaganda that exploited the prejudices of the "civilized" against the "barbarians." In any case, at least one mitigating circumstance should be acknowledged for the "barbarians": unlike the "international community" of that time (and, indeed, today's "international community"), they did not glorify their own atrocities as praiseworthy deeds of defending civilization from barbarism.

Archaeology has nonetheless confirmed some of Herodotus' allegations, in particular those pertaining to the Scythians' funeral customs. Let us recall one of them: the custom of carrying the deceased in a cart for a whole forty days after death, during which the deceased was given abundant funeral feasts (the Slavic "*trizna*"). The importance of this period of forty days has been completely preserved in the Orthodox rite, whereas for Catholics, as far as we know, it is of no significance. Serbs and Russians have also preserved the custom of memorial feasts, or "*dacha*", as notorious to their neighbors of other faiths as towing the deceased to their final destination in a cart. One could see a concession to "civilizedness" in the manner of modern Westerners in the fact that today Serbs transport their deceased in a closed coffin, and this "civilizedness" obviously did not entirely pass over barbaric Scythia.

***

DALMATIA[44]

The mountains were bare, or with very little vegetation, and there was even less as we drew nearer to the sea. To the south and to the west, in the indescribable poverty of the landscape, mountains were reduced to a mere skeleton, the skeleton of karst rocks lacking soil.

The same was the case with the human settlements: the villages there are only modest hamlets composed of but a few dozen scattered houses. On a neglected pathway, we saw a peasant who strolled along lazily with a saddled donkey.

The proximity of the Mediterranean pointed itself out to us in the mysterious change in the air, which was full of the scent of aromatic herbs, and with each second the barely detectable fragrance of the sea grew clearer. We have left the Balkan Mountains and their dense forests far behind us. Before us is a small valley full of red earth, whose strange image is thrilling in the heat of summer. We should make one last effort to climb the naked hills so that our eyes will make contact with the clear blue Adriatic Sea.

This was the *Limes* border, one more durable than that established by the old Romans. We were in a no-man's-land separating two worlds, dividing the land from the narrow coastal area and the continent from the Mediterranean, the empire of the olive from the kingdom of the oak tree. It was this border that corresponded to ethnic boundaries and divided the two peoples - the Serbs from the Croats. This was also the border between two cultures, two different and perhaps irreconcilable experiences of the world: one

---

[44] Featured in the first English edition of *Return of Myth*, first published in Serbian in Boris Nad, *Nemi bogovi* [*Silent Gods*] (Belgrade: Žagor, 2008).

expressed in stone, in the glories of cathedrals, and the other in temples that are noticeably smaller and made entirely of wood. The first was a culture whose element is Sea, and the other - that of Land. The civilization of the Sea does not heed the "memory of blood": for example, the Serbs of Dubrovnik embraced the sea, and with it a new religion, very quickly forgetting their origin and faith. The differences become even more clear if we listen to Dalmatian songs, the melancholic music of islands and shores, and Serbian heroic poetry sung in accompaniment with the *gusle*.

We now live in an era of the dominance of Sea. It now floods across all the old and well-established borders. But can one ever doubt the enormous, persistent, life-giving power of Land?

***

SLAVONIA[45]

The machine gun rattled from the top of the high silo, which was like a monstrous tower of macabre. The strange flames threw lights upon the plain. That evening, two bombs hit the silo and the grain began to burn. Other, weaker fires smoldered in the city, and their reflections vibrated on the surface of the sluggish, lowland river, smooth as oil. These were, after all, the only lights in a town which had lived for two days without electricity – they looked like some kind of demonic illumination. Here and there, in back streets, it was possible to see the bodies of dead boys which police in blue uniforms loaded onto trucks. A tragic autopsy followed by laughter and swearing.

The smoke in the night blew without any breeze, in an almost straight line. In the wheat-bearing fields, the frantic gunfire of infantry rekindled. Flashing from the dark of the woods, artillery shells spewed forth into the air with a strong roar. Monotonous roaring came from tank engines which, like clouds of cotton, suppressed all human voices. The landscape and the night took on a terrifying new visage.

No one had any hope that the fires which blazed that night could be extinguished by anything but blood. No one knew that the war which had just begun would take the next four years and leave behind pillaged, burnt villages and deserted towns. It would end with a long column stretching for miles, full of crying children, women, and men with faces tanned by the sun in tattered camouflage uniforms. This history is describable as a circle that has closed, finished with

---

45 Featured in the first English edition of *Return of Myth*, first published in Serbian in Boris Nad, *Nemi bogovi [Silent Gods]* (Belgrade: Žagor, 2008).

the defeat of a people forced to leave their homes not by death, but by migration.

The oak forests rest in peace, disturbed only by the muffled thunder of distant explosions. Mist from the River Danube is raised by the wind, bringing the feel of fresh water. Under the shady trees, in the night, there are armies. The burned city once had a picturesque name – Palina. There ran, as always, the Limes, the border, the Military Frontier, and not just during the Austro-Turkish wars, but in the era of Byzantium and Rome as well, and possibly much earlier. In this sullen ground lie silent graves.

No one has ever written a proper history of the kingdom called Slavonia.

***

AMERICA (THE UNITED STATES)[46]

The following is a sort of modern pilgrimage.

In the gray, dirty, neon twilight you pass a huge boulevard. In its immediate vicinity lies the White House, with its dome, its sterile, always damp lawn, white fence, swarms of discreet guards, and place for the press conferences of American presidents, secretaries of state, and their spokespersons. This is an almost mystical, disturbing place, a center of world power as enigmatic as prophecies at Delphi. There is the silhouette of the Library of Congress, resembling the shrine in Abu Simbel, presided over by Abraham Lincoln, a black shadow made of stone.

The Founding Fathers.

Egypt, a kind of modern Egypt, or perhaps Babylon and, at the same time, the promised land of Canaan. The modern Israel that worships Mammon and the Golden Calf as much as its only god, Yahweh.

The twilight, sunset, perhaps some kind of magical dawn, lends everything in sight a hallucinatory, spooky, almost monstrous look.

The howling of police sirens, electric discharges in the atmosphere, twinkling lights, spacious boulevards, traffic lights.

Oil fields, dragon's blood.

Supermarkets, shopping malls, manna falling from the sky and always a magical, paradisal abundance.

The night drowns in a golden glow. Melodious music.

---

46 Previously unpublished in Serbian and English.

America, with its McDonald's, Statue of Liberty, Mickey Mouse, bombers, and aircraft carriers. With its records, cosmetics, and sports all in plastic packaging.

New York, stinking ports and narrow streets, skyscrapers, traffic jams, airports, and yellow taxis.

Uncle Sam points his finger at you.

Democracy for all, without exception, for both black and white slaves, for grunts and warlords, for shepherds and pharaohs.

Plastic Christ and gospel. Banks, the most powerful in the world, and Wall Street. His majesty the Dollar. TV preachers broadcasting the message of the coming Judgement Day and the ascension of the righteous, the rapture, and the war that will be fought at the End of Time. Here the host is replaced by the hamburger, the holy wine of communion and the blood of Christ by Coca-Cola.

And you, like every inhabitant of the planet, are invited to participate in its mysteries.

This is a completely new eschatology, a new Gospel. America is now addressing all of humanity.

America, land of outcasts.

America, land of the free, land of opportunities and promises. Land of the dead, the mystical Atlantis miraculously raised from the ocean floor with its phantasms: Walt Disney and Star Wars. Hollywood.

You are a complete stranger here.

Faces on billboards. Commercials, TV shows. Bulky buffalo chests. Indian shadows, cemeteries, military cemeteries with thousands and thousands of identical white crosses.

Two towers going down in flames.

Cyborg-warriors equipped with unimaginable weapons, aircraft carriers stranded in warm seas somewhere off the Persian coast…

Explosions, ominous mushroom clouds rising over the Pacific Ocean.

The empire which did not want to be, so different from all the others, with the flag of night. A History so different from anything humanity has ever seen.

Good and Evil. The Devil and God, the one in whom America believes.

A force that decided to conquer the world and lead the last of all wars, the war against war. This is the final showdown, Armageddon. The Holy War for the End of the World.

And Jihad.

This is on the horizon now. America, your dream will finally come true. The hurricane you started is now hovering over your sky. But you just wanted freedom. And justice for all.

America, alone against all.

A miraculous country, an isolated island in the West of the world. Thousands of miles of empty roads, the red mountains of Nevada and Arizona. The warm, bloody sky of the South. The poison of the desert. Drums and fires at night.

Wet dusk. Whiskey bars.

America, obsessed with morality, faith in God, Good and Evil, you are just a misunderstanding. You are a misunderstanding of history and faith, of faith in God, of faith in history and its meaning, the crooked point of a wrong union. Your face is both the innocent mask of Good and the mask of pure Evil. You have no soul, nor could you ever. You are cruel in your striving towards the Good, and infinitely sensitive in accepting Evil. Good and Evil, in your case, mean nothing.

You have never been weak and you will never be strong. You are not an empire; you are not part of history. You are an anomaly, an anomaly in the eternal cruelty of history. That is why you are not a winner and you cannot be defeated. Your so-called moral values are your weakness. As long as you strive towards the Good and moral, you shall be breeding Evil, and as long as you strive towards unity, you shall be breeding division, you shall be breeding death. Your ideals are your evil. Your moral values are your curse, your doom; your decomposition is your life and the last chance for humanity - or at least what is left of it at the moment when your death is more than certain.

America, flag of freedom! Try to understand. Your freedom is not for you, but freedom for others. For those who shall rise upon your corpse, for those who shall feast on your flesh, for those who shall quench their thirst with your blood. That is why you have to fall. Your death is freedom – freedom for you and freedom for others. In fact, you are already dead, and therefore perfectly free. You once believed that you lived beyond time and history, and that is why awakening from your dream, a dream that is not life and that is not a way of life, but only a way of dying, will be bloodier, more painful and more difficult.

You are dying. Actually, you are already dead, without even knowing it.

There is no awakening from your dream of freedom, just as there is no awakening from death or a deep coma.

***

THE GOLDEN FLEECE[47]

One day, in some unspecified age much earlier than the Trojan War, at least two generations before, an unspecified number of heroes joined forces on a quest. This is one of only four tales to be told over and over again, in various forms, until the end of time.

The story claims that they embarked on a voyage to find the Golden Fleece, yet their pursuit could just as well have been for the Holy Grail or the Kingdom of Prester John. What is certain is that on one grey morning, most likely at the crack of dawn, the heroes boarded a ship and sailed away. According to legend, their dangerous quest was successful, and they returned to their homeland. As an almost contemporary author added, in ancient times all stories had a happy ending: Theseus slayed the Minotaur; Odyssey returned to Ithaca after roaming the seven seas; the quest of the 30 birds to find the bird-god Simurgh was ultimately successful with the birds' revelation that each of them is Simurgh and that he is simultaneously each of them.

The epic of the Argonauts is one of the oldest Greek stories. Thus, it is not surprising that many different accounts exist, even to the point of contradicting each other's narratives. "Homer and Hesiod, the two earliest Greek poets whose works are still extant, both knew of the voyage, and Homer speaks of it as 'on everyone's lips.'"[48] Many more recent sources, like the ancient ones (apart from fragments found in Homer's Odyssey), are forever lost. Nevertheless, there is no doubt that this epic cycle relaying the story of Jason's Argonauts and their

---

47 Previously unpublished in English. First published in Serbian in Boris Nad, *Nemi bogovi* [*Silent Gods*] (Belgrade: Žagor, 2008).
48 Robert Graves, *The Golden Fleece* (Hutchinson, 1983), p. 447.

voyage to Colchis to seize the Golden fleece from King Aeetes, is one of the oldest Greek epics.

As we are reminded by Graves, "Pherecydes of Athens, in his mythological work, which has survived only in short quotations, was perhaps the first writer to record the story as a consecutive whole; and the Boeotian poet Pindar in his Fourth Pythian Ode (462 B.C.) gives a brief summary of it, the earliest to survive complete."

The supposed age of the Argonauts' adventure – two generations before the Trojan War – is contentious, as is the crew list and count. It is certain, though, that the story itself is older than is generally assumed. This is confirmed by particular episodes in Jason's life. For instance, according to Robert Graves, Jason being on the verge of death in the jaws of a sea-monster is a motif attested in Etruscan art. Both Heracles and Theseus clearly belong to a much earlier period; the story in its entirety abounds with inconsistent, relative interpolations.

Similarly disputed is the route taken by the Argonauts. Colchis is today known as Georgia, a recent combat zone, while the Phasis River is known as the Rioni. It is certain that the return journey of the Argonauts included traversing the Danube Delta, then sailing upstream, and consequently through the territory of the present city of Belgrade. The journey continued along the River Sava, to the "top of the Adriatic (sea)", where Circe's island is actually the island of Lošinj. It may have resumed along the River Po, then across the Mediterranean Sea to the shores of Libya, further to the (now drained) lake of Tritonis whose shores were inhabited by cavemen, to finally conclude in Jason's native Iolcos. This is the circle in which history will play out in most famous episodes for many centuries to follow.

Particular episodes of this story deserve to be mentioned. One of them is the encounter of the harpies, the birds persecuting Thrace's king for disclosing the future to mankind. The harpies always arrived to devour the greater part of the king's food and befoul the remainder. By beating swords and spears against their shields, the Argonauts chased the birds away. "Harpy" means "snatcher" in Greek and Borges's *Book of Imaginary Beings* adds that they were originally wind-deities. According to other opinions, harpies are marsh birds from the Danube Delta, who carry and spread disease in their plumage.

The episode with the sorceress Medea is the most intriguing and, furthermore, could be said to represent the key to the story. Medea is more than a sorceress; she is the chthonic, female divinity, an eminent goddess, like Isis or Lilith, and just as relentless, unconscientious, demanding and resolute. Notable is her skill at taming snakes, as is her ability to prolong the life of heroes with magic potions, which is in turn reminiscent of Celtic myths. Jason's tragic destiny is, hence, not surprising. Long after the quest has been successfully completed and the Golden Fleece has been taken to Iolcos, he will, as an old man and after many travels, return to Corinth and to his old ship, the Argo. There, Jason will attempt to hang himself, only for the bow of the Argo to suddenly break and crush his skull. The Golden Fleece disappears without a trace; Jason dies not as a king, but as a refugee and impoverished exile.

This is the tragic end of Jason, the leader of the Argonauts, still remembered as the one to tread with only one sandal - an old custom of Aetolian warriors was to sandal-clad only their shield-side foot in order to easier navigate mud and to allow for more powerful strikes. Even today, the left leg is considered hostile. One departs to war with the left foot, but does not cross a friend's doorstep with it.

According to tradition, unlike Jason who for some unknown reason fell out of favor with the gods, Medea did not die. She ruled the Elysian Fields and married the great hero Achilles, the one whom she could neither subjugate, deceive, humiliate, restrain, or vanquish.

***

The Reawakening of Myth

PART II:

A TALE OF AGARTHA

"And darting upon the paper, with eyes bedimmed, and voice choked with emotion, he read the whole document from the last letter to the first.

It was conceived in the following terms:

In Sneffels Joculis craterem quem delibat
Umbra Scartaris Julii intra calendas descende,
Audax viator, et terrestre centrum attinges.
Quod feci, Arne Saknussemm.

Which bad Latin may be translated thus:

'Descend, bold traveller, into the crater of the jokul of Sneffels, which the shadow of Scartaris touches before the kalends of July, and you will attain the centre of the earth; which I have done, Arne Saknussemm'...

"This is my decision," replied Professor Liedenbrock, putting on one of his grandest airs. "Neither you nor anybody else knows with any certainty what is going on in the interior of this globe."

- Jules Verne: *A Journey to the Center of the Earth*

O Dieu, purifiez nos coeurs!

- Ezra Pound, *Night Litany*

The Secret of Secrets

Searching for Paradise in the East

The history of peoples is made by the unwritten history of great travels and world travelers - a history that began long before Herodotus or Marco Polo, in the Neolithic or even earlier, in some fantastical age of mankind. Perhaps even at the dusk of the primordial Golden Age, with glaciation or flood, and with the first in a series of catastrophes faced by the human species.

Then followed eras of the migrations of peoples and races. If we believe Plato, then the Atlanteans were the first colonists in the world, and they came from the West. Others say that their ancestors were the Hyperboreans, who fled snow and ice in the Far North of the continent. Over the course of subsequent history, peoples would move from North to South and from East to West - and not otherwise. This constitutes their course through history - a path of aging, degeneration and, at times faster, at times slower, of inexorable decline. This is how great conquests began, those that encompass immense regions, entire continents, and this is how great wars start, like the one that raged under the walls of Ilium - or was this only a shadow of some mythical war waged in the far deeper past, during the mythical age of the Earth? Perhaps at the beginning of time, "*in illo tempore.*"

They did not rush towards unknown and exotic lands, but towards their lost homelands, towards mythical lands of the beginning, towards the riches of the Golden Age. Towards primordial, Edenic abundance. Towards Paradise Lost, such as the Biblical one, which we have not stopped searching for here on Earth even today.

One Islamic mystic, Suhrawardi, claimed that after death the soul returns to the homeland, for merciful Allah himself commanded this, and this would not be possible if he had not previously resided in it. This mythical homeland is to be found somewhere in the "spiritual East." In order to find the strength for this, we must start from the spiritual West, the "Western wells of exile."

The true journey, true adventures of the spirit, this Sheikh taught, start in the West. This is a place like a grave, a stockade of the burial-place. Arriving on the soil of an unknown continent, Christopher Columbus thought he had discovered the New Earth mentioned in the Apocalypse of St. John. The famous seafarer believed he was in the Gulf of Paria, and in its fresh currents discovered the origin of the four rivers of the lost heavenly garden, Eden itself. "God made me the messenger of the new heaven and the new earth, of which he spoke in the Apocalypse of St. John, and before that through the mouth of Isaiah," Columbus proclaimed to King Juan, "and he showed me the place where to find it."

The end of the world, as it is written in the *Book of Prophecies*, is preceded by the discovery of a New Land, a New Earth, the conversion of unbelievers, and the destruction of the Antichrist. Evil will be destroyed on Earth once and for all.

What is the link between Agartha and America? Is it the same thread that interconnects all continents? Could their appearance, or rather re-appearance, on the horizon of world history represent a sign of the "final times", the "End

Times?" The "secret" of America was known to the Vikings, the Egyptians, and the Phoenicians even thousands of years before the Portuguese and Spanish seafarers.

Esotericists and the adepts of secret societies, mystics and conjurers, astrologers and neophytes, the followers of secret cults and obscure conspirators - they are all still weaving their dark webs around Agartha and the deep mysteries that hide this underground kingdom.

America is not only the land of the Apocalypse – a story that speaks about the end of the world and the last revelation. The first newcomers identified America with paradise, where even the trees and plants spoke the "hieroglyphic language of our Adamic or primitive state." The New World was for them a projection of paradise on Earth, by which God baptized his chosen people - the New Israel. Here the attribute "new" has the meaning of "godly." Others identified America, on no lesser grounds, with Atlantis, whose downfall was described by Plato. Failing to observe that the Greek philosopher was precise in the details he gave, and that, besides the island of Atlantis, he also mentioned a "land in the West surrounded by ocean on all sides." This, there can be no doubt, is the North American continent. America is only its shadow, its projection in the Far West, the "false Atlantis."

Herman Wirth spoke of the vanished land of Mo-Uru (the Biblical Moriah where Abraham wanted to sacrifice his son), an isle in the North-West Atlantic, a lost sacred continent. The land of Mo-Uru is the real Atlantis.

The India of the Middle Ages and later, towards which world travelers were drawn, is just as much or even more so a mythical land and not a mere geographical fact. Brazil owes its name to Hy-Brasil, a mythical land of Celtic legend. Why did Siberia ultimately become the "sacred soil" of the Russian Empire? To Yesenin, Russia is paradise, or is even more important than paradise. Taken together, Russia and Siberia, or their Far North, are according to some researchers the actual mythical Hyperborea - the ancestral homeland of present mankind, or at least part of it, the homeland of god-men, the divine race of the Golden Age. One researcher thought he had discovered in Russian Lapland the ruins of the temple dedicated to Hyperborean Apollo and the mythical Thule - the Ultima Thule in which the ancient Greeks believed.

America is, of course, not the mythical island of Atlantis that vanished in the Atlantic Ocean at the very dawn of history. It is actually the Green Land, the Land of the Dead, the "Kingdom of Shadows" in the West that is mentioned in the legends and myths of many peoples. America is Trans-Atlantis. What is the meaning of the reappearance of a dead, sunken continent, on the horizon of world history? In the same way, Agartha is also a "land of the dead" which, as prophecy holds, is still to be discovered in the depths of the underground. In historical times, this reportedly was realized by some travelers and seekers. One of them was a Mongolian hunter who could not keep his secret, and thus had his tongue cut out by lamas. The Lama Djamsrap spoke of this in his book. Another was an illiterate Norwegian sailor who claimed to have lived in Agartha for several years. The reader will see that these fleeting mentions are not without grounds, and that America and Atlantis are closely connected without the topic of Agartha, the mysterious kingdom hidden in the everlasting dark, deep underground, and deep in the past. It is closely connected with the worlds of the dead and the past - with the past that refuses to die. And it verily conceals many secret histories of the human race.

At any rate, there is no single land, island, or continent in the world that is a mere geographical certainty. The whole Earth is a sacred text, a holy book written in special signs - or at least this is what mystics and esotericists believe. The words of this text, it is thought, were written by God himself. Every journey is, in fact, a pilgrimage, for we are always walking on sacred ground. Every land and landscape, far and near, possesses hidden meaning and secret significance - spiritual, symbolic, eschatological, and even profoundly mystical. A landscape is at once both a physical and spiritual reality. This is the domain of a secret, mysterious science - mystical and sacred geography - whose knowledge, as happens, has been lost forever over the course of centuries or millennia.

If the discovery of America, or rather the return of America to history, triggered such unrest among peoples, then what will happen if the prophecy of the end of the world is fulfilled and the secret Agartha becomes known to all of humanity? It is prophesied that the people of Agartha will once more come out onto the surface of the Earth. And likewise, Paradise, the Garden of Eden, is hidden somewhere in the East. It is in the East of the "wise sages of Tatary", Swedenborg claimed, that we should search for the "long forgotten word." Others say that we are in Hell, and that paradise, the Biblical one, is hidden in the same place.

Legend claims that somewhere, in the depths of the Earth, in dark caves and secret passages, there still lives a secret, mysterious people, one hidden from the sight of others, that this is known to only a few chosen ones on the surface, and that this knowledge is a strictly guarded secret. Or maybe it was until recently.

This secret kingdom, as we have already said, is called Agartha. This legend is ancient and comes from remote prehistory. Agartha is spoken of in the legends of diverse peoples - white, red, and yellow - in both East and West.

Travelers who have set their minds to find it have whispered about it. Caravan merchants have told exhilarating tales of it in inns and on mountain trails, in deserts and in remote corners. It is known to Tibetan sages whose teachings nourish monks and lamas.

The common crowds, meanwhile, ridicule and laugh at such tales as the superstitions of the uneducated and gullible.

***

The Two Faces of Janus

I don't remember the exact moment when my search for Agartha began. It must have been in the early days of my childhood. I surmise that everyone's childhood is marked by dreams that we later forget or hold in contempt in our mature age. In those days, I dreamt that I owned an underground castle led to by marble steps, and that some joyous event opened the path to the castle.

A secret is buried deep in the ground. The secret door that led to the castle was in the foothill of some giant tree, in a forest in the vicinity of a town, a forest which extended to our estate outside of Moscow. The entrance to the castle was hidden, and its ancient stone steps were covered by soil and dry leaves - the dreg of many centuries. The underground castle comprised countless, fabulous chambers, and was reminiscent of the caves of the island of Monte Christo. Whoever steps inside would be transformed into an enlightened being wreathed in glory rather than plenitude. The first of the magnificent chambers rested in semi-darkness and imperial purple. Torches hung on the walls, and if I lit the first one, then diamonds and pearls would scatter across the stone floor. Rubies glistened in chests. I was in possession of unsurpassable wealth, wealth not even of this world: golden coins forged by the hands of sorcerers or dwarfs. They were my servants, my reticent helpers. The underground world is inhabited with beings who are not human.

No one could guess my secret. Whom could I even entrust with such a secret? The silence increased my powers.

In January I turned 70. January is the month of the God Janus, the God of beginnings who has two faces. One looks towards the East, the other towards the West. One, as Ovid said, looks forward, and the other behind: into the past and into the future. One is happy, the other is sad. The moment of triumph, the moment of the fulfillment of our boldest dreams, those upon which we have based our whole preceding lives and to which our reality is subordinated, contains the bitter taste of our defeat: our highest hopes are extinguished with it. This was felt even by the greatest favorites of the Gods, such as Caesar or Alexander, in the moments of their deaths, if not before. Joy is passing and short-lived. Loss, on the contrary, is final and irrevocable. That is why our lives are reminiscent of passing through a valley of tears.

In olden times, I was in all likelihood a very spoiled and unbearable brat. The guilt for this was no doubt shared by my grandfather and governess. The governess' name was Aglaia. Aglaia Prokhorovna - that is how we were to address her, but for me she was just Aglaia. My world consisted of books and strange stories, mostly those given to me by my grandfather. Among them were luxuriously illustrated novels for boys, such as *The King's Messenger* by Jules Verne, or his *Journey to the Center of the Earth*. I would often spend the afternoon hours in his library. That is one of those magic places we remember from our childhoods.

I would interrupt him in the evenings or late afternoons while he was working at his writing desk. Such privileges were not enjoyed by my father, or my mother - his daughter. This was in his house in Saint Petersburg. In August, under aslant rays of sun that did not set even at night (like in the mythical

Hyperborea), his library was truly like a cave, and he looked like a monk, or a druid, a hermit with a beard, similar to the hermit I saw in Optina Pustyn.

At the time I had a black cat who followed me everywhere, and I gave him the name Behemoth – the name of a beast, a Biblical one, a land-monster who fights Leviathan, the monster from the deep sea. This black cat would come back to life in our literature, such as in Bulgakov's novel, which must be well known to you. It would bear the same name.

He was my companion in adventures which I am no longer capable of describing. He spoke with a human voice and reminded me of the Puss in Boots of children's stories. That fairy-tale cat, one scholar of myth claims, is in fact a god from the Neolithic, from the younger Stone Age, who over time receded into the guise of a fairy tale creature, the famous hero of children's books. Maybe he existed only in my imagination.

In my imagination, I was that enigmatic child - a miller's son, the youngest of three brothers. In Russian fairy tales, such a boy is usually called Ivan. A similar boy is also a king's messenger, one who carries a secret message, upon which depends the fate of the kingdom and the happiness of millions. The messenger arrives at the last moment. In that last and decisive moment, I would whisper secret words in the ear of the Tsarina, or would put a secret letter, sealed in wax, into her hand. She would praise me with a smile and a soft kiss on my forehead. In that moment, her eyes would be filled with tears. By virtue of this, I became a favorite of the court's ladies-in-waiting. The king himself looked at me with gratitude, and firmly clasped my small hand.

Hiding under the crinolines of those ladies-in-waiting, there is no doubt, was my mother, my sisters and cousins, distant and closer, and my governess. Between my mother and the governess there was a visible, insurmountable rift, unfathomable to a child's mind. The beauty of my mother was delicate, the sophisticated beauty of a refined and disdainful aristocrat resembling Botticelli's models. The beauty of Aglaia Prokhorovna recalled the beauties of Rubens' paintings. It was the sensual and healthy beauty of a rounded peasant, a Russian woman. The same one smiling today from Soviet posters, the beauty of the *kolkhoznitsa*, the peasant, or the worker.

Above these imaginary portraits stood a portrait of my grandfather - a cruel face with small eyes and high, almost Mongolian cheekbones, and an overgrown beard, similar to those of the Old Believers. He was Yusupov, an incorrigible Tsarist, killed in Moscow in the summer of 1918 under unclear circumstances. Finally, there is my father. A strict face with deep blue eyes. A well-groomed blonde mustache, and a rubashka the color of soil. Or at least that's how he was in my memories. He died in an unfortunate incident in Kerch, Crimea. I see him, as if in a dream, as he walks in marching steps. My chest is filled with pride. Everything in these dreams is so clear and natural.

It is summertime. The sun is bright. We are standing in some wide yard - all streets in Russia are wide, and buildings are monumental. Golden and multicolored turrets in the shape of a bulb. Ringing bells, maybe from the church of St. Basil the Blessed. Lions in stone several times bigger than an average man. At the entrance are griffins. A stone dragon with unfolded wings is visible on the facade. It could fly away at any time.

Somewhere in the vicinity is the Emperor himself, the Tsar, the real King of the World. The ruler who stands still, whose face is akin to a golden mask. Such are also the faces of the officers, guards, and cadets who surround him. In my memories and dreams, the emperor looks more like a monument in bronze, or stone, more like a bronze horseman from a poem of Andrei Bely than a man of blood and flesh.

The warmth of the chest under the white shirt is that of my governess. She hugs me closely. I can feel her excited heart beating. Russia, the Mother-Land, is in my head connected with her, not my mother.

Such are my earliest memories. She lifts me up, not too high, but enough for me to see the face of the Tsar, which appears as if cast in bronze or granite. Maybe only his eyes are smiling at me. His eyes are alive.

My life starts as a fairy tale, as an idyll. In childhood, life is just an endless adventure. Idyll and tragedy are actually one and the same play, one which we watch everyday in the theater of the capital city. And in this play, in every character and plot, there is duality. Wherever we approach the essence, everything splits into two.

This is the face of Janus, the God Janus, who is at once God of the beginning and God of the end. And here the first step depends on the last, and the last on the first.

Seventy years of age is a chance to put accounts in order. My life, this is quite clear now, has been marked from the very beginning by one secret mania: a search for the world hidden underground, or rather in the dark of time, in the past, which is dead now and will remain such forever. Only we can make it come alive. Once, a long time ago, I was born and grew up in a magical kingdom.

This is a pursuit for the lost Golden Age. Yet our only golden age is childhood, as we recognize at the end of our path. In it, and only in it, are hidden our deepest secrets and our Gods – the Gods of childhood.

No effort will bring it back, except our memories. There, and only there, in the past, like the shadow from Greek Hades of which Homer sang, wander our ancestors, our father and mother, our closest loved ones, those who persecuted us and those whom we have persecuted. Friends, and traitors, the saved and the damned; convicts and executioners, sinners and blessed, heroes and cowards. Reds and whites, Bolsheviks and Tsarists, communists and fascists, agnostics and believers, and above them all, our Lord God, whom we address in our prayers. Every one of them whispers their own history. Thousands and thousands of years of history of which we know nothing.

Over the years we inexorably near our end, our physical end, and at the same time we return to our beginning. This is the snake, Ouroboros, who ceaselessly devours his own tail. What happens after death, said the philosopher Heraclitus, who is remembered as "the Obscure", people cannot anticipate.

Ouroboros is only time, an endless ocean in which we were thrown in, not knowing where we came from or where we are going. Not knowing who we are. We comprehend this only in the hour of our death.

It is morning, early morning. The sun illuminates the windows of my flat in Moscow's outskirts. The sky is clear and endlessly blue. Once upon a time, centuries ago, people did not see the sky as blue. The world changes with the times, and everything in it, even the colors, has its own history. The blue-colored sky appeared in paintings only much later, starting in the Renaissance. It was not blue for Homer and his heroes, but some darker green or purple, the color of wine dregs.

I think about how, in the meanwhile, I have become a face without a name, as nobody has called me by my real name, the one I received at baptism, for years - no one besides a female kiosk worker who sells me a newspaper every morning. We hide our real faces under the masks of alien names.

I go down the stairs, as the lift is out of order, and then, after a short walk, I go back up the same stairs and drink my tea. In front of me is a still unopened issue of Pravda. I light my first cigarette as part of the morning ritual. The smoke rises up in a nearly straight line. The windows are wide-open. A stranger on the other side of the street, in a blue shirt and a tweed jacket, is trying to stay unnoticed - but this detail betrays him.

The one-bedroom apartment is of the size of a cell, whether a monk's or a prisoner's. This is my space of freedom. The room is filled with books, and a writing desk in disarray and buried in papers. In one red folder is all that is left of the documents I've collected. I burned most of them in 1938, in some Berlin hotel. The rest I am burning now, slowly, piece by piece, in a Chinese pot made of jade, while I write these notes.

I am going through my memories. Memory is unstable and deceptive. Where to begin the story of Agartha, the world disappeared underground? Why would this story arouse any interest in the reader? A story of a world that lies much further than 20,000 feet under the surface of the Earth? Somewhere, in its warm interior, like a hidden heart. I do not know if that heart is alive or if what we see are the shadows of Homer's Hades. Some of them, they say, are as old as this world, or even older.

This book – although I hesitate to call it a book – is probably never going to be published, and certainly not during my lifetime. Maybe these notes are not destined to see the light of day. In fact, this is almost certain. In spite of this, I am trying to write down a story so incredible that it seems as if it were a fantasy of the imagination, a darkened mind, delirium, or drunkenness. But still, it is true. I dare to say that it is authentic, word for word, as far as my unreliable memory has not distorted it. Or perhaps it is a dream, a mirage similar to what travelers lost in the desert experience.

Immediately after my death - I am completely certain of this - unknown people will enter my apartment with expressionless and indifferent faces and meticulously remove any trace of my life on Earth. Some of them will be my old acquaintances. Let the reader - if there is one, and a reader who is not just looking for superficial entertainment - forget the names and years. I am writing these notes as I remember them. The reader should not waste their time with visiting archives and libraries to verify everything I claim here. The names here are false for reasons that will soon become clear. Only those who already know the secret of Agartha will understand them, and therein lies the paradox. This story is not for anyone but the reader who is predestined for its symbols. It will come to life only in their hands.

There is one episode with which I would like to begin this story. It played out in 195* in the valley of the Uburtelin-Gol.

***

Here are the Gates of Agartha

In the year 195* a Soviet archaeological expedition approached the valley of the Uburtelin-Gol River in the Mongolian Altai; the name of the river in Mongolian means "the river of black abysses." The convoy of vehicles drove through beaten paths with difficulty, kicking up clouds of red dust behind it. There was a larch forest to our left. The treetops were motionless. We could feel the sultriness. The air was heavy, humid, without a whiff of wind.

A vast valley lay below. There was a red hill towards the North, standing lonely under the horizon, called the Devil's Hill. It belonged to the Khangai mountain range, a range, as the Mongols described it, made of dragons' teeth and stone turrets. It resembled a mirage, at once unreal and clear in every detail. A white cloud appeared anchored above its top. The cloud had a rosy lining.

When we reached the valley, overtaking huge rocks resembling cyclopean walls - or perhaps they were the actual walls erected by the Ispolins, the Nephilim, and the Titans of Greek myth – we dove into a sea of fog. The strands of fog were pierced by the sharp and smooth stone blocks of the Khangai.

Near the river, we noticed huge columns of red granite and their reflections on the motionless river surface. Even lower in the valley, green mounds, tumuli, showed themselves. On top of each stood a granite tombstone about two meters high with some kind of rune-like inscriptions. The whole valley was occupied by high mounds, overgrown with green and yellow grass. These mounds belonged, as we were told, to prehistory, to some undetermined period as remote from us as the mythical, bygone tales of the Earth.

While the expedition was getting ready to set up a temporary camp, five of us set out towards those columns or turrets of red granite. We passed a circular necropolis of a perimeter of some thirty meters, which the archaeologists planned to examine. There was a pile of stones in the middle of the center; stone blocks rose up on the rim of the outer circle, marking, as it seemed to us, the four corners of the world.

We stopped in front of them. We were amazed by their monumentality, something we did not notice when looking at them from afar. In one place we caught sight of simple drawings carved into stone: angled lines and circles, letters similar to runes. Then we discovered a few narrow passages, cave entrances, some of them too narrow for a man to enter, similar to vertical splits, crevices, or cracks in a wall of stone.

We left the exploration of these tunnels for the following day. The first inspection showed that descent would be possible. The equipment for this would have to be simple: strong ropes and torches would have to suffice. My idea was that we would leave a few people at the entrance to oversee our descent. The next morning, we chose one of these tight passages, fastened our ropes and started our laborious descent. I say "descent", because very soon we discovered within the rocks a real labyrinth of interconnected dark corridors, which would constrict in one place and extend in another. This lasted for an hour, or maybe longer.

We stopped to take a breath. My face was covered in sweat. Inside the chamber, there was a constant air flow. It was not completely dark inside. The ceiling was high, and mostly not touchable by hand. For a moment it was colored in rays of light. A shimmer, at first barely noticeable, swept the place. It was dark inside the cliff; a continuous, but not complete night reigned. Some kind of light was emanating from deep underground. The walls were scintillating with an opal shine. We switched off our flashlights, waiting for our eyes to adjust to the darkness. The shine of gemstones that covered the floor of the gallery became brighter. It seemed as though we were walking on a stone floor through which electric currents flowed, generating a soft interplay of weak lights.

The archaeologist Yefremov was closely examining the cave's walls and ceilings. The movement of his torch left traces akin to the light of a firefly, issuing reflections in unexpected places. After maybe a quarter of an hour, he let out a holler. On one wall of the cave he had found a row of complex lines, perhaps a full inscription in complicated signs, which he called runes. I stopped to take a look at the writing. What I saw forced me to recoil - I have seen similar signs before.

While he was copying the signs, drawing in his notebook, something else attracted our attention: at the south side, the gallery floor was crumbling, leaving a shape like a crater and finishing in new, narrow cracks. Some were the size of a hand, the others such that they could let a man pass through. Some of them were blind niches carved into the rock, the others were leading down, even deeper underground. The shine of light also emanated from there, more intense than that which we had discovered in the gallery.

We felt excitement, as if we were at the threshold of a great discovery, as if we had broken into a dragon's cave in which the shimmer came from a hidden treasure.

In such a spirit, we no longer felt tired. We wanted only to continue our descent into lower chambers. What did we expect to find there? This is the fever that sometimes overcomes explorers, like the gold fever felt by gold miners.

Yefremov was quite fiery. Perhaps he expected to find more evidence of human presence and be rewarded for some special discovery, whether fossils, cave drawings, or tools from the Stone Age. The geologist was examining samples; he slipped chosen ones into his backpack. The others were intensely investigating the walls and vertical gaps, occasionally throwing glances towards the depth beneath our feet that looked like a dense grid. At that moment, I suggested we stop our search. The day was nearing its end, it was late afternoon.

The leader of the expedition, A.I., gave a nod; we started preparing for the return. Yet in each other's glances we could recognize disappointment. The zealousness suddenly subsided. Still, there were reasons for that decision. We returned to the surface after almost two hours of climbing, as though we emerged from the unknown, from some other world, beyond the ordinary. The Mongols in our attendance were waiting for us, sitting on the grass and smoking.

Once more we returned to the entrance to the underground, hidden by the highest of the red turrets. This was maybe a month after our first descent. This time, there were only three of us. It was happening almost in secret. There is no official report or record. Below the first gallery, we discovered, there was a much larger space, huge cavities within the Earth's crust. They were connected by a whole tangle of underground passages, some of which, according to Yefremov, must have been dug by human hands.

We were amply rewarded for our boldness. Earth, the Great Mother, opened up for us one of her secret treasuries. First we saw a stone ceiling, an immense ceiling whose end we could not fathom as it dissipated in the distance of murky, fragile green light.

We passed an area of stalactites and stalagmites that formed beautiful halls, and some of them looked as if they were made for dwarfs, and the others for giants. We entered a crevice within the rock wall. A magnificent scene appeared beneath our feet.

Had we stepped into a chamber that still preserved the opulence of the Golden Age, or at least memory of it? We beheld a crystal forest, made of monoliths, crystals and the shine of amethysts, emeralds, agate, opal - a forest that came to life under the beams of our torches illuminating our path, revealing itself in a spectrum of colors and trunks that suddenly assumed a phantasmagoric shine. After a long time in darkness, this marvelous play of light blinded us. We felt dizziness and then pain in our eyes.

What geological theory would explain this miracle that entered into our view deep inside the Earth? For what eyes was this spectacle made? Perhaps no human being had set foot in these marvelous chambers for thousands of years.

Closer to the cave wall, a passage opened up through which there appeared to be a path. The path was covered in some kind of crystal dust beneath which were visible miniature crystals and colored pebbles. I noticed one stone with a ruby shine and placed it in my pocket. The wall, however, looked like rock burnt by fire emanating from deep within the Earth, or even the Cosmos. Such fires only burned during the age of the world's creation. In some places the stone had been transfigured by the flames into glass, while in others it kept the black and gray color of rock.

On the surface of the wall were inscribed letters, 12 in total. They were pressed in or engraved onto the hard surface. I ran my fingertips over them as if trying to curb my disbelief or excitement.

The archaeologist leaned over them, speaking disjointedly about runes, some unknown script, a lost language and an unknown people. Or were they some abstract drawings, incomprehensible symbols from which would emerge, over the course of centuries in some indeterminate proto-historical age, the oldest human script?

"Would you like to know the exact meaning of the inscription?", I asked Yefremov, not taking my eyes off the inscription. "I have already seen this inscription. They are not runes, but the letters of the Vattan alphabet. The literal meaning is: 'These are the gates of Agartha.'"

The archaeologist stared at me in disbelief. He thought that what I had just told him was a joke.

"Agartha is an underground world," I said calmly, "A world inhabited by people or beings very similar to humans in their embodiment, a world that lives its own independent life and of whose existence today's mankind is unaware. From one explorer of Antarctica I heard a legend of Ningens: beings similar to humans, but of a height up to thirty meters, humanoids who suddenly resurface from the ocean depths only to dive back down again. This is the only comparison worthy of the inhabitants of Agartha. In fact, the Ningen beings also inhabit Agartha. Who, after all, can actually presuppose what secrets the depths of the Earth hold? Agartha still influences all happenings on the surface in its subtle, invisible way, and these influences are sometimes benign, sometimes malign. This hidden centre, the invisible center of humankind, directs the flow of the history of the world.

"Its existence was, until recently, one of the jealously kept secrets of the East. In the interior of the Earth, there are numerous passages dug out, making a unique web that connects lands and continents. They existed even in the Neolithic and, according to many opinions, even much earlier. Some time ago, the entrances were sealed. But even if there were no entrances, the influence of the underground kingdom on humankind on the surface of the Earth would be no less significant.

"Their enigmatic ruler has the power to peer into the mind of every human being. His whisper penetrates men's consciousness and controls their actions. He is listening to what we are saying here, and he can read our minds."

***

A Tale of Agartha

Let the reader forgive me this scholarly introduction, written by the hand of a scribe.

The tale of Agartha reached the West from two independent sources.

Agartha is a kingdom hidden underground, populated by a people gifted with miraculous powers, a people that lives in wisdom and immense wealth. But Agartha is even more than that: it is the spiritual center of mankind ruled by a hidden ruler, the head of its initiatic hierarchy. His title is "King of the World."

"Saint-Yves d'Alveydre's posthumous work *Mission de l'Inde*, first published in 1910", René Guénon informs us, "contains a description of a mysterious initiatic center called Agartha."[49]

In the book *Beasts, Men and Gods*, published in 1924, Ferdynand Ossendowski reported his tumultuous trip throughout Central Asia during the years 1921-1922. There is a moment, Ossendowski claims, when stillness overcomes the world, when wild animals stop in their run, horses stop to listen, birds stop flying, and travelers stop in their tracks. Hordes of sheep and cattle and yaks crouch down to the ground, and dogs cease their barking. The wind subsides into a slow trembling of air, and the Sun stops in its motion. For a moment, the whole world sinks into silence. An unfamiliar song penetrates the hearts of animals and people. This is the

---

[49] René Guénon, *The King of the World* (Hillsdale: Sophia Perennis, 2004), p. 1.

moment when the King of the World speaks with God himself, when tongues of flame in the letters of the Vattan alphabet erupt from his altar.

Legend holds that this supreme spiritual and metaphysical center of mankind, Agartha, has not always been hidden underground, nor will it stay there forever. This condition corresponds to the fallen state of humanity, the age of darkness and confusion which, it is said, has lasted for the past 6,000 years. In 1890, the King of the World allegedly issued the following prophecy in the monastery of Narabanchi: "The time will come when the peoples of Agarthi will come up from their subterranean caverns to the surface of the earth." The prophecy continues:

> More and more the people will forget their souls and care about their bodies. The greatest sin and corruption will reign on the earth. People will become ferocious animals, thirsting for the blood and death of their brothers. The 'Crescent' will grow dim and its followers will descend into beggary and ceaseless war. Its conquerors will be stricken by the sun but will not progress upward and twice they will be visited with the heaviest misfortune, which will end in insult before the eye of the other peoples. The crowns of kings, great and small, will fall...one, two, three, four, five, six, seven, eight... There will be a terrible battle among all the peoples. The seas will become red... the earth and the bottom of the seas will be strewn with bones . . . kingdoms will be scattered... whole peoples will die...Then I shall send a people, now unknown, which shall tear out the weeds of madness and vice with a strong hand and will lead those who still remain faithful to the spirit of man in the fight against Evil. They will find a new life on the earth purified by the death

of nations. In the fiftieth year only three great kingdoms will appear, which will exist happily seventy-one years. Afterwards there will be eighteen years of war and destruction.

The name Agartha, according to the French esotericist Guénon, means "imperceptible" and "inaccessible" (and also "inviolable", since it is Salem, the "Abode of Peace"). Moreover, this author associates Agartha with the "Light of the East" of Islamic esotericism.

The Light of the East, however, is none other than the "Light of the North", the "Gold of the North" mentioned by classical writers. In other words, Agartha is only one of many projections of the Pole, the North Pole, Hyperborea or Paradise, which has shifted over the course of history from the North to the West and from the South to the East.

There exists, to name it, the Absolute Pole. Agartha is an Eastern projection of the Absolute Pole. We cannot seek this mystical Pole above the surface of the Earth, at the top of Mount Meru as it was in the Golden Age or in the Hyperborean cycle, but only underground - not in the polar ice of the Arctic, but in the East of the Eurasian continent. Emanuel Swedenborg issued the mysterious pronouncement that in our age the "lost word" is to be found only among the wisemen of Tatary and Tibet, i.e., in the East.

Some authors claim that contact has been maintained with this center during almost all of the historical cycle of the West. This contact was at all times direct and realistic. But the final projection of the North Pole - the sanctuary of the sacred King of the World in the East - has become more and more inaccessible and mystified. It was interrupted only in late historical times. Guénon states that this happened soon after the Thirty Years War, more precisely in 1648, when the "real Rosicrucians", 12 in total, left Europe and withdrew to Asia, to Agartha.

Guénon explains that Ossendowski wrote the name of this underground kingdom as "Agharti", whereas Saint-Yves used the form "Agartha", "the latter being known to have been in contact with at least two Hindus." The fact that this mysterious legend from the East reached the peoples of the West in two different versions is explained by the fact that Saint-Yves was inspired by Hindu sources, while Ossendowski was informed by Lamaist ones. This legend is, in fact, known in two different traditions of the East: the Buddhist and the Hindu, remaining alive but hidden to this very day.

A book published in the 17th century in Leiden mentions a city by the name of "Agartus Oppidum" reportedly located in the Nile Delta of Egypt. This fact was unknown to Guénon. Lucius Ampelius, a Latin author from the third century, claimed that in this city stood a statue with hands of ivory and a bright emerald on its brow. This statute, it is written, incites panic and fear among animals and people, and especially among barbarians. The word *oppidum* in Latin means elevation, fort, or hill. The meaning of the word Agartus is unknown and has no meaning in Latin.

It is also recorded that long ago, in Medeia, near the Southern coast of the Caspian Sea stood a city called Asagarta. Ptolemy added that the inhabitants of this land called themselves Sargartians, and Herodotus claims that 8,000 Sargartians (inhabitants of this lost land) were present in the army of the Persian King Darius.

Asgard, the mythical city of the Aesir or Aryans, was the capital of the Sarmatians and Roxalana. Some researches equate Asgard with Agartha. Others think that Agartha was exactly that city mentioned by the Roman Lucius as lying on the banks of the Nile. This is a mistake - the very same mistake committed by some in regards to Atlantis or Thule. Agartha is in fact Thule, one in a chain of Thules which appear at different times in different meridians. The same is true of its mysterious inhabitants, who at times come out onto the surface of the Earth.

The name Agartha has been known since ancient times, since the very beginning of history, and it can be found everywhere, from ancient Egypt to Bactria, in its projections, in its representation on Earth, in its secondary variations, just as every Thule, including even Atlantis, is only a projection of the primordial and original Hyperborean Thule, the one erected by the hands of man-gods at the dawn of time.

The King of the World's plenipotentiaries still wander the world today. Once, in ancient times, they were kings, holy men, princes anointed by God, prophets, and spiritual teachers. Today, the masses no longer recognize them or understand their words.

***

A Conversation with a Knowledgeable Lama (A Tale of Agartha Continued)

"One Mongol tribe was once fleeing from Genghis Khan", Djamsrap told me as we were sitting in his ger, "and found an entrance into the underground from which they never returned. It was near the River Amyl."

We had this conversation in the summer of 195* in the Uburtelin-Gol river valley, during the expedition in the Mongolian Altai presented in the beginning of these notes.

"Some lama saw an inscription on an inaccessible rock in the Himalayas which he could not interpret. Only just before the end of his life did he discover its real meaning. It is written in the Vattan script: 'Here are the gates of Agartha.'

"One hunter found gates leading to this underground kingdom. When he came back and spoke of what he saw there, lamas cut out his tongue. In old age he returned to the entrance of the mysterious cave and forever disappeared into Agartha."

These words of the lama were articulated to the young archaeologist Yefremov. There was nothing new or unknown to me in what he said. It was as if he was speaking my hidden thoughts, those which I found hard to convey to anyone. And this was only the beginning of his story.

"*Some time ago (tens of thousands of years ago),*" the lama continued in his calm voice, "*after a catastrophe that befell the* mankind of that time, some ancient peoples found refuge deep underground. Legend conveys that this happened after the flood, the worst to have ever befallen the Earth, followed by earthquakes and fires. This is the flood spoken of by the philosopher Plato.

"They were very different from today's men, about as much as today's men differ from animals. These ancient people were more like Gods or their descendants: 'The earth's daughters', the sacred books say, 'in that ancient time commingled with the Gods, and bore sons and daughters.' It is futile to waste our words on describing their physical strength, which enabled them to handle the strongest beasts. They were gifted with what are to us inconceivable powers. Telepathy was one of them, being in that time so ordinary as is the gift of speech to us. They knew even the forgotten language of the birds, which today only the angels speak, that language that still lives on in poetry - poetry in its highest sense - and can be sensed in the rhythms and consonances of sacred books.

"But above all else, these people were in possession of knowledge that made them wiser than our contemporaries. Deep underground, they continued to cherish teachings which are largely lost today. As strange as such may sound to our contemporaries, all knowledge and science originated from Agartha, albeit in distorted, profane form. But some of that knowledge can still be found in diverse legends and secret teachings on the earth's surface, teachings which we call tradition. I say secret teachings not because they are intentionally hidden from today's mankind, but because the majority of people are incapable of recognizing or understanding them. They are those pearls thrown in front of swine mentioned in the Gospel. Did the Apostle Paul not speak of this in his Epistle to the Hebrews?: 'About this we have much to say, but it is hard to explain, for you are dull of hearing and understanding.' Agartha and the people who populate it still possess highly developed technology, inherited from the civilization of the Atlantis, which disappeared some ten thousand years ago.

Agartha is not only a kingdom, but a spiritual center - a center that has existed forever but has become hidden to our days. Tradition says it is hidden somewhere in the East, in inaccessible and faraway lands to which no paths lead. The path to Agartha can only be found by those who are called and invited to it. Their sovereign is the King of the World, who is today invisible to ordinary people; from time to time he appears on the surface, and walks unnoticed among mortals. Sometimes, the King of the World voices some of his prophecies.

"The King of the World is, namely, a ruler like no others: he is before anything an instrument of Providence. He is the executor of the Divine thought and a superior of the spiritual hierarchy in place since the beginning of the world. The King of the world is Melchizedek, God's anointed one, the king of righteousness. He is the legitimate descendant and heir to the sun dynasty, a king and a priest at the same time. Agartha is therefore the spiritual and religious center of humankind. Its influence is for now obscured, but the agency of the King of the World is not interrupted even in times of great confusion and darkness. In fact, only his actions maintain the world, although in our time such is like the light of a single candle in the night. It is little, but just enough. It is said that even the three wise men who came to greet the newborn Jesus were emissaries of the mysterious kingdom of Agartha. They alone came to greet the coming of the Savior, the true Son of God, the tenth and last avatar.

"How has all of this remained unknown to present-day mankind, which never ceases to speak of the progress of science and *the increase of knowledge? If there are so many peoples on Earth, and if some of them still live in the interior under the rule of the King of the World, then how is it possible that this is unknown to modern science and that no evidence has yet been found to testify to their existence? How is it that so many ancient, sacred civilizations disappeared from the face of the Earth without a trace, without leaving behind at least some remains accessible to the excavations of Western scientists and eventually becoming a subject of interest?"*

Saying this aloud, the lama was posing the question which the archaeologist wished to ask him. The lama was, I thought, reading his thoughts.

"In discovering ancient civilizations and bringing their remains into the light of day, present-day archaeologists are releasing forces which they are unequipped to handle. They do not even suspect the existence of such forces - forces which are far beyond their modest capacities. These are not mere artifacts of ancient civilizations, dead remnants of past historical epochs, but souls of the dead, dead objects and humans capable of becoming powerful magical means, especially in the hands of magicians. Even when they are hidden or destroyed, they serve goals which transcend them.

"Unfortunately, today's scientists are not aware of this, as they do not possess any knowledge of the objects of their findings. The pyramids, for example, are constantly attributed to Egyptian civilization, and today's scientists see in them only tombs of pharaohs. Nothing is more untruthful and erroneous than this. The pyramids are sacred objects of ancient Atlantis, and they are found scattered across virtually the whole world. They do not even grasp that hidden under the paws of the Sphinx are forgotten histories of mankind. The Sphinx, the secretive guardian of suprahuman power, a beast with the body of a lion and a human head,

does not stop smiling at us and giving us its riddles. Its ill-omened laugh was heard by King Oedipus. Moreover, it is little known that it also appears in Hinduism, in the temples dedicated to the God Shiva, where it is known as 'Purushamriga', as the 'human beast.' Its paws conceal underground chambers harboring libraries carved in granite, books that reveal the most ancient past of humankind. I am talking about the secret Chamber of Notes. It is strange that this has been missed by all the explorers of ancient Egypt and the mysteries of the old world.

"How could this happen at all? We should bear in mind that the world has changed its appearance several times between ancient times and the present. This is not accidental, superficial change caused by some external culprits, as scientists from the West would have us believe, but change in the depths, penetrating the very structure of the world. Not only have the earth's external conditions changed, but so has the world changed fundamentally. We can say the same of people, as both stand in direct connection. Modern mankind does not bear any likeness to the old races. Even in the physical sense, modern man is just a sad caricature of the ancients. The fallacy of modern man is that he looks everywhere but in the end only sees those who are similar to himself.

"Hence the opaque veil that falls upon the past. Six thousand years is roughly the limit beyond which their sight can no longer penetrate time. This is the beginning of the final period of the fourth and last Yuga, the Iron Age or Dark Age. Destruction is looming over humanity today. This is the era of the reign of the Antichrist spoken of in Christian holy books, your Scripture, which we have studied with great care."

The Lama paused for a moment, covered his high forehead with his bony palms, and added a few more strange remarks: "*Once upon a time, in the ancient age, according to legends, precious stones were scattered all over the Earth, whereby diamonds were something quite ordinary, like the coarsest gravel today. But these same legends warn us that treasure in the hands of the uninvited turns into coal, into worthless, ordinary stone, and brings them the most terrible misfortunes. No one can appropriate gold for themself. You are searching in vain for El Dorado and the Garden of Eden.*

"*The peoples of Agartha will come out on the surface again. Thus has the King of the World prophesied, and he can speak with God himself. This will happen. Until it does, however, until the time comes, Agartha will remain hidden from the eyes of the unworthy. Agartha does not want to be discovered yet.*

"*For this to happen, for the peoples of Agartha to come out on the surface again, the world must change, and change in its deepest foundation. After all, if they were to come up to the surface today, the inhabitants of Agartha would dissipate into dust and ashes. The world has since become coarser, while their bodies have remained subtle and fine. Such is also the case of the mind of the ancients, the Firstborn, compared to ours. The precious stone has disappeared from the surface of the earth, leaving only coarse gravel, but it has not disappeared in its depths. Only the coarse man of the modern age can withstand the conditions that currently prevail here on Earth, on the surface.*"

***

The Dark Brotherhood

The Pueblo Indians believe that their divine ancestors came from deep within the Earth, a place connected to the surface by a large opening in the North. Navajo legends also teach that their ancestors came from underground. These ancient people, it is believed, possessed supernatural powers, and a great flood forced them to abandon their homes. When they found themselves on the surface, they transferred their knowledge to the human race and later disappeared in pursuit of their old shrines. The Eskimos in the Far North also know of a race that lives deep within the Earth's core.

I heard this from a Navajo shaman, who told me other, equally incredible tales. It was in the summer of 1937. We were sitting on the ground in front of his hogan, a house built of timber and mud, on the Navajo Reservation in Northeastern Arizona.

"Some time ago, an archaeologist from California was staying here, wishing to explore the old cities that could be found starting from here and stretching all the way to Utah. I was trying to dissuade him from the idea; I did not like it. He described to me an episode which he experienced a few years before in Yucatan.

"Together with six friends he climbed down into Loltun Cave. Its name means "flower stone." The cave is huge, with many corridors and narrow passages attached to it, so it was not unusual that they got lost. In the end, their exploration became a panicked ramble in the dark labyrinth. They thought they were finished when they caught sight of a weak light. They spotted a torch in the hands of a hermit, who was approaching them with shaky steps. Can you imagine their astonishment when they realized that the old man was completely blind? He told them that he had lived for a couple of years underground, deep under the Loltun Cave, and that he seldom went to the surface. He claimed that he is second-sighted, and that he found them with the help of his inner sight. He was carrying the torch to illuminate the path to the lost. All of this seemed unbelievable to them, so they asked him how he acquired food and drink.

"He answered that he was taken care of by friends who lived even deeper, in a magnificent underground city. He showed them how to return to the surface, and disappeared back into the cave like a magician. I think that this old man met the inhabitants of Agartha, whose cities underlie all continents, and that they blinded him so as to hide their secrets. The Apaches claim that their ancestors came from an isle in the Eastern sea which had cities and ports. Afterwards they lived in underground tunnels. The Votans were kings of snake-people who arrived from the East, through passages dug out underground. The wise-men of the Zapotecs teach that their tribe, in the times before the Great Flood, used to live in splendorous cities-caves.

"Not far off the coast of Florida, on the bottom of the sea, rest the remnants of some great civilization; stone cities and pyramids whose trails can be followed up to the Caribbean and Cuba. There are similar things to be found off the coasts of Europe and Asia. Something similar can be found in the mountains of Peru, on the banks of Lake Titicaca, at three meters above sea level - cyclopean buildings that look to modern humans as if they were built by giants. Their antiquity - if it is at all sensical to compare their time to human ages - is measured in thousands of years. Now *these cities and temples of the ancients rest on the bottom of the ocean. This is a consequence of the Great Flood, that which in the old times changed the face of the Earth, the one of which our legends speak. The story of the Great Flood is known to the White people as well, and not only them. The fires and floods desolated the world of that time, bringing a wave of death to people and animals, flooding vast areas, whole continents. This lasted until the world acquired its current shape. That is how the ancients vanished. The pyramids on both sides of the Atlantic allegedly hide entrances to that underworld.*

Today the new masters of America pride themselves in their buildings, the tallest and largest in the world, overlooking the fact that throughout our continent there are traces of these much older buildings that have withstood earthquakes, fires, and floods for thousands and thousands of years. The capabilities of moderns in which they take so much pride are no match for the powers of the ancients. Today's builders of skyscrapers and builders cannot reproduce the endeavors of the pyramids. What's more, they are overlooking something else as well: the silent presence of these monuments stand as warnings to modern people. This was well understood by our ancestors, who shunned cities and lived the simple lives of hunters, warriors, and nomads. White people remember a similar myth: the construction of the Tower of Babel.

"More than 10,000 years ago, a highly technologically developed civilization really existed, and it spanned across a large part of Earth, over many continents. Caves with the tombs of these people can be found deep in mountains. By our terms, they were veritable giants, over six feet tall. You call this Atlantis, we remember it by a different name, Aztlan, and it is remembered by many other peoples on both sides of the Atlantic.

"Yes, giant men once walked the Earth, and there were huge cities and machines, their society being much more advanced compared to the inventions of the modern West. Moreover, their weapons were incomparably stronger than all present ones, with rays that could cause immediate death and destruction, earthquakes followed by fires, wreaking destruction across the face of the Earth.

"The decline of this civilization began with a loss of internal equilibrium, with a spiritual eclipse which caused new animosities or spurred old ones. Some say that the Dark Brotherhood emerged within this ancient civilization; others mention divisions that had their roots in the even much deeper past preceding the establishment of Atlantis itself, from the time of the creation of the human race, of which we better not speak. Either way, the war which the ancients waged started suddenly, and reached its culmination just as quickly, threatening the annihilation of all of humankind. The great flood was only its consequence. One day, the sky turned blood-red and then became dark. Countless lightning bolts ripped apart the sky. The seas and land turned red with the blood of the giants. The Sun hid behind the clouds - clouds made of smoke and ash - and this lasted for several years. Many animal species went extinct. The surviving people returned from deep underground, and the surface of the Earth was populated with a new race: the race of the present-day humans, the most worthless of all.

"Today, White people are creating a new Atlantis on the soil of America, unaware of what they are doing. It does not matter if they are doing this out of blindness, ignorance, or if they are possessed by the demons, ghosts, and spirits of that cursed world that disappeared under the ocean waves. The fate of that ancient civilization will be repeated. These people are tools in the hands of others. Weapons of mass destruction nearly as potent as the ones of old have already been created. The world which we see before us now will sink into the ocean, the Earth will open and release fire from within. The impending catastrophe could be prevented or stopped only by the ancients, whom I have already mentioned. But the old divisions amongst them persist with the same flair. The fate of our world will depend on the results of the spiritual struggle that has already long been waged between initiates on the surface and the inhabitants of the underground kingdom. Ordinary people are not aware of this at all. And this struggle is as brutal as wars amongst men. The lives of millions do not mean much, or anything at all, to the ancients, for whom we are like insects aimlessly crawling around the Earth."

The following words he said in a much quieter voice, as he was confiding in me a strictly kept secret: "Deep underground, above Gods and humans, there is a secret kingdom ruled by the King of the World. Little is known about him, and even less is known for sure. Even those initiated into the deepest mysteries only whisper about this. In the legends of many peoples, we find cautious allusions to his existence. However, only the rare, only those who have climbed the spiritual hierarchy, are able to understand the whispers of the King of the World. His obscure words are understandable only to them."

The sun was setting. An Indian woman passed between hogans with a child in her arms.

On the road leading to the small town of Window Rock a whirl of red dust lifted up.

The face of the shaman, the medicine-man, was showing fatigue and indifference.

"The world has been created five times. We live in the fifth one. But it is nearing its end. The fate of people is uncertain. We will remain in the underworld.

"I wish to believe that the King of the World and his devoted helpers are watching over the fate of humankind, and that their secret operations will stop the Dark Brotherhood that has been directing the fate of our world in an ill-fated manner for thousands of years."

***

The Secret of the Red and Yellow Lamas

In Yarbul, in the Valley of the Kings in Tibet, the knowledgeable Lama Robsang spoke to me once about a tightly sealed door that led directly into the belly of the Earth. Heavy smoke reportedly gushes out of it in a constant flow. It has its invisible guardians, and everything about it is shrouded in superstitious fear. He was confiding in me a well-kept secret.

It seemed as if I was drawing close to solving a thousands-years-old enigma (tens of thousands, as Djamsrap corrected me with a voice that denied any objections). I had thought about the worlds hidden underground, about the opening of the Earth opened at the Poles, about the underground Sun of Agartha whose blessed aura warms the caves and secret passages where no humans have set foot. Lama Robsang was, in fact, telling me of an underground paradise, or rather the real Eden which has been situated under the surface of the Earth for some time. I thought about the "Hollow Earth" of Edmond Halley, astronomer for the English Crown, with its rotating spheres, and how the underground is lit by two suns called Pluto and Proserpine.

I also thought about the ancient peoples and tribes, unknown or long forgotten in the West, which were ruled by a mysterious Brahmatma sitting on his high throne made of stone, surrounded by thousands of incarnated gods. Around his throne stretched magnificent palaces of Goros who ruled over all earthy forces, visible and invisible. Under their commands, the lama claimed, grass and trees grow and the dead are resurrected.

But, above all, I thought about the vanished plenitude of the Golden Age. It reveals itself to us today in such wonderful images as vaults full of precious stones and lumps of gold hidden in the bowels of the Earth. This is the "secret of secrets" about which the Red and Yellow Lamas chant and Tibetan monks whisper with pious humility. They believe that our thoughts predetermine events and can be read like an open book. And that the King of the World does this every day, determining the fate of every human, every people. He has the power to raise them up or destroy them. Only he is allowed to read from the Great Book of Destiny.

This is one of the most carefully guarded secrets of the East, known in the West only to a fair few.

Not far from here, he said to me, the Tibetan kings were raised up to heaven. In a much later time - when their time was up - they disappeared into the underworld, opening that tightly sealed gate of which the revered lama spoke. Should I have believed this?

Two days earlier I had noticed wheel tracks and feet imprinted in the snow, in places where there is no way they could have possible gone.

The wind, an eerie, cold wind, was freezing my bones and the blood in my veins as it blew over the plain.

It was bringing snow, hard dust, and a smoky smell which stung my eyes and pinched my nostrils. There was a Tibetan village not far from here, around which were raised black tents.

I was able to hear a shot, or its distant echo.

I was treading the frozen ground, skidding on smooth stone between rocks with sharp edges.

The barking of dogs could be heard in waves. Something was unsettling, or scaring them before dawn, in the grey twilight. Maybe a Goro's shadow? Or the presence of beings more terrifying than the Ningen?

I was feeling severely nauseous and dizzy due to the lack of air. At dawn, a thick fog settled, and through this gray curtain only the Tibetan mountains were visible in dim outline...

***

One Important Note

The French esotericist René Guénon, who wrote about Agartha much earlier, claims that a Russian translation of Saint-Yves d'Alveydre's famous book *The Mission of India* never existed. From this erroneous premise stem a whole series of important - and equally erroneous - conclusions. One of them is that Agartha is a secret of the East (exclusively Eastern), and that it has been unknown to the people of the West.

A Russian translation of this book did in fact exist. I held it in my hands as a boy in my grandfather's library, where some time later I also discovered the original French edition from 1886 (a piece of information which I am not able to verify now): *Mission de l'Inde*, or *Mission de l'Inde en Europe*.

I read it at the age of 15, before the revolution swept the Empire, and somewhat later in French (French is my second mother tongue).

At first glance, this note is not of great importance.

However, it is precisely this fact, as well as taking into account other errors that plague Guénon's work entitled *The King of the World* (*Le Roi du Monde*, published in Paris, 1927), that calls into question some of Guénon's claims, especially the allusions that he was acting as someone's plenipotentiary.

René Guénon never accomplished any real contact with the King of the World and the mysterious underground kingdom, so he could not speak in its name. That is undeniable.

Over time, my writing desk has come to overflow with various notes left by travelers, scribes, wanderers, and adventurers, reports and travelogues, chronicles and annals, the speculations and suspicions of both fantasists and sober people, which I am now trying to put in order. I realize that this is completely futile work. They all speak of Agartha.

Here is an account, not too long, which I am copying almost word for word. It bears the date of 25 January 1966. I wrote it down in Moscow. The manuscript has undergone minor changes. Some parts are missing. I will add a few more details to this short description at the end, although I do not know whether they deserve to be remembered or forgotten.

***

Descent into Agartha

My First Wandering

My full name is Maximilian Rupert Dietrich Sikorsky.

My persona does not bear weight on what I am going to describe, as this is not my own personal story. I was present in it mostly as an observer, someone who recorded what he saw and heard while participating very little. Yet I want to say that I am by heritage Russian and Balt, not German. I lived in America and Asia, and then Soviet Russia, just as long as I lived in Germany, if not longer. I am not of any political persuasion, and politics and religion have always left me indifferent (perhaps this is true of the religions of our age). I have no wish to convince the reader of anything, even of the truthfulness of the story which I will describe here. The truth is obvious. He who reads this short story to the very end might understand why.

I was born in the Russian Empire, where my father served in the military. After the Revolution and Civil War, my family shared with so many others the unfortunate fate of White emigrants. Until then we were wealthy and belonged to the aristocracy. After a period of abundance came a period of scarcity and humiliation. Similar to the immigrants who entered New York Harbor, we were also homeless and refugees, but we were not greeted by the Goddess of Liberty, the one standing on the island at the mouth of the Hudson with broken chains under her feet.

I spent my youth in the Weimar Republic; those years were marked by misfortune and poverty. Perhaps it was my recklessness and predisposition for adventure that led me to leave Germany in the '30s first for Africa, then to India. Those were my first journeys. I described my trip to Africa in a small booklet. If I had stopped my adventures then, after these first wanderings, it is certain that I would have lived a very ordinary civic life. This, however, did not happen. I was the traveler, Ahasver, just looking for the opportunity to wander.

Before leaving, I had the occasion to be acquainted with National Socialism firsthand. It was not difficult to presume that it would soon win over the fragile democracy of Weimar Germany. And not only Germany, but the whole world at the time was seized by a strange unrest. An unforeseen cataclysm was in the making.

In 1938, I participated in a German expedition to the Himalayas which today has been overshadowed by the notorious organization, the Ahnenerbe. Immediately after I returned from the United States I gave a series of, I dare to say, very notable lectures throughout the German Reich. I say notable because, apart from the press, several influential people from the state and party leadership showed interest in this expedition.

***

On the Roof of the World

There is, after all, a photograph that caught my handshake with Heinrich Himmler and was then published by several daily and weekly newspapers, including the major party paper *Völkischer Beobachter*. I received high state decoration from the hands of Himmler. All of this would cause me much trouble later, and almost cost me my life. On my next expedition, I went as a member of the SS with the rank of Untersturmführer.

I will repeat: I did not decide to participate in the German expedition for any other reason - whether loyalty to Germany or party ideology, towards which I have always been indifferent - than the fact that since my last return I proved incapable of thinking about anything other than the Himalayas.

I have spent a certain amount of time in these mountains, which are popularly called in the press and television the "roof of the world" without any sense of the meaning of this word. "The Himalayas are a land of demons," the English writer Alexandra David-Néel said, "and they reside in the trees, in the rocks, in the valleys, lakes, and springs", being able to take on many shapes and forms so that every traveler finds themselves face-to-face with them.

The American expedition in which I participated could only be described as a complete failure. It is not even remembered in the history of the conquests of the Himalayas except for small side notes in passing or a minuscule footnote. It did not leave any important trace, and it could not boast of any noteworthy results.

A series of ill-omened and unexpected events brought the expedition to the point that it began to fall to pieces. Some of the participants perished in avalanches or succumbed to frostbite, the others just simply disappeared in the snowy whiteness. More frequent were cases of madness that would onset overnight.

A few months later, I was living as a beggar, traveling from one monastery to another, each of them populated by orange-robed monks who were benevolently welcoming despite their own lived poverty. During this time, I was actually living off of their charity and under their protection, for which I owe them tremendous gratitude.

I returned to India a year later in the company of some English adventurists to whom I managed to sell one reel of my footage from Tibet.

A prolonged stay at high altitudes brings a kind of inebriation. I am now inclined to believe that it is not lethargy caused by exhaustion, lack of oxygen or starvation, but a threshold of higher consciousness with which we become aware of inexplicable, superhuman existence - some would say of gods, some of demons.

But in the impossibility of us completely leaving this earthly existence, we can still see the possibility of passing into inhuman worlds, as if we are looking through a half-open door, unable to see clearly what lies on the other side.

***

An Expedition in the Yarlung Valley

Be that as it may, subsequently I did not need to worry about money, public lectures, or choice of collaborators. Behind me was always standing the powerful and secretive Ahnenerbe, and above it the even more powerful and mysterious SS. The leader of the new expedition, however, was not myself, but a certain SS colonel, Zur Linde. Thus the expedition would be remembered. I presume that the reason behind this was, besides the general suspicion of non-party members, the very pragmatic assessment on Himmler's part, or somebody close to him, that I am, at my core, an unreliable dreamer and adventurer, that I had not yet proved my loyalty, and that I was returning from an increasingly hostile country. Nor did I hide my heritage, which could hardly be regarded as Aryan: too much Asian blood runs in my veins. Nor did I show any jealousy towards my superiors. And why would I?

I had already drawn up a map and made a precise plan for the trip, approved and signed by the Reichsführer himself. These plans included the Yarlung Valley, and the chances of the plan changing were slim, or even less than slim. The preparations were going according to plan. A mighty machinery was put into action and showed its efficacy with each passing day.

Our real adventure started in the spring of 1938. Besides starting a little bit late due to the unwillingness of the colonial authorities in India to issue the needed permits, everything was unfolding according to plan.

Sometime in early September, we reached the Yarlung valley. I do not have any available notes, my diaries were lost, and I am writing all this from memory. The reader should excuse small errors.

The rest, however, is well-known, especially the triumphant return to the Third Reich by the next year, where Colonel Zur Linde received decoration from the hands of the Führer himself.

I did not participate in the continuation of the expedition, nor could I take the credit for its triumph. My name was, as I surmise, deleted from the official reports. In the end, all the glory went to Zur Linde, an agile, refined and somewhat mean Saxon, fond of cognac and opium, who, as I found out later, ended his life in 1942 or 1943 under English bombs in Munich.

In the Yarlung Valley we had our first and last misunderstanding - after that we did not meet again. I remember the day we welcomed emissaries from a nearby Tibetan village. The elders were admiring the swastika on our flag; we exchanged gifts and niceties and then conversation, for which I was the interpreter. They told us the legend of how the first king of Tibet descended down a rope from the Celestial Kingdom and landed not far from here. This is the same place where the kings of Tibet would climb up the rope to heaven. That rope finally tore after being used for many centuries, and since then all their kings have died like all other mortals.

***

A Tower in Ruins

rinking brandy and suddenly becoming cheerful, the elders added that there were ruins of some old tower. If we wanted, they could find us guides from their village.

Colonel Zur Linde quietly dismissed all of this, despite my repetitive reminders of their offer. I added that the Yarlung Valley was the cradle of Tibetan civilization, and that the ruins of the city - city, I emphasized, instead of mere tower - was probably the oldest site that could be seen in Tibet. I added a few racial arguments: I referred to one of the ideologists of the Ahnenerbe who spoke of the Aryan roots of Tibetan civilization. The colonel, however, in his grumpy manner, sharply responded that the goal of our expedition was something completely different, and that our efforts to go there would be a waste of time.

I raised my glass to give a toast, said a few words in honor of our hosts, as was expected of me, and added a few more that surprised our tribal patriarchs. They stopped for a moment and, exchanging glances with one another, carefully nodded their heads.

Not waiting for the morning, some time after midnight I left the tent and headed for their village alone. The trip was tiresome and took longer than I anticipated. It was dawn when I finally spotted it. The houses were small, built from stone, and surrounded by even smaller dwellings; they were organized in three or four rows with narrow paths between them.

Somewhat lower I noticed a series of black tents, but did not know what their use was. I remember that a cold wind was blowing, bringing fine, dry snow, and that there were no signs of life around besides the smell of smoke and some weak light. That is how my contribution to the expedition of Zur Linde, the most famous venture of the Third Reich in the Himalayas, ended.

Nine years later, I was leaving Inner Mongolia with a nomadic tribe. We were nearing the Soviet Trans-Baikal on horses, bypassing the Mongol capital in a broad curve.

It seemed that my unusual appearance attracted the attention of informers. I was wearing Mongolian attire customary for shepherds and sported an overgrown, long, russet beard streaked with grey hair. We stopped for some time at one of the stations along the way to engage in the usual exchange of goods. The next day, I fell into the hands of NKVD investigators.

***

A Trip to the Moon

Now it is 1966, a year of great expectation for various circles, and I live the unnoticeable and quiet life of a pensioner under a new name in a very modest apartment in Moscow. Every morning I get newspapers from a kiosk. While going through my change, consisting of only a few kopeks, with the rosy shopkeeper, I am glancing at a front-page headline with definite uneasiness. I think she notices my nervousness.

Here, economic successes and socialist construction, and, on the other side of the Iron Curtain, the miraculous and paradisal blessings of the "free world." I fill the short time I have left with books.

Next to my bed lie the books of Jules Verne, Bryusov, Lovecraft, and Poe. I am also enjoying the old editions of Merezhkovsky. There is also a novel with the title Solaris by a Polish author about a mysterious being, an ocean on some faraway planet, a being that has the power to materialize our hidden fears and dreams. This reminds me of the Inner Ocean illuminated by the pale sun of the underground world that mysteriously glimmers in the belly of the Earth.

People are smiling everywhere today - in deserts, in taigas, sprouted towns, cosmodromes, research and industrial centers. Advances in technology and science, in living standards, while multinational companies measure their successes in millions of dollars. I put the newspaper down and my face frowns a bitter smile.

At first glance, everything appears to be determined and predictable. Things are going their usual way. We believe in the inevitability of progress, in the impending fraternity of all of humanity. Yet ahead of us, I know for certain, lies a whole series of very disturbing events. One of them is the Moon landing. Humankind will receive the Moon landing as a triumphant act, one more victory of logic and technology over the forces of nature and the force of the Earth's gravity, like a fulfillment of an ancient human dream. What a misapprehension. Or maybe not?

During my sleepless nights I stare at the pale, dead face of the Earth's only orbiter, the one always facing us. The arrival of people on the Moon, the steps taken on its lifeless surface covered in cosmic dust, will awaken and stir both the dead and the living. But this is only an illusion, the true meaning of which will be made clear only later.

Across from me is a heap of apartment blocks completely identical to the one I live in, with the same concrete entrances, yellow-painted lifts, small balconies overladen with flowers, and the same stairs in eternally dimmed light with a pleasant timber handrail. Hundreds and thousands of lives, existences, all set in seemingly stable forms. Everything suggests permanence, given immutability. While sipping a cup of hot tea and slowly enjoying the inhalation of cigarette smoke into my lungs (a ritual sporadically interrupted by strenuous coughs), I feel immense pleasure in beholding the clear, cold sky. Beyond it are unreachable worlds inhabited by myriad beings, unknown and incomprehensible to us, and a reality of which our mind cannot even conceive. The hypothesis of the cosmic, alien origins of man - let us call it a hypothesis - seems to me in such moments to be the only logical and unquestionable truth. Somewhere, in the depths of the Earth, thousands of feet under the surface, between gray walls of rock, lie the ruins of giant machines, resembling cosmic shipwrecks of vanished races, about which even the Firstborn knew little.

My eyes, I repeat to myself, have beheld the pale sun of Agartha.

I breathed that air circulating the subterranean passages and I saw the gently rippled surface of the Inner Ocean. I saw the magnificent places of the Goros, surrounded by the unfathomable in the dream of the submerged Brahmatma.

***

20,000 Feet under the Earth

The tower is high, immeasurable, but not because of its physical size; from afar it looks like a slanted stick stabbing into the sky. There is something contradicting Euclidean geometry in its architecture. It would be wrong to say that it rises above the Earth; it would be more correct to say that it grows up out of the surface into the clouds that move quickly around it, driven by strong currents of air.

For a moment, it seems to me that the tower is standing in the midst of a stormy whirlwind, a hurricane. I see myself standing at its base, surrounded by complete strangers speaking their barely recognizable language of guttural consonants and syllables that are difficult to repeat. I feel dizzy, which is probably a consequence of the very thin air.

The tower's height is actually around 200 feet. Its walls crumble under the touch due to old age. A pile of rubble rests at its base.

This is only one of those ruins whose age no one can determine. Whose hands raised it? Perhaps the hands of those giants who built Asgard, the City of the Gods?

A guide is showing me something below with his hands. His words carried a sharp, cold wind. The absurdity of my situation makes me helpless, vulnerable, and weak. The guide says to my ears that there is an entrance down below that leads into the tower's interior. Inside, there is a spiral staircase that originates in the depths, in the very core of the Earth. Nobody really knows where it actually leads, but its depth is certainly no less than 20,000 feet.

Twenty-thousand feet under the surface of the Earth. No one who has attempted to enter here over the past hundreds of years has ever returned to the surface. In ancient times, only shamans descended the staircase; only they could return. Legend says that the passage has secret guards, and that no one uninvited may enter.

I sat down, either at the foot of a wall, or against a rock eroded by time. Around me I saw stern faces, slanted eyes, high cheekbones, dark, gray, and expressionless. An attempt to have a smoke ended in nausea and vomiting yellow mucus. I drank bitter tea offered to me by an old man, a priest or a shaman. For the hundredth time, I stubbornly persisted to try to think rationally. The food supplies I carried with me, if I treated them sparingly, were enough for at least seven days. The situation was different with water supplies. But this shouldn't be a problem in the bowels of the Earth. There was also a Walther, whose cold grip I could feel in my pocket, and a supply of a hundred bullets in my rucksack, in addition to the rifle I carried slung over my shoulder.

I arrived at the staircase, and what I saw reminded me of a Roman well, like the one I had once seen in Belgrade. Hearing unclear, excited voices around me, I started descending the steep, dark staircase, walking faster and faster and running out of breath.

***

In the Depths of the Abyss

Soon enough, my descent turned into a mad run and tumble which I could not stop at will. I was falling, or rather floating in a space with no gravity, ever lower and lower, being careful not to smash into a rock wherever I put my feet. I felt several strong blows to my arms and chest around my heart. Finally, I slipped and lost the ground under my feet, suddenly disappearing into a dark abyss, in a whirlpool that forcefully sucked me down. It is impossible to say how long this lasted. The last thing I remember is the thought, or feeling, that I have stepped out of everything real and predictable, that the laws of physics and gravity no longer apply here, and that something terrible will happen soon. At last, I thought, I had found my grave.

What woke me was a very pleasant feeling. I was lying on a soft, silky bed of wet grass, or maybe young fern. Above me shined a diffused, yellow light. Lukewarm rain fell on my face and hands in tiny and persistent droplets. I saw a low cloud above me, through which a dim sun shined. I thought of Captain Edmond Halley's talk of rotating spheres and subterranean suns. I got up with difficulty and immediately felt sharp pain. Dark, almost black blood streamed down my arm. All around me, in a pleasant dimness, rose bare, grayish, smooth rocks. I thought I was somewhere beyond, perhaps in hell itself. I laughed. I was lying at the bottom of a giant cave, a terrifying abyss of unfathomable depth, hidden in the womb of the Tibetan mountains. This was, truly, my grave. It is quite certain that I will end here, peering into the unreal reflection of a sun shining through a vertical cleft in the rock. If anyone had walked this path before me, I thought, as the Tibetan elders and lamas claimed, I will surely find their bones here.

The rain was from the watery curtain of an underground waterfall that touched down on dark stones. I stroked the grass with my hand; it was soft, pale, and unnatural, like human hair. Then I noticed something resembling a steep path leading down. The sight of it made me cringe in horror. I searched for my rucksack and rifle in vain, and gave up. I found myself trapped with no escape. But at the moment of coming to this realization, I suddenly felt a strange indifference. To fill the short time I had left, I started down the path that opened beneath my feet.

***

Walking above the Abyss

I was advancing easier than anticipated, walking almost effortlessly, like how we walk in dreams. Suddenly, I realized that I was walking above an abyss, and a huge valley stretched out all around me. The rain had stopped, but the yellowish-gray cloud still hovered over my head. The non-reality, or rather impossibility of everything I was seeing leads me to a ridiculous thought: I am experiencing a hallucination caused by the shaman's drink. One effort of will would be enough to wake me. Either I will soon see the same yellow faces around me again, or I will die, trapped in this dream-vision for eternity. I recall sitting hunched over with my head buried between my legs for a long time, but the nightmare persisted and I was unable to wake up.

I climbed some sort of a platform made of material which gave off a silver shine. I touched an inexpressibly cold railing or fence consisting of curved metal bars. Beneath my feet lay the same abyss, but it now looked much larger than before. Over these gloomy landscapes rose a light, transparent haze whose drift constantly gave the landscape below a new and different appearance. I remember seeing at one point some kind of metal body. Inside of it was a cogwheel with a diameter of at least two fathoms, but this did not draw my attention or arouse amazement.

Then the platform unexpectedly moved, and I noticed that I was standing on a large metal disc whose bold arch rose, I suppose, up towards the vault of the cave. The light, that same light that had previously shined ever dimly through the clouds, suddenly blinded me. When I opened my eyes again, I almost screamed in surprise. Deep down below me, I saw mountains and valleys, a dark river, and several almost black lakes, and then an entire city surrounded by quadruple ramparts, in whose center what must have been a miraculous temple stood tall. It also seemed to me that I saw in front of the temple a statue of a god who, perhaps because of the trident he brandished, reminded me of Poseidon. The flight landed in front of the wide-open gates of the city and I hopped off the disk, which was still slightly vibrating. Not even that, however, drew my astonishment.

***

A Man Stood before Me

Memory of such wondrous and bizarre experiences as this one does not fade over time. It stays alive in each and every detail, to come back to us in waking consciousness and in dreams. Sometimes I find myself, like in a nightmare, once again in front of this same city gate, and I feel once again that cold touch of metal.

I am sitting at the kitchen table, in front of me lies a still unopened issue of *Pravda*, and next to it a cup of hot tea. I feel the whole building trembling as a tram passes down the street. I am thinking of the caves I passed through, and the ancient mines. In fairy tales, such places are inhabited by dwarfs amassing their treasures. I inhale the cigarette smoke and a severe attack of coughing hits me. It is a sunny day, the beginning of August, and in such moments I feel almost primordial joy.

I am thinking about how everything which we think and see around us could be just an illusion, a dream that will soon become a nightmare - terrifying, naked reality. About how we are mere unreal shells of being, and about how somewhere, probably at our very fingertips, are those who fully determine reality. To them, our lives and our passions have no meaning; we are but pawns in a game whose meaning and persistence escape our understanding.

I arrived at the gates of the unknown city. Symbols and letters were drawn on them. The gateway was not made of stone, but of some kind of metal emitting a dim, reddish glow. I ran my hand over its coarse surface and thought that this wall was ancient, thousands of years old, much older than anything I had ever seen in my life. Older than the pyramids or the Sphinx, older than the cyclopean cities, older than the temple at Halicarnassus. I stepped into the shadow and passed under the arch of the gateway, and at that moment I was left speechless in amazement.

A man stood before me. He was of unusual height, perhaps as tall as two fathoms, with deeply cut facial features, long but sparse, dark hair, a bit like a North American Indian. Instinctively, without thinking, I reached into the pocket of my leather jacket and felt the cold handle of my Walther.

I stood before him, unable to move or speak. I stared intently into his face, which had an unpleasant, gray-yellow tint in the dim light. I saw him move his lips. The words which he uttered softly penetrated my consciousness. Trying to lean in to hear him, I inadvertently took a step or two backwards.

What he said to me was, roughly, the following: "*It has been half a century or more since any human being has stepped foot in the underground kingdom of Agartha.*"

***

The Temple of the Moon

The underground kingdom of Agartha...

I laughed loudly, like a madman. The stranger did not move, his face was expressionless.

I was looking with my eyes at what I thought was a myth, a superstition I had heard from the Tibetan monks, a fairy tale from books, a product of the fantastical imagination of writers, a ghost created by fantasists and illusionists.

I recalled Baron Ungern von Sternberg, the mad "bloody Baron", who three times sent a young prince to look for it. I recalled Saint-Yves d'Alveydre, who spoke about this underground kingdom, and I remembered the verses from the Indian Ramayana describing how the great avatar Rama appears on a magical aircraft as an envoy of Agartha. I remembered so many others speaking of Agartha with such passion, so ecstatically painting it in incredible colors, such as the young ideologists in the Ahnenerbe. But what I was seeing now simply didn't resemble their fantasies.

It took me some time to regain the power of speech. I did not feel fear as much as disbelief or genuine astonishment. Through my mind raced a whole whirlpool of thoughts, many of which were not my own. Everything was happening in one moment. It seemed as if I could quite clearly see in front of me things of which I had never even conceived, and as if I was hearing forgotten and lost words. Finally, I told him - I must have spoken in an insecure voice, likely stammering - that I had found myself here by accident, by an unfortunate series of circumstances, and that I would leave Agartha immediately if he could show me the way out, and that I would keep the secret to myself forever. That was nonsense. In Agartha, nothing, not even earthquakes, happens by accident.

The stranger beckoned me to walk with him. I heard what seemed to be akin to muffled laughter from the chest of the giant. He spoke to me slowly - and, it seemed to me, with some effort - as if speaking to a child: *"No one reaches Agartha without being called…without the call of the King of the World, and no one leaves the underground kingdom without his permission."*

I was thinking that I was his prisoner, and that the weapon I still had could be used as a last resort. The giant could read my hidden thoughts like an open book. They did not deserve any answer, obviously.

As we were walking down the city street, I saw huge houses of dark marble, monumental constructions resembling the caryatid-adorned Acropolis, and then something that looked like a temple. I instantly knew that this was the Temple of the Moon in the heart of the city. I saw several shadows of equally tall people who sped around corners at the speed of spies, and I felt the immense loneliness, almost desolation that reigned in this city hidden in the mountain depths. I thought about the loneliness of the Gods, the solitude that they feel even in the company of their own kind. I had found myself at an immeasurable depth where no human being had ever set foot. Yet everything I saw around me gave the impression of abandonment, of sad desertion, as if it was all finally abandoned in the face of inevitable decline after thousands and thousands of years…

I nearly tripped over the ruins of walls, stones, and rubble left lying on the road. The stranger opened a gate made of iron, or some kind of almost black metal, and we began to climb up the spiral staircase of a tall tower under dim, smoldering lights, like pale candle flames, which barely allowed us to not stumble along the way…

***

The Underground City

We reached the top, where I leaned over the parapet between its jagged ramparts. What I saw first was a landscape on the other side of a low embankment, and fields of pale grass that looked as if they were silk-woven. Then I saw forests of ferns and conifers, or plants like them. In some places, I spotted herds of animals similar to tapirs and lamas. All of this dissolved under the same yellowish light into some kind of gray semi-darkness. I saw a canal, a river, and several lakes whose water was black and shimmered on their surfaces. I turned towards the panorama of the city engulfed in a transparent haze betraying domes and hundreds of curved towers with massive, heavy bases.

I saw the same shadows in the streets, no more than 10 in total, of people approximately the same height as my host, dressed in long tunics, robes, or dresses made of leather. Their gender could not be determined from this distance, but still, it seemed to me that at one point I caught sight of a woman of supernatural beauty, reminiscent of a goddess, and I unconsciously uttered to myself: "Athena." The streets lined up at right angles and were full of long, dark shadows like those cast of the evening light.

I remember feeling a cold breeze at the top of the tower. But the breeze did not bring a breath of freshness. It was the stale, cold, damp air of clefts, caves, and dark crevices in rock. I thought of how an immense mass of rocks rested above our heads, from which I suddenly began to feel anxious. I envisioned myself buried alive, never again to see the Sun or a starry night above. I felt weak, and I might have fallen onto the stone floor if my host had not offered me a goblet from which I took a few sips. The liquid had the consistency and taste of blood, and at the same time resembled a bitter, heavy wine. I thought of the soma of the Vedas and the haoma of the Avesta, and in that second I felt the beneficent drink flowing through my bloodstream directly into my heart.

Then, all of the sudden, I believed I was dying.

**

The Shadow of Dawn

I woke up the next day at dawn, at the dawn of that cursed land called Agartha. I say "dawn", but such was just the apparition, the shadow, the idea of dawn, like the shadows in Plato's cave, and not the dawn that exists on the Earth's surface.

The pale sun that had just yesterday radiated through the clouds and fog had a somewhat stronger glow now. Then a light rain fell, and the landscape once again disappeared behind the morbid mist.

The stranger told me his name was Mani, and he was, like all the inhabitants of Agartha, hundreds or thousands of years old. His existence was incomparable to the duration of ordinary human life. From a human point of view, he was immortal. From the point of view of the Ancients, his life lasted no longer than an instant.

"Who are the Ancients?", I asked, listening to my own voice, "And who are the Immortals?"

"Who are the Ancients?", he repeated.

His voice sounded expressionless, mechanical, robot-like. And yet it had a depth and mellifluence that no human voice has.

"*Gods, demons, extraterrestrial beings, cosmic forces or entities, beings without names and individual traits, it does not matter, whatever you would like to call them. They are all our futile attempts to imagine something that cannot be described by words or any human language. We see them only in their human form - a form that only remotely and vaguely resembles that of people and is, by all accounts, just one of many. Beings, omniscient and omnipresent, which we pass by every day without noticing them in reality. According to some, they reside at the bottom of the ocean, according to others they reside on the inaccessible tops of the highest mountains, or deep in the belly of the Earth, much deeper than Agartha. What we see are only their unclear projections or shadows. I have never seen them in their original forms. To be able to do so, we would have to become like them. The King of the World could tell you more about this if he finds you worthy of an answer."*

***

They Came from the Unknown

This is the story which Mani then told me. This is its meaning as I understood it, not his words. This was, in fact, a conversation which we held for many days and nights, sitting among the shadows on the top of the tower under the pale sun of the underground kingdom.

In the beginning, there was the Golden Age. In the beginning, there was pure Thought which manifested itself in the Word.

There were the Ancients, who came from the unknown, mighty and sovereign, disinterested in the lives of the animals under them. We do not know if their arrival, their descent to Earth, was sudden and unexpected, the result of some cosmic catastrophe, or some premeditated plan. We do not know what it was they sought on Earth, nor do we know if they found it. Why did they stay here? We do not even know where - at the bottom of the ocean, or in the hot core of the Earth? Only the King of the World knows - maybe not everything, but at least something about this. Only he can talk with the Ancients. They are the oldest among the Gods of the world.

As it happened, this was also the beginning of the human race, uncertain as any other, for it too has a very long and complex prehistory. This is not spoken of, because it is forbidden to speak of it, for it is the object of cults and religion, the primordial mysteries - and those before them - shrouded in the veil of true mystery which mortals cannot and must not know. Ordinary human reason simply cannot penetrate its logic.

Up until then, the laws of evolution were in force. Since then, since their appearance, however, time has acquired a new course, a completely different, opposite trajectory. The wheel inexorably and unstoppably turns backwards - involution, not evolution, is in force. The evolution of man-beasts ceased once and for all, and a new human race appeared against it, the race of man-gods.

***

The Race of Soft Bones

They created the first humans. The appearance of the man-gods of the North in their corporeal, material form, with perfect features, was connected to some sort of error, fall, and their materialization was, in the beginning, incomplete. By virtue of some kind of physical weakness, these first people would be remembered in tradition as the "race of soft bones." Some intermediate forms which preceded them, beings quite alike humans, and some animal forms were perhaps the result of unsuccessful attempts at embodying man in physical form, to finally materialize him in a physical body.

In the beginning of their existence, the man-gods inhabited the Far North of the planet, the North Pole and surrounding areas. This was a land of eternal spring, moderate climate, huge hordes of cattle, deer, and mammoth roaming the steppes. Insurmountable barriers such as mountain masses and glaciers separated two worlds: Arctogaia and the Land of Night, which has since come to be called Gondwana. These man-gods did not know of death, and they served pure thought - thought in its elementary, effective, creative state, mightier than any magic or technology. When they resort to technology, this will be the consequence of degeneration, of fall. Their actions are ritual, each of their acts is more of a divine ritual than ordinary human life and everyday doings.

These primordial humans - we call them "human", but they were obviously more like gods – spoke a magic language which tradition remembers as the "language of the birds" from which all later human languages would develop, which testifies to a status much closer to divine or angelic language than human language in the present sense of the term. From that angelic language, the language of the birds, the language of the Gods, from its mysterious rhythms and meanings, would develop all true science and knowledge, and its last echoes would be the rhythmic languages of sacred books and poetry whenever it approaches its sacred ideal and moves away from the profane. Poetry, in this elevated meaning, is the last trace of that lost and forgotten language of the birds. All later, derivative languages would signify new phases of degradation, of human decline, just as the emergence of ethnos and race marked the split of primordially universal man.

***

The Man with Arms Raised

This pre-stage or proto-phase of history did not mark the actual appearance of the man-gods in history; they still lived in isolation and manifested themselves only sporadically, or indirectly, without leaving obvious, clear traces. They did not build civilizations, but lived in their enlightened, divine simplicity, something that we could call "proto-culture" - and all later cultures would be the consequence of the degradation, deterioration of this primordial heritage. An occasional petroglyph, symbol, or rune engraved in stone are the only traces of their existence. Two of the most important such signs were the man with raised arms, being a symbol of dawn and ascension which reminded them of their divine origin, and the deer, the true symbol of the North, the animal with proudly raised antlers.

The divine race dwelled in the Far North and had its counterweight in the man-beasts of the South, Gondwana, the descendants of Lemuria. The latter erected cities with masses of people and followed the Cults of Mother Earth, the Moon, and Night. If there was any contact between these two, then it was rare and excluded mixing. Sacred books recall the ancient prohibition on mixing between races. Why did this nonetheless eventually happen? The interbreeding of the people of the North, Arctogaia, with the semi-beasts of the South would become the milestone of the next cycle of involution, the Silver Age, as a consequence of a new fall or, according to some opinions, it was this mixing of races that began the first cycle of involution. This was preceded by cataclysms which destroyed Arctogaia forever, shifted the Earth's tilt, and covered their homeland with snow and ice, thus setting into motion the first migration waves of the people of the North towards Gondwana in the South.

At the beginning of time there were the Firstborn. Those who followed them, the Secondborn people of the Silver Race, were still man-gods, but with diminished powers. These were followers of the Moon, the inhabitants of Atlantis, the paradisal island in the North-West Atlantic. One of its names was Mo-Uru. The Secondborn were a product of the genetic engineering of the man-gods and the semi-animals of Gondwana, or perhaps the mixing of the man-gods with the ancient races of Lemuria. The Adamites were the product of a similar technology. As it is said in the Book of Genesis, "*Elohim*" is plural, and they created the Garden of Eden and the first humans in today's sense of the word.

It is not possible to say what happened to the man-gods during their contact with the races of the South and the crumbling of their civilizations. From this contact was born a civilization of the West, Atlan or Adland, which the human race remembers as Atlantis, no longer illuminated by the light of the North and Sun, but by the light of the distant nocturnal reflection of the Moon, and the primordial joy was replaced with melancholy and fatigue. The moon, it is said, is just an elevated and transformed Earth that only reflects the light of the Sun.

***

At the Beginning of History

The Golden Age did not know a priesthood, for life itself was holy and sacred, and humans and gods were alike. The lunar age gave birth to the female priesthood which maintained the sacred fires, and with it death appeared for the first time. Life was distorted and spoiled. There appeared illness and aging, which are just other names for death. This was an age of decline and fall, in the beginning imperceptible, but later all the more obvious and rapid. Language changed, becoming more discursive, thus facilitating the appearance of the sciences, at first magical, and then mere technology born out of magic. This was, among other things, the consequence of contact with the animalistic languages of Gondwana and its perverse sciences. They established the first highly technologically developed civilization on Earth, a heritage which is still preserved in the kingdom of Agartha.

With the Silver Age began the proto-history of humankind. From the island in the West began the first migrations of the man-gods to the East and South, to warm seas and different lands, paths along which they left clear and unambiguous traces. This island-continent in the West was also called Moria. There followed migrations from the last remaining islands of the frozen Arctogaia, forming a complex network of intersections and migrations. This was the beginning of the first human races in history. New races came from the West in the form of almost perfect, divine human types whose remnants can still be discovered in the caves of Cro-Magnon; this was a race of seafarers and farmers, conquerors and warriors who, whoever they appeared, changed the remnants of the degenerate, dying races of Gondwana. Along the paths of their migrations sprouted the civilizations of the first city-fortresses and monumental temples, ports and sacred centers, the first centers of the earliest cults and writing.

Their center was a vast island, the Atlantis reported by, among others, Plato. A city straddled this island with fortified walls and surrounded by embankments through whose channels triremes constantly entered and departed. Their capital was Thule (but only a reflection of the primordial Hyperborean Thule). The Atlanteans were colonizers, sometimes benevolent, sometimes ruthless and cruel, who served their equally cruel gods and goddesses. First among them was mighty Atlas, who worshipped Poseidon, the god of the wide-open blue sea. The Deer of the North was replaced by the cult of the bull with its sacred games, and the appearance of death brought with it the establishment of the first cults of the dead. On both sides of the ocean and throughout the Mediterranean, complex techniques for mummifying corpses began to be cultivated to enable the survival of the soul for at least some time after the body's death. In connection with this arose witchcraft and the ritual significance of blood, the color red, and the fiery principle within the human body.

The people of the Silver Race would degenerate into the Bronze Race remembered in legend as the Titans. They were giants, the Ispolins, the Giants who seduced earthly women and then tried to conquer heaven, committing violence against the divine - in other words, against the people of the Golden and Silver Races. This was a race of cruel and unrestrained lords, giants of insatiable greed and lust, rampant and hot-tempered giants which the Jewish tradition knew by the name *Nephilim* - those who would try to storm Olympus and assault the "Father of the Gods" himself.

***

The Wars the Titans Waged amongst Themselves

After a few thousands years, the Titans found themselves on the brink of extinction, waging continuous wars against the people of the Golden or Silver Races, from whom they descended, or amongst themselves. The repercussions of these wars were, among other things, floods and fires that all but completely destroyed the Earth. An end was put to this by the Heroes, also members of the Bronze Race but "better than their fathers." Yet it was too late for them, too: the Titanic race was almost extinct entirely. They were replaced by the people of the fourth and final race, the Iron Race, today's worthless and greedy, weak and frightened humankind. All the previous races and their remnants withdrew deep under the surface of the Earth, to Agartha, although up until recently some of their descendants could still be found in various barely accessible places.

The wars of the Titans left a wasteland and caused the extinction of many peoples and races. For the sake of survival, the citizens of Agartha made a kind of pact, a tacit agreement: all future conflicts were to be waged outside, on the surface, using the peoples of the Iron Race as mere tools, while in the interior, at least seemingly, harmonious peace would reign under the rule of the King of the World.

The balance was fragile, maintained only by cautious skill, or rather the superhuman power of the King of the World, one of the few surviving Firstborn. But even he had to take into account the complex relations between the antagonistic sides and, above all, the wishes of the Ancients, whom, for some reason, the extinction of humanity did not suit. The end of the world was postponed - we believe, only for a while.

An attempt by the Firstborn to restore the Golden Age, the Last Thule, under the leadership of the King of the World and to assemble all other races under their flag and solar cult ended in defeat. Things followed the same direction as they had on Earth for thousands of years. The priests of the cult of Poseidon and then of the Moon evermore openly disputed the spiritual rule of the King of the World.

Then, into the light of day - meaning in the conflicts still taking place outside Agartha, by means of the people of the Iron Age - the Titans, or what was left of that ancient race, resurfaced, and then the Heroes as well. History repeated itself with equally devastating consequences, albeit this time around its protagonists, the people of the Iron Race, were largely unaware of what they served. The eternal sacred principles of supra-history were translated into the cramped, limited language of the greatly degraded humanity of recent times - the language of the religions and political ideologies of the modern age.

It was only a matter of time until those wars, titanic in character and scale, would make their way to the underground kingdom. At first almost imperceptibly, with seemingly coincidental accidents, deaths, or assassinations, followed by the persistence of ever stronger earthquakes suggesting the use of the most destructive tectonic weapons, and then open but still limited conflicts. The already sparse population of Agartha was decimated. The power of the King of the World was weakened, he looked more and more like the Wounded Fisher King from the legends of the quest for the Holy Grail (the quest for lost sacred unity), and his underground kingdom increasingly resembled a wasteland.

This lasted for maybe three or four thousands years. In the end, the unity that remained was only seeming, superficial, but this was only a pale shadow of what was underway, what was already taking place on the planet's surface. The underground kingdom of Agartha, the only stronghold that could unite humanity, bring peace, or at least prevent or delay extermination, was counting its final days. Or so it seemed to those who refused to believe in the spiritual, intangible, and incomprehensible authority of the King of the World.

***

The Pale Sun of Agartha

We descended from the bronze tower and strolled through the almost empty streets of the ghostly city. An occasional shadow would skip alongside the dark walls and dwindle in semi-darkness. I was looking at the windows and terraces, some of them warped from old age and on the verge of collapse. Everything was built in grandiose, exaggerated, unnatural proportions unsuitable for humans. Walking through this city, a person of our times, someone from the surface, would feel like a stranger. I felt both admiration and concealed terror.

We were stepping over ruins and piles of stones that had fallen over the thousands and thousands of years of this underground kingdom's history. Stairs would rise suddenly and just as suddenly end without gradation; arches and aqueducts stretched along bridges and roads with no evident order only to disappear into the abyss beyond the city's walls. The absurdity of these buildings confused me, or rather caused discomfort, horror, and froze the blood in my veins as I was taken aback by deep trepidation.

We stopped by the Temple of the Moon again, where I witnessed priestesses dressed in white - priestesses of supernatural beauty, like Westphalian maidens, but with empty, numb, lifeless gazes. An observatory-like building stood - without purpose, I thought, in an underground kingdom - not far from the temple, surrounded by obelisks and magnificent dolmens.

We passed through another set of city gates, entirely alike the previous ones, and after some time we began to climb up some kind of hill or small elevation. The sun, the pale sun of Agartha, was shining as always with the same weary but uneclipsed light.

We climbed up the same disc that had brought me to this haunted city, and a slight jerk brought me back to reality. We were flying high above the dark landscapes, resting in a constant twilight above dark forests that reminded me of the forests of the remote geological period of the Tertiary. A strong wind forced tears to my eyes. Then I noticed that we were losing altitude; I knew that our trip was nearing an end. In a clearing, I saw a group of very large lizards, a sight which I attributed to hallucinations of my overstimulated mind. I caught sight of the walls of another city in the distance. As we flew lower, I could see the leaves of giant ferns and the shimmering surface of a creek or mountain stream.

In that moment, I let out a scream of shock. I saw apelike beings, humanoids like Australopithecus or Java man. They were watching us, unstartled and almost indifferent, as if they were accustomed to such encounters, and held primitive weapons, sticks or spears, in their hands. Because of this sight, so similar to the drawings of textbooks on evolution, I suddenly felt relief. I wanted to shout into Mani's ear, to point them out to him. Their form, it seemed to me, contradicted everything I had heard from him, all that nightmarish history of thousands or millions of years. Man-gods, the noble heralds of Arctogaia, could not have existed. These troglodytes mathematically, irrevocably discredited the "Ancients" and "Immortals", the people of the Golden and Silver Ages, the existence of the Nephilim and Titans...

We descended very slowly, a lightened breeze finally allowing for conversation. Mani turned to me and said clearly: *"Did you see those wretches? They are the last remnants of the ancient races of the South, ancient Lemuria, of which we know very little or almost nothing. They are not a product of evolution, as scientists of the final age believe, but of the last stage of involution. They inhabited Agartha long before us. And even before then, they resided on the surface of the Earth. Encountering them invokes terror in us, for they betray the inevitability of decay, degeneration in its final stage. For a long time we discussed what to do with them, but then we realized that they are dying off on their own, slowly disappearing, going extinct. They are almost harmless. It seems that there are no more than a few thousand of them left, or maybe just a few hundred. They will completely disappear within a few thousand years. They are now at the stage of troglodytes, mindless and blunt animals near death. All attempts to make contact with them or at least exchange thoughts have proved unsuccessful. If their existence does not end in cataclysm, then this is the fate of the last Iron Race of the fourth age."*

***

Ultima Thule

The city whose gates we were now passing through was not like the one before. First we flew over the concentric ramparts surrounding it, and I saw boats and triremes made of black timber drifting in dead canals. It seemed to me that the water was just as black and dead. Their sails hung like rotten, wet rags.

Stopping at the open gate, I ran my hand over the red-glowing, rough metal of which the gate was made and remembered once again Plato's description of Atlantis in his *Critias*. "Orichalcum", I whispered to myself.

"*Orichalcum*", repeated the giant after me, as if straining to recall the name, "*the red-glowing metal made by the red man of Atlantis - Cro-Magnon, as he is called by scholars of the present age. The age of seafarers, farmers, and conquerors in which, alas, began the steep fall of man ongoing to this day. However, it was still a happy age for us..*"

"Some time not long after the Golden Race failed to rebuild the original Thule, the red men, the people of the second, Silver Age, raised the Thule of Atlantis, a secondary Thule of the red continent faithfully described by Plato according to a tradition borrowed from the Egyptians. The King of the World designated the underground Thule, a shadow of a shadow, as his capital. This very act, since he was one of the Firstborn, signified the acceptance of failure, a tact acknowledgement of defeat - the defeat of the man-gods. This replica is, as you can see now, literal and faithful. Since that age, each of the human races has claimed equal rights to the throne of the King of the World. Relentless struggle was waged around it. This painful history ended with an agreement that the future King of the World could only be one of the Firstborn.

"But the view which you have today no longer evokes the greatness of that underground Thule of gleaming buildings and walls, ramparts and towers, temples and mighty gates, embankments and canals…Once upon a time, in ancient times, we also called it the Land of the Court Masters. It was divided into four powerful kingdoms modeled after the primordial Hyperborean Thule."

I noticed that this Thule leaned up against a sea, and he told me that this is the Inner Sea of Agartha, a remnant of the ancient, mythical seas of Earth whose flora and fauna had changed over tens or hundreds of thousands of years. We were to walk along its rocky shores now.

Large, wet stones scattered along the shore creaked under our feet, some of them were undoubtedly gems and semi-precious stones. Far off stood sharp, black cliffs. Somewhat further, I noticed dry trunks strewn about, either discarded or thrown around by some cataclysm. As we approached them, I saw a tree that had begun to turn to stone and was already half-fossilized, its entire structure still intact.

We then passed through a forest of giant mushrooms, three or four times the average human height.

***

On the Coast of the Proto-Ocean

The streams, rivers and lakes of Agartha were almost black; the sea, however, had some kind of a cheerful, azure color, but only in its shallow parts. In the depths, it was dark and threatening. Along the coast itself, the water was clear and transparent.

Mani said that no one had sailed this sea since the most ancient time of Agartha. As it turns out, sailing was fraught with too many dangers. Triremes were thus left to rot in the shallow canals of underground Thule. Hydras, antediluvian monsters, ichthyosauruses, plesiosauruses, and giant sea worms, like those living in the waters of the River Kali, fed on human fodder, and mythical typhoons, sirens, and phantoms met sailors on long journeys - everything, he said, was there and posed a threat to seafarers. The dangers that followed sailors have grown in proportion to the decline of human powers. This was all the more obvious evidence of the degradation of the human race, of all its races, to the point that even the Firstborns had given up on sailing the proto-Ocean.

The Inner Sea of the underground kingdom was reminiscent of the dark subconscious of the human race, with all the dangers that lurk there and, without a doubt, we should add to this list all of those magical powers possessed by the quarreling parties, primarily the Silver, the race of the Moon, and its malevolent first priestesses. They were the only ones to retain some of these powers in the end.

I listened to what Mani was telling me, lying on a sandy bank, refusing to believe all of this, staring at the calm sea surface, on which there was almost no breeze, no movement, no waves. The surface of the ocean resembled a mildly creased mirror, skin with thousands of tiny wrinkles, and it seemed to me that from its depths a gentle light was still shining. It reminded me of the pale sun of Agartha, only more dim, almost invisible, resembling the reflection of metal thrown into the deep. I could hear its noise, almost calming, amplified by high air pressure and perhaps a stone vault that had evaded my view. The ocean water was salty, bitter and lukewarm; I was looking at that dark open sea with a feeling of faintness, almost fear. I saw the shadow of a pterodactyl, or perhaps some giant bird, flapping its wings high over the sea and a few fish that looked like sharks passing through the almost clear water of the shallows.

***

A God with a Fish Head

We were returning to the bridge across the embankment, myself trailing a little behind, and Mani, who did not know fatigue, looked back at me as he strode forward with always the same, unvaried step. We crossed the bridge, meandering over the embankments and canals, and slowly approached the walls shining like dark gold.

I knew that inside these walls, in one of the tall, black towers, stood the King of the World, surrounded by his invisible servants who were "people" to the same extent as my enigmatic companion, and surrounded by Goros, whose words, as the lamas believe, revive trees and humans.

The sky above us was dark, darker than usual - I remembered that this was the pale night of Agartha. I say "sky" while being perfectly aware that this word is inappropriate, that expressions such as the vault of the cave or tomb carved into stone are just as suitable.

The streets, not wider than a stadium, were half-dark, full of dark shadows and the outlines of temples and observatories which, as I have now begun to understand, depicted the positions of the stars and celestial bodies in some distant time.

Winds, one rising up from over the proto-ocean and one carrying the smell of decay and damp caves, met twilight, the eternal dusk of Agartha inhabited by the shadows of the dead - shadows that walked among the living and visited the outside world evermore often.

We spent the night in some abandoned temple full of statues of gods with fish heads and tridents in their hands, which must have been forgotten for tens of thousands of years. Mani told me that he did not even remember their names, that they must have been the gods of the red people, the oldest among the Secondborn.

I was woken by some kind of scraping sound, perhaps the sound of a heavy iron door being opened. I was lying on a cold, marble bed, my limbs numb from the cold, and I was heartened to see a pale flame in one corner, over which I barely warmed my hands.

Mani was not around. I ate a few bites of the food he had left while I was dead asleep, food which reminded me of dried fish as such is prepared in Russia, and I took a strong gulp of wine from a black jug.

This restored my strength and sharpened my senses. I heard, quite clearly, slow steps steadily approaching from stone stairs. It could have been Mani, or anyone whose age is measured in thousands of years. I thought of an executioner or an apparition from the world of the dead. But at that time I did not feel fear, only sadness, endless sorrow that I would end my life here, so far beneath the surface of the Earth, that I would never again inhale fresh air to fill my lungs, nor see the Sun...

I also remember that at that moment I thought that ordinary human life, compared to the lives led by the inhabitants of Agartha, was filled with joys which either the wisdom or longevity of the Firstborn could not replace.

Indeed, what could gladden the hearts of the inhabitants of Agartha, those who passed along the streets of Thule or were imprisoned in their towers like silent ghosts?

I was taken away from such thoughts when Mani entered the room again, in the company of someone who looked to me like a priest...

***

Face to Face

We were descending long, spiral staircases, then endless corridors illumined by that same pale flame. At last, we settled in a cave, five or six fathoms tall, with black walls illuminated by electrical-like lamps. The inside of the chamber reminded me of the interior of a spaceship. On a catafalque of black marble, I saw lying the body of a man much taller than Mani; he lay motionless and lifeless, and it seemed to me that he was really dead, that he had been lying here for hundreds or thousands of years.

He was dressed in some kind of black skirt, made of leather or some material resembling it, stretching all the way down to his ankles. Next to him I seemed to be a dwarf, a midget, since I barely reached his waist. I stared into his face, seeing an eagle's nose, high forehead and cheekbones, in which I did not find much human, and it was impossible to determine the color of his skin or its age, the lines on it strained to inscrutability.

As he opened his eyes and spoke to me, I suddenly realized that I was standing before the King of the World, and that I was hearing his words reverberating in my mind.

I stood face to face with the King of the World, the one who could talk to the Immortals and the Ancients, and perhaps with God himself, as the Buddhist legend claims, and for whom, it is said, every human mind is like an open book. I stood face to face with the one who had the power to elevate me or destroy me. I thought of how the King of the World could kill or revive me with one single word. Then I saw how he opened his eyes and his lips moved gently.

"You see Agartha, the underground kingdom, at the time of its decline – it has not always been so. Once upon a time, the streets of its cities resonated with joy, Agartha could still hear songs sung in the language of the birds; I am old enough to remember it. Then the time of decline began, and it started right here - the time of division and discord. The conflicts that started between people, and continued between the Firstborn and the Secondborn, were difficult or impossible to overcome.

"Two or three times we tried to restore the Last Thule, and every attempt we made was futile. The divisions were then transferred to the surface of the Earth, and each disaster was worse than the previous one - the last one in the series has just begun, and it is not excluded that it will lead to the extermination of the human race.

"The Ancients needed time, and time is what is now escaping, ceaselessly accelerating its flow. The darkness is progressing.

"However, the time will come, as the ancient prophecy claims, when the people of Agartha will come out onto the surface of the Earth to bring wisdom, righteousness, and goodness to the peoples on the surface.

"Looking at the desolation around you, the obvious signs of decay which not even Agartha has managed to escape over tens of thousands of years, you are now wondering whether this will ever be possible at all.

"The reversal will be spiritual. And it will inevitably come. It is already underway in Agartha and on the surface of the Earth.

"The beast will be destroyed", he added - I distinctly remember this very word, "beast." "The triumph of being and spirit will occur at the very moment when everything is lost, or when it seems to be so - but not before. And if that does not happen, the world will be extinguished forever and external darkness will prevail.

"Yes, the people of Agartha will once again emerge onto the surface of the Earth. This will happen because the cycle is closing inexorably. Nobody knows the exact day or time - but it will be the time of the sudden return of the gods, the return of the dead to Earth. It will be the return of the Immortals - a time of sudden recognition, horrible revelation, and purification which, there is no doubt, will bring death to many, and to many others their desired liberation…"

***

Flames Rising from the Altar

I do not know whether this is a literal record of what the King of the World said to me on that day, or whether this is merely a reflection, an echo - the echo of an echo - awoken in my mind by his words. Let it be the latter.

I thought of the Greek Hades, the Christian Hell and the Jewish Sheol, of the Egyptian Ammit, the "Devourer of the Dead", and Anubis, of the dreadful things of which the *Tibetan Book of the Dead* speaks, about the Apocalypse and Swedenborg, and about the worlds of the dead which are unexpectedly but unavoidably revealed to us in their nakedness.

But above all this, there was one single thought which I was trying to suppress, to conceal the whole time, as if this was possible at all, from the irresistible, all-seeing eye of the King of the World: namely, that these gods had been disfigured over the long course of time that they had been away from humans, that over the course of thousands of years they had acquired new, hitherto unknown and terrifying traits. Some of the details of the statues in the temples - the stern look in their stone eyes, their jaws clenched too tightly, the haughty indifference reflected in their face - spoke in favor of this.

On the other hand, compared to the inhabitants of Agartha I was like an animal or a child, a being incapable of truly understanding their words, unable to understand what the King of the World was saying.

"Who are the Ancients?", I uttered, somewhat overwhelmed by my own question, or rather the boldness of directing it to the King of the World, "and why do they not prevent the schism that is threatening such cataclysm?"

"There is no way to describe them", the King of the World said, "except, perhaps, in the language of the birds that is largely forgotten today.

"Who are the Ancients, really? We think of aliens from outer space, of gods or demons, or of the fathers of gods, like Saturn or Cronos, the gods of the Golden Age who, since the Golden Age ended forever, have slumbered in dead sleep in some hidden place. We think of mysterious beings, as large as mountains, asleep in the sea, in glaciers, or deep underground. Beings which, at the dawn of time, came from the stars. There are countless ways to answer your question. And they are all, without a doubt, equally wrong.

"Really, why do they not end the rift and stop the extermination? According to some, the Ancients have fallen into dull indifference and are essentially uninterested in the world of men. This contradicts the fact that they are the fathers of men and that they actually created the human race, or at least the mankind that we know today. Since they are, in a way, responsible for the present situation, it would be logical to liberate people from their rule of terror and to let people rule themselves in the future. Members of the Dark Brotherhood, those of the lineage of Cain, call for great revenge against the Ancients and are preparing their destruction. But they are not aware of where such actually leads. They threaten to forever extinguish the great fire of being. Our world could not exist for an instant without the presence and invisible influence of the Ancients.

"In the opinion of others, the Ancients need human help, just as people depend on them. Their absence is only illusory. We live in times when the Ancients are silent, they do not respond to the prayers of the people, and they no longer hear the words addressed to them, or so it seems. Overwhelmed with helplessness, many people perceive that all is lost, since the Ancients have fallen into a dead dream or have long since died.

"But from time to time, they awaken. The polar light shines over the wastelands, fjords and gulfs of the North Sea; then the flames rise from the altar and the King of the World speaks with them. Birds stop in the field, wild animals in the woods, and a dead silence falls upon Earth for a few moments. Shepherds stop their flocks to gaze at the sudden darkness of the sky and listen to what is around them. This does not last longer than a moment or two. Then, everything goes on as usual. No one, almost no one, ever realizes what this moment actually means."

"One day, the hour of their return will come. They will appear among people, just as at the beginning of history, in the Golden Age of mankind, like the gods walking among the living - and no one knows when exactly this will happen.

"I can tell you no more of this. Remember, however, the following words: 'The Ancients are those who truly are (more than you or I or any human being), and who will one day renew the Golden Age on Earth."

***

In the Orichalcum Tower

I thought that it would be much better if I had not seen or heard anything of the sort, if I had never seen Agartha, this sad kingdom of the dead, a kingdom in decay, and its, so it seemed to me, wounded, powerless, gravely sick king.

But he stood directly in front of me in all his greatness, godlike in his appearance, so that even Mani looked small beside him. Calm and self-confident, he raised his hands and continued to speak, and everything he spoke was more and more suggestive. It was like listening to the voice of the long-disappeared gods, the last voice that the man of our time could still hear. Contrary to reason, it resonated strongly with something in my mind or in the deepest interior of my being. I suddenly felt ecstasy and deep passion.

The time of our conversation was coming to an end. In the end, I saw him standing in front of the altar, his back turned to me. His words were still echoing in my consciousness; I wished it lasted much longer. However, when Mani made it clear to me that our time has expired, we parted without final words.

I asked Mani what all this really means, but he showed me with his hand to be quiet and said that I was one of the few mortals to have had the opportunity to see the King of the World and to speak with him.

I was, therefore, as he said, chosen. My arrival in Agartha was not accidental. This event was just a fateful consequence of countless other, seemingly insignificant and unconnected events, such as my expedition to the Himalayas. But, taken together, they made the precise fabric of this world, composed of thousands and thousands of thin threads. What all this meant, Mani said, would be clear to me one day. One day, when a fateful event will change the face of the world, or perhaps will not, if things take an ill-fated course for the King of the World and his subterranean kingdom. The King of the World, he reminded me, had the power to speak to any human being at any moment and to read their thoughts effortlessly.

I was thinking about all of this during the night which I spent in the orichalcum tower, as Mani once again drowned me in a state that resembled catatonia more so than a dream. I lie with my eyes open, staring into the void. Outside, as far as I could see, it was quiet. Only that same noise, the roar of the underground ocean, the wind slightly bending the branches of the forest of giant ferns, reached us. I thought of the troglodytes wandering through it, and I thought I could see the reflection of red fires in the distance. My position was, in essence, hardly different from theirs. I thought of how, in my opinion, I had the same dull, indifferent look of a troglodyte, and how in Mani's eyes I was no different from an animal.

Everything that I recognized, everything that I saw and heard, seemed, at first glance, absurd. It clashed with everything in which I believed and everything which I believed I knew. Yet the obviousness of what I experienced was undeniable.

One day, I will return to the real world and, over time, I believe, I will forget this underground kingdom just as one forgets a nightmare…

***

Departing from Thule

At dawn the next day - I say dawn, but it was, again, only a pale reflection of dawn - we departed from that gloomy, underground Thule which was also but a reflection of the polar or Atlantic Thule, or perhaps both, through which the same man-gods, or only their shadows, still walk.

We passed under the open gates, and for the last time I looked back upon the walls that shined with red-glowing metal. It must have been years since I first entered Agartha, where time had its own peculiar flow, completely different from the one on the surface of Earth.

We were standing on the same disk, floating above the forests of ferns, while the underground ocean, pale fields, and black lakes and rivers disappeared from my view, and then, very suddenly, the disc stopped on a cliff and I followed Mani down a path that led to an entrance to a dark cave.

I understood that this was to be the end of my stay in Agartha, and that I would soon again find myself in the outside world, in the world of people. That thought brought me some kind of relief. We climbed some narrow platform so fast that for a moment I felt faint.

When I opened my eyes again, I saw the top of a mountain, I felt a strong blow of wind on my face and small snow covered us in waves. I found myself once again on the surface of the Earth. This brought me short-lived joy.

Next to me, Mani was standing slightly bent over. His face, red-skinned-like and bearing an eagle's nose and deep-seated wrinkles descending almost to his chin, seemed to me even more monstrous in daylight.

Before I set off down the path which he showed me, I extended my hand to him and he gripped my elbow in his strong fist. I realized that this was a gesture of parting and wondered if I would ever meet him again. He paused and said very quietly, his words muffled by the wind: "*I must be very old, and my age must be measured in tens of centuries. I remember the walls of cities which you have not, nor will you ever have heard of, and I remember the time when many continents were empty. I remember a herd of mammoths running, and the roar of a saber-toothed tiger at dawn. I saw ships arriving from the stars. Ordinary human life is but a fleeting moment. We might meet again in some unexpected and unimaginable place - in the shimmering mists of Orion, or on some gloomy plateau of prehistoric Asia.*"

We then finally parted, not looking back, as each of us simply went our own way.

All day long, I descended down a dangerous hill, pausing to take a sip of that intoxicating wine of Agartha. In the evening, I saw the walls of a monastery built into the rocks. I had found myself back in Tibet.

The Earth's face had changed irrevocably over that short time. The outside world was inevitably changing, and my stay in Agartha certainly changed me. I remember being taken inside, almost frozen, and being laid on a bed from which I would rise several days later.

***

The Uprising of the Titans

In the years that followed I traveled through China, seized by revolution and war. The news that reached me since I had left Tibet was scarce and uncertain. A mosaic was assembling around me, revealing a frightening picture. There was no doubt that the whole world had been hit by catastrophe, one of the most destructive in all of its existence - a catastrophe comparable only to the destruction of Atlantis. Piece by piece, the gloomy prophecy of the King of the World was being confirmed. I realized that within a short time, only a few years, millions would be wiped off the face of the Earth.

The conflict was already titanic in character: the atomic attack on Hiroshima marked the beginning of the final uprising of the Nephilim who would destroy Agartha. I was expecting the war to continue. That night, I heard the voice of the King of the World again and left my remote Chinese village to reach Mongolia. I passed through the Gobi Desert in the company of nomads. The thought that I would soon find myself in civilization seemed impossible and even comical. Years of exile, my stay in Agartha, and the wanderings throughout Central Asia that followed had estranged me.

About a thousand years ago, a number of members of the Titanic race began their rebellion in Agartha, the last rebellion against the spiritual authority of the King of the World. Dramatic changes on the surface ensued. They renounced fidelity to the Immortals and conspired against the Ancients. They were joined by a number of members of the Silver Race who, following their selfish goals, immeasurably increased the power of the conspirators. They were opposed by the last members of the heroic race, who joined forces with the remaining people of the Golden Age. When their rebellion was quelled in Agartha, they disappeared on the Earth's surface. This significantly weakened the power of the King of the World.

The technology now at the disposal of the Iron Race approaches in its destructive power that possessed in Agartha. The last spiritual centers on the surface are either destroyed or will soon be destroyed, thus rendering the position of humanity truly tragic. Today's mankind resembles a sleepwalker who walks along the edge of an abyss. The Titanic spirit of blind rebellion pervades ubiquitously, and the people of the Iron Age, whether intentionally or not, indulge in it. I remember the words spoken by the King of the World himself: "The great fire of being is threatened with being extinguished forever."

The Titans' goal, it is said, is the destruction of the Ancients. Their clash with the Immortals will be merciless, it has long been underway in the dark labyrinths of Agartha and now, more or less openly, on the surface above it. Both the Titans and the Immortals look at the people of the Iron Race with the same disdain. For them, the people of the Iron Race are like insects crawling upon the surface of the Earth. The ancient war will undoubtedly continue, and with new force.

***

The Voice of the King of the World

In early 1947, I crossed over into the Soviet Trans-Baikal with a group of nomads. Soon after, I was deprived of freedom. Before the NKVD investigators, I pronounced a name which acted as a password. Today I believe that I owe my life to the mysterious power of the King of the World, which extends to each and every, even the most distant corner of the planet.

Those were, I repeat, the years in which the final cataclysm openly loomed over humankind. After a while, unexpectedly to me, signs of calming ensued, and before our eyes took shape the world as we know it today. I would like to say that I contributed to this. But we are mere pawns in a great game of chess that has lasted thousands and thousands of years. Media transmit messages that belong to others and perform, or do not perform, tasks set before us by others. Their true meaning eludes our understanding. As I said, I was more of a silent observer or messenger than a real participant in all of this.

What I know, what I saw with my own eyes, is only a small part of the truth. The truth is fully known only to the King of the World. I wish, however, to never be awakened by his voice again, and as the years pass there are less and less chances that I will ever hear him again.

Over the last decade I have been an associate of the State Geographical Institute in Moscow. Tense relations with China postponed, or prevented, my participation in a long-prepared

Soviet expedition to the Himalayas. I was happy about this, for I wished to never return there again.

***

The Return of the Immortals

My days in Moscow flow by monotonously, without excitement and without passion, and I am grateful to God that this is the case. I am aware that this is just another name for a long dying, for a slow death, but that is what is happening all over the world - slow dissolution, gradual transition to entropy, into nothingness, a journey for which there is no end. We can still hope for a painless death. Mountains are crumbling, just like the walls of ancient towns or our worn-out bodies resembling starving ghosts, and nothing but fire itself will be able to restore the purity and innocence of the Golden Age. Even the Immortals die. The number of people of the Golden Race is now only symbolic. I do not know if this is true for the Ancients.

From time to time, I remember the King of the World's promise that the people of Agartha will once again come out onto the surface of the Earth.

I believe that this will actually happen in the end. What reversal did he have in mind? I ponder the moment in which people will behold the Immortals face-to-face. Will this be the time when the Ancients will finally awaken, the time of their long-anticipated return?

For so many, this is the last hope for humanity to be able to unite, for a period of wisdom, justice, and prosperity to finally come - that prosperity promised by ancient prophecies.

I believe that day will be completely different from what many imagine. What we see today is contorted and distorted, like in a mirror, and we will see clearly only then. It will be a moment of truth, when the veil finally falls from centuries of hidden secrets. It will be the time when the dead will overflow the Earth and the living will become like the dead. An ancient horror will emerge, and we will know what we have known for a long time: we are not able to look at the bare truth; just one glance might blind us, or kill us. The Kingdom of Agartha extends beneath every continent, which means that its inhabitants will appear on Earth everywhere at the same time.

Will their appearance bring the human race obliteration or a new era of prosperity? Or do the Immortals feel only indifference towards humans? This will - and only this is certain - be the final end of the world which we know today.

We will never see the return of the Ancients, for it is not we who will experience it. Only the Immortals, those made of Gold, and not of Iron or dust, can see it.

Only the King of the World and a few of the Firstborn who will then stand tall around his throne.

***

Epilogue

A Few Words at the Very End

My story about Agartha and the story of my journeys, the life of Ahasver the wanderer, ended when I left China. This ended my exile from my fatherland that lasted nearly three decades.

Odysseus's wanderings lasted shorter. Thirty years is the life of one generation here on Earth. Upon setting foot on his native land, Antaeus, according to myth, renewed his strength. And Odysseus ultimately returned to his home of Ithaca, not as a king but as a beggar. He returned to his homeland, where no one recognized him. Introducing himself as "nobody", he did not enter his homeland under his own name. According to Homer, only faithful Penelope awaited him there.

All that remains is for me to add just a few more episodes which mostly relate to my stay in America as a kind of humble epilogue to this story. They are also about legends, fairy tales, and myths. The past is unattainable to us; it is hidden, as one writer put it, like a snake in the grass. The past, especially the distant past, is a foreign country whose language we do not know or have forgotten. These are tales of man-giants, immortals and gods, who supposedly once walked the earth; of the goddess of freedom who still guards the entrance to New York Harbor and illuminates the world with her torch; of the winds that ceaselessly blow from the East, from Asia and Scythia, bringing new people to the West; and of one god-traveler who brought disturbance with him everywhere. The reader, I fear, will hardly be able to believe in this. All of it will look like the product of a disturbed, sick imagination. Or like a story for simplistic, gullible people devised to entertain the ignorant and spiritually poor.

As I write these words, on my desk lies a gemstone from among the underground treasures in the Mongolian Altai, shining with a red glow. It is the only treasure I own. I described how I found this gemstone at the very beginning of this short story. And that story was equally incredible. A few official notes are burning in my Chinese jar of jade. This is a precautionary measure that is almost irrelevant; someone, after all, will already try to blur all the tracks that lead, or could lead, to Agartha. The truth about it will remain hidden for some time. When we remove the names and dates from a story, and as time erases the real protagonists and their memory, there remains only a story, a legend. And that is what is important, what will be remembered and repeated over the centuries.

Over the past few years, there have been several insignificant expeditions - insignificant for these memories - over the course of which I have always found signs of the Forbidden Country, and they are, as the reader has already noticed, scattered across all continents. In the meantime, the idea of a Soviet expedition to the Himalayas was brought to a halt. Such a decision was completely correct.

Signs leading to the Land of Underground Fire, also called the Land of Miracles or the Land of the Living Gods, are written in the letters of a secret alphabet and in the languages of countless peoples. The whole world, in fact, is covered by the secret network of Agartha. This network is made up of its devotees who have been waiting patiently for centuries for their moment. And this time will dawn sooner or later.

On the surface of the Earth, time flows fast, but this vortex that leaves behind corpses and ruins does not scare the inhabitants of the underground world. In the shadow of the palaces of the Goros, centuries and millennia are no more than a prolonged day. The voices of the inhabitants of the underground world are their whispers. They are listened to by sages and hermits in their caves, in the West and in the East, from Palestine to Mount Athos all the way to Tibet.

From time to time, however, the Earth trembles in its core, and the Sun, Moon and stars change their path. The giant Gong-Gong, says Lao Tzu, breaks the celestial pillar and the Earth's axis changes its inclination. The pillars of the sky break.

The whole universe stops in confusion. The Earth opens up to pour out water and fire that flood the continents. Peoples drown in blood and the sky assumes a crimson-red color. This is what the lamas and Buddhist wisemen teach, and they are inspired by Agartha's quiet wisdom.

After one such world cataclysm came years of fragile peace. The beast that momentarily emerged from the abyss was finally defeated, even at the cost of 60 million human lives. This was the beast mentioned by the King of the World.

The Third Reich was demolished, in blood and ashes, and behind all these events, in all likelihood, stood the adepts of the Dark Brotherhood. The throne of the sublime ruler, the immaculate King of the world, was shaken. Then there was silence, full of terrifying horrors. It is little known that in opposition to the Dark Brotherhood stands another, even more secret society whose motto is "Order above Chaos."

It is now quite certain that in the near future there will be a much more terrible disaster, and that the peace that occurs in the interim will be but a short-term truce, a short pause before the storm. Humanity is blindly rushing towards this cataclysm, similar to the one in which ancient Atlantis disappeared in water, smoke, and fire into the ocean. No human, and no human beings will be able to stop this. Such is beyond human powers. This is a war waged by the Immortals amongst themselves.

People's hearts are horrified. Under their masks, their true faces are revealed - the faces of the Immortals and the Titans. We are now looking at them with astonishment. One rabbi recognizes Biblical beasts in them, and Christian fathers speak of them as apocalyptic horsemen who will suddenly emerge on the horizon at the end of time. Who will claim victory in this apocalyptic battle? The fierce war of which we speak here has been ongoing since the beginning of history, since Rome and Carthage and much earlier, since the beginning of the world. We have seen only its pale glare. This is always the same battle, that which takes place at the end of the world. Everything depends on its outcome. Only in it, the King of the World said, will the fire of being be reawakened.

The Titans, "those of the line of Cain," forced their way to Olympus in rebellion against the Father of the Gods. In the heavens, as the Church Fathers taught, the two armies are always confronting one another: the demonic legions and the legion of angels led by the Archangel Michael brandishing a flaming sword. In the Bible, we find the prophecy of the hordes of Gog and Magog which are "as numerous as the sands of the sea." The Apocalypse, the book of Revelation, contains a prophecy about the last battle with the armies of Antichrist. The second army will be led by Christ himself. Plato also speaks of this battle in his report on the divine Atlantis, its man-gods who came from islands in the West to rule the world. Muslims believe in the coming of the Mahdi, the prince who will oppose Dajjal, while Zoroastrians hope for the return of Saoshyant the Savior. The Hindus are expecting Kalki, the tenth and last Avatar. I voraciously await God, his Second Coming.

I think that thus it has always been, and thus it shall be until the Sun extinguishes and the Cosmos plunges into eternal darkness.

We live in an age of darkness, in which the darkness is so thick that no one even remembers light. The defining characteristics of modern humanity are blindness, cruelty, and irresistible greed. These are the men of iron, the least valuable of all human races, who are destined to live in the Night of God.

Blinded by greed and an insatiable hunger for gold, Francisco Pizarro destroyed the ancient Inca Empire. The same was done by Cortés in Mexico with the Aztec Empire. Julius Caesar conquered Gaul to seize the gold mines and monetize Gaelic gold. For Caesar and Rome, gold became loot. Gold would soon be found in the hands of traders, usurers, and speculators. The old order was finally toppled. The touch of their hands darkened even the glitter of gold. This irreversibly extinguished the divine light, and together with it faded the sacred authority of the King of the World, and with it the authority of every ruler on earth. A period of impotence began.

For what is gold if not the Sun's light that once, at the beginning of time, turned into matter? There has always been a sign of equivalence between rulers, the Sun, and gold. Therefore, gold, as well as sunlight, cannot belong to anyone, to any king, to any man, or even to the King of the World. Trying to take something of it, only for one's self, is usurpation of what belongs to all. Whoever appropriates even one nugget of gold has committed something intolerable, the most serious crime: he has stolen from people a ray of light. The first usurpation was committed by the king who reached for gold as wealth (and not as a symbol). Then everyone else did the same. Everyone, even the saints on the street, tried to seize gold exclusively for themselves.

The age of darkness is an age of wandering. The era of great geographical discoveries was a time of general hunger for gold and feverish searching for the golden kingdom of El Dorado. Obsessed with the unrest of "gold rush", people left their homelands and turned into Ahasvers, into greedy, insolent, wandering thugs. These are all signs foretelling of an unfortunate, impending storm.

The lines that follow were written in the late 1930s, when the author of these notes was in America and then in Europe, in Germany, when it was ruled by Nazism, when the whole world was shrouded in the frost of a terrible winter like the one that bound Hyperborea with eternal ice.

These final notes constitute a kind of farewell, a closing word - a word pronounced at the end, or a modest epitaph.

***

Giants Walked the Earth

"The Zuni Indians believe that their ancestors came from underground, and that the ancestors of other nations also once lived in caves in the interior of the Earth", the Navajo shaman said, "and the Aztecs thought that they were one of seven tribes that one day came out of the Aztlan Caves."

"Hopi shamans say that even today there is a cave in the Grand Canyon that represents the entrance to the underground world," the elder spoke, trudging through the red soil with his bare feet, "and the Apache claim that on their reservation there is still a tunnel leading into the underground, which is populated by mysterious tribes who are not people like us at all."

These people of the land of Aztlan were, allegedly, real giants, and the shaman also spoke of giant graves that can still be found in the mountains. "All this is well known even to the White people. The graves of giants have been found in Arizona and Ohio and in many other places. We could barely measure up to their waists. The Whites came to wonder about this, write about it, and then the skeletons of these giants suddenly began to disappear overnight. Why? No one can remove the traces of their existence, because such traces are scattered all over the planet. This is also evidenced by the cities which they left behind. Indian legends claim that giants could still be encountered in some parts of the United States just a few hundred years ago, and that such people lived in Patagonia and the South of the continent up until recently."

I told him that our sacred books knew of giants and their ancestors, such as the Didanum race and the giants of American soil, as well as the reports by seafarers of much later periods. Pigafetta, the chronicler of Magellan's expedition, reported an encounter in Patagonia with one such giant who sang and danced before the explorers and threw sand on his head. The sailors were only as tall as the giant's waist. Something similar was claimed by the sailor Francis Drake, as well as John Byron, the grandfather of the famous poet, who was also a traveler and sailor. Patagonia has been called the "land of giants." All of these testimonies were later dismissed as false.

"Not only humans, but animals as well enjoyed gigantic growth in the past. The bones of prehistoric animals are sometimes found mixed with the bones of giant humans. There are (or were) dwarf races alongside them. The peoples of Aztlan were giants - at least for our notions - and the remains of these races still inhabit the interior of the Earth. Why have giants retreated from the people of our time to the point of finally, completely disappearing under the surface? I think that these are only the remains of old races whose time has expired.

"One cycle of time closes for a new one to begin. The Mayans knew much about this. But this does not happen all over the world at the same time. Surviving races gradually disappear as new ones take their place. Thus it was centuries upon centuries ago. America has long been a world in the shadow of the land of Aztlan, of the surrounding world in the West. I am talking about many thousands of years ago, which no human on Earth today remembers. And now its time has dawned again: the return of the ghosts from the land of Aztlan. Many old peoples will die out and others will disappear underground, just as so many old races before."

***

Liberty Enlightening the World

This old America, the America to which the Navajo shaman belonged, was long dead, and over its remains, over its dead body, a completely different and new America had risen: an America that does not cease to amaze and captivate, one towards which head processions of pilgrims from all parts of the planet, from all continents, unaware of what they are actually doing. What deity have they worshipped? Were they not slaving for demons?

The new American nation is a nation of refugees and pilgrims, of all those who wanted to escape from their past. Those who came to its soil thought that they had left behind not only their country of origin, but the "Eastern sin" with all its consequences: evil, sickness, poverty and death. There, on that happy island, as they imagined it, wolves and lambs would live in peace alongside each other. There, free from history and its delusions, they would ultimately build the "Shining City upon a Hill", the New Jerusalem. Something without precedent in history.

But who can escape their past? Who can escape from themselves?

In the summer of that same year, I walked along the banks of the Hudson River and I gazed at the panorama of the tallest skyscrapers in the world. Here, too, I was obsessed with the ancient past of that continent, that past before the first white colonizers stepped foot, before those who came from across the sea, from the East, on ships, to start a completely new history. The Toltec capital was called Tula. Quetzalcoatl was their mythical hero, a person with a beard and light skin who came from the East by sea to return to his homeland.

Did the Indian shaman know what he was talking about? Is modern America not the real New Atlantis of Francis Bacon, with all its miracles? An Atlantis equipped with all the innovations of new technologies, gunships, planes, submarines, deadly and destructive weapons. An Atlantis that is once again readying for world conquest, for a victorious campaign in the East to bring the light of the one new civilization?

In the age of the European discovery of North America, its original, red-skinned inhabitants were called "Indians", and they still lived according to their ways, in forests and on plains, in the Neolithic. They did not know metal. Could these original inhabitants really be connected with Atlantis and the Atlanteans, the "red continent" spoken of by esotericists and researchers of the Earth's mythical past? Is it not, in the end, pointless to think of the future of one people, one land, and one continent in terms of ancient myth, following a story of undetermined origin and even more indeterminate antiquity?

These descendants of Europeans today despise their former homelands, because they believe that they live happily on their island, in prosperity without rival, and that they have forever broken with the past and history - a history which is only one of dishonor and ignorance from which they will henceforth be exempted, as if God himself has chosen them.

They believed their mission was to bring the flame of freedom to the whole world. That freedom is burning in the torch of the proudly raised hand of Liberty, Liberty Enlightening the World - on Bedloe's Island at the entrance to New York Harbor.

***

The Seven Spikes of Her Crown

Once upon a time, the first thing that arrivals would see in their approach to New York harbor, if they were traveling at night, was the flaming light of the torch in the hand of the Goddess of Liberty. Like the Colossus of Rhodes, one of the wonders of the ancient world, Liberty was a beacon.

The feet of the Goddess of Liberty rest on broken chains.

The seven spikes of her crown symbolize rule over all of the seven seas and seven continents to which America offers its freedom and which it illuminates with its unknown light - the light of some new, hitherto unknown radiation. The one who created this unique land of utopia and "republic of virtue", its mythical founding father, is believed to have risen to heaven, in Masonic uniform, to become one with the gods of ancient Rome - this is depicted on the interior of the dome of the American Congress building. Its name is "The Apotheosis of Washington."

But what is this tradition shining over the seven seas and seven continents?

For the first colonists, for the Puritan pioneers, their departure from their old homelands was quite like the Biblical exodus of the ancient Israelites' escape from Egyptian slavery. The Atlantic was their Red Sea and Sinai Desert, and the New World was their Canaan, the promised land which the Old Testament Yahweh intended for them to populate. In some places, he is even called the "God of Britain."

"Knowledge, like the sun, set out on its path from the East," claimed one of these pilgrims, "and then crossed over to the West, where we enjoyed its light for a long time." This resembled the journey of the three wisemen who followed the star of Bethlehem.

America, virginal America, has been held by others to be the true earthly paradise. This earthly paradise somewhat later becomes the mythical Atlantis, miraculously raised from the ocean. The world of the dead who bring gifts to the living. Until then, America was hidden; behind the fact that she was finally discovered, that she emerged from the sea in one moment, there must have been something miraculous, some divine secret, Divine Providence itself.

The America that I came to know in the 1930s, however, was at the time dedicated to feverish labor and did not at all resemble the magnificent empire of the Puritan imagination moving West. She was obsessed with records, with a cult of youth, with sports and newspapers. This was, in fact, the path of American salvation; their way of living and dying, the path by which Americans and those who follow them reach bliss - a bliss similar to that acquired by good Christians or Muslims in paradise.

Yet, behind the semblance of this ultra-rational and ultra-modern America, the image of an almost mythical continent dimly peered through. It appeared to me for only for an instant, in the blink of an eye, but in the future this would be obvious to all.

America, with its wealth and power, did not have a worthy competitor in the world even then, they believed.

This barbaric country which rose proudly in the West was almost like Plato's Atlantis. The Western Hemisphere, one half of the world, was already theirs; others were forbidden from interfering with it. This prohibition was forced by moral reasons: the corruption of the Old World, the decay of Europe already ruled by the Antichrist. Such an America, in the beginning, had to be fenced off by an invisible wall which would protect it from the hordes of evil, from Gog and Magog. It just couldn't happen.

Americans already see themselves as the newly chosen people, blessed by the Lord himself, predestined by him to rule over everything and everyone else. This is where an entirely new human race has been created.

I thought about this in a building on Eighth Avenue in New York. There was a kind of pleasant semi-darkness in the room. On a small table, like an altar or shrine, a seven-pointed candle burned.

Out of somewhere came the heavy, stunning smell of smoke of plant resin that was, among other things, stronger than the smell of incense. All of this contributed to an atmosphere at once magnificent and disturbing, full of anticipation, as if something extraordinary were to happen at any moment.

Captain Hastings spoke of a secret history of America and a new race that the New Age would bring about thanks to the spiritual evolution of humanity. Like Blavatsky, he spoke of a mutation governed by Divine providence. History, he believed, was going according to plan.

I presumed that we were in a Masonic temple, in one of its chambers, intended for the teachings of the "brethren."

The wall was filled with a variety of symbols, among which stood out an inverted pentagram - the sign of the Kali-Yuga, the dark age, with two spikes pointing upwards, which, as the adept explained, is a symbol of human sorcery unmistakably revealing the position of the "left hand." Then there was a swastika and a rose-cross, followed by a series of allegedly Egyptian symbols, including an Egyptian Ankh of gilded metal. High above all of these symbols was a depiction of the Great Architect of the Universe, a grotesque sculpture, as if carved from polished ivory, no taller than up to the elbow. It was a horned, hermaphroditic creature, like a sitting goat, with its legs folded and wings relaxed, one arm raised and the other outstretched downwards.

Today, as I am writing this, it is even more obvious than it was then. The eyes of humanity are turning towards this, until recently, remote country. America, an island that threatens to drown in the sea, has its own theology, its own, albeit farcical, gospel, a message which it heralds to all of humanity in both hemispheres. By participating in its mysteries, the believers of this new cult worship the unknown god.

Believing in their own exceptionalism, it is only natural that Americans have tried to shape the rest of the world according to their template. The despised East has to be turned into a colony - East meaning the whole world inhabited by numerous and diverse peoples on all seven continents. They believed they represented New Israel, and during that time the world was covered by the shadow of something growing behind their backs: the shadow of the dead continent, the shadow of Trans-Atlantis.

Its rise will mark the return of the dead, the resurrection of the dead ancestors who bestow rich gifts upon everyone, bringing them abundant Eden, or at least its promise. It seemed to us that millions of people have marched around the world, led by their blinded leaders, but in reality, they were the marching dead, resurrected from the bottom of the ocean. The seven spikes of the crown of the goddess enlightened the whole world, threatening to burn it to ashes.

***

Wotan, the Traveler, Awakens

Even now, I believe, in remote places in Germany, in taverns and villages, one can encounter an interesting and peculiar representation of Christ: he is like a mysterious traveler, a mysterious visitor riding on a white horse. A wanderer arriving from afar out of wind and rain on a stormy, dark night.

Towards the end of the Weimar Republic, a strange restlessness enveloped German youth. The god-wanderer was back and announcing a storm. Blonde boys and girls began to wander "from Nordkapp all the way to Sicily", as Carl Gustav Jung said, "armed with rucksack and lute." Their wandering only seemed to be aimless.

For "Wotan, the traveler, is awakened."

Wotan-Odin is the god not only of intoxication, but also of initiation into the secrets and mysteries of the occult, and he is the one who knows the runes. He is the one who hanged himself upside down for nine days and nine nights in order to drink from Mimir's Spring, the Spring of Memory.

He is accompanied by an uncertain restlessness and the whistling of wind, that wind which accompanies Nietzsche's Zarathustra and "suddenly casts open the gates of the castles of death." At first, several sheep were sacrificed to him. Then millions.

This tidal wave moved thousands, and soon hundreds of thousands, including both the old and children. All of

Germany was raised to its feet to hail the unknown. Who directed this movement, and was it not the same fire that erupted two decades before in the East with the Bolshevik Revolution of Red October?

Around 1933, this movement transformed into a march of millions. But then, like Ahasver, the eternal wanderer, I had already left Germany, thinking that I would never return. What I saw in the fall of 1937, and not only in Germany, I beheld with astonishment and disbelief. The whole world in those years was in agitated motion and shaking, and not only America, Germany, or Russia. The Far East, Japan and China, were also shaken, plunged into the bloody chaos of civil war. The great cities of East and West were shaken.

The period between the two wars was an interim. We looked at the time before it with melancholy. Is it any wonder, then, that in such a world we have sought another foothold elsewhere, turning to ancient epochs or, even further, rejecting with contempt everything that bears the mark of modernity?

***

The Wind that Blows from Scythia

Germany has always lived in fear of one primal horror: fear of the East, of the steppe, the ancestral homeland of the Scythians and the Huns. Formerly, Germany was separated from Sarmatia and Dacia by "an impenetrable wall of mountains and mutual fear", as Tacitus said. Now, weapons were rattling on both sides of the wall and millions-strong armies were gathering. The same horror, however, also paralyses the British, but for them the Germans are the "Huns", the barbarians drinking from human skulls.

For Westerners, this is always the same Asian endlessness from which new peoples and ideas that shake the world are constantly emerging and rising. The wind which blows from Asia and Scythia, reaching as far as Thrace and Germany and beyond, carries with it, like dry leaves, whole peoples to the West.

On the eve of the war, that uneasiness, that primal horror, bore a new name: Bolshevism. The "Red Danger." In the East, Soviet Russia rose, ruled by the Red Emperor, the same Russia that the German townsfolk feared so much - the fourth Russian Empire, which was destined to bring peace to Eurasia, at least briefly. Before then, the Third German Empire must fall.

Only then could the conflict of two worlds follow, that of East and West, the concluding battle of history, the *Endkampf*, the battle that is yet to come. The West was the true enemy for the East, the New Carthage to be destroyed and its fields seeded with salt. It is the sea monster, Leviathan, that must be cast back into the ocean depths.

Behind both of these forces stood others, even more secretive, each of them possessing their own strongholds in Agartha and basing themselves on its, albeit distorted, teachings. The devotees of the Dark Brotherhood operate in and through both of them.

The goal of the King of the World was to re-establish the Solar Empire of Ram, which would restore peace and bring prosperity to peoples. Prosperity to all the nations of the earth.

I did not see this clearly back then. These are the subsequent thoughts of an old man who has survived a world cataclysm, the most frightening of all that human history remembers. At the time, I thought that an agreement was still possible, that we were only a step away from reaching it. Two years later, Hitler committed his fatal mistake.

Either way, the collision of worlds, titanic in scope, seemed increasingly imminent.

The gates of war were once more opening wide before us.

In 1937, Germany celebrated Christmas in a still idyllic atmosphere, with Christmas festivals and trees - *Eine deutsche Weihnacht* - with costumes and traditional songs about the Christmas tree. Only now, somewhat dissonant tones intertwined with the melodious tunes. *Eine deutsche Weihnacht* began to resemble the Scandinavian Yule, the ancient festival in which Yule logs were burned and the flames of winter were dedicated to the god Thor, who shined brightly from afar.

I observed the New Year of 1938 in Dresden with champagne, at a ball that brought together various Nazi officials. One of them was Heinrich Himmler. The way to the top, to the roof of the world, was wide open for me. The path to the underground kingdom of Agartha presented itself to me.

An adventure that would bring many surprises and events that would change the face of the world.

***

Red Star above the Kremlin

Just at first glance, my days are monotonous. The monotonous life of a pensioner, dedicated to his habits and vain rituals.

I devote my time to thinking and prayer, recording my memories along the way. That work is now nearing its end.

Moscow is the city of my earliest memories. And childhood, as said at the beginning, is our only golden age.

Sometimes, I take short trips in my leisure time. My grandfather's house is a public library today – I find this fair. The forest in the suburbs which I remember so well from childhood was turned into a cemetery. I stand over my grandfather's grave, over which a winged angel of marble rises today. Leaves flutter over it, the breeze is pleasant and fresh. I visit galleries, such as Tretyakov, to view portraits of famous people with particular interest. This is how I make quite unusual discoveries.

Age prevents me from venturing out on longer journeys. I no longer feel any desire for them. The journeys I dreamed of at an early age are terrifying and frightening to me today. After many wanderings, I returned home. We come home, tired, to finally find our peace.

The Moscow I see today, however, is no longer the one I remember from childhood. No one, says one philosopher, has stepped foot in the same river twice. I no longer look at it with young eyes.

This is a Moscow of high, cold walls, golden sun, red flags, and deep shadows. Just a few hundred meters away I find an old Moscow: wooden houses warped by age, through whose cobblestones shoot up blades of grass. Then follows the Moscow of lavish palaces, emperors, and aristocrats: the Third Rome built on seven hills. Above it rises the Moscow of the Stalin era, more monumental than the others - Moscow of the Fourth Empire. The next, the fifth, will rise on its ruins. These are events that are yet to come.

Above the Kremlin shines a single red star. I walk through Red Square, feeling both amazement and pride over it. These are monuments of the heroic age, an epoch that is now rapidly approaching its end. The New Great Age, the one yet to come, will also rise from blood as red as the flag fluttering before my eyes.

I head to Kolomenskaya Station and pass through the golden park to descend down to the river bank. It is autumn. Boats pass through Moscow. A path leads me over a wooden bridge. Now it is late afternoon. The sun is shining over the water. At this time of year, evening descends quickly.

Here, between numerous apple trees, rests the Church of the Ascension of the Lord. Raised by King Vasili III in honor of the birth of his son, Ivan, who would later come to be remembered as "the Terrible." Its dome has the shape of a tent resting on the vaults of facades and stairs. It all belongs to an already vanished world.

A few sentimental memories bind me to this place.

I sit on one wooden bench for a long time. Here, one name is engraved in the bark of a tree: Anastasia, which means Resurrection.

During such walks, I feel an almost endless loneliness. Among the masses that flood Moscow's squares, this feeling brings me endless pleasure. I feel safe and protected within the endless crowd, my face here is just one among thousands of others, one that goes unnoticed or will soon be forgotten.

These long walks are reminiscent of my farewell with other dear places.

Sometimes, in these aimless wanderings, I am moved by an image I see suddenly, like in my old childhood fantasies. At the bottom of the garden is a secret gate. Where does it lead? Below modern Moscow lies in silence an entire secret city, an underground Moscow, built over hundreds or perhaps thousands of years. Here, they say, in one of these underground chambers, is the lost library of Tsar Ivan the Terrible. Even deeper below lies a secret network of underground corridors, some leading to other cities and countries and some to distant continents. There are also cemeteries and ossuaries. No one knows whose hands dug these underground passages. There are innumerable links connecting peoples and continents. Some of these pathways undoubtedly lead to the Land of Underground Fire, Agartha.

At my fingertips lies not one castle, but an entire hidden kingdom, one in which there is neither disease nor death, but on which time still leaves its mark. The walls bend under the burden of years, covered in a red-glowing metal. The ivory ramparts crumble and disintegrate. But the life of its inhabitants is so long that we can count their peaceful souls as immortal.

Countless are the paths that lead to this hidden place.

I could say that I am slowly preparing for my last journey, the one that leads underground. It is inhabited by shadows like those that wander through the Greek Hades, visited by Odysseus, looking both into the past and into the future.

***

Afterword: Sikorsky's Mission

"A book is a thing among things, a notebook lost among notebooks populating an indifferent universe, all until it finds its reader, a person destined for its symbols."
- Jorge Luis Borges, Personal Library

The manuscript in front of the reader is incomplete. It consists of several different parts which had either been cut, were irreparably damaged, or whose text was interspersed with very harsh interventions. Certain parts are undoubtedly missing. It is signed by a certain Maximilian Rupert Dietrich Sikorsky, but it cannot be ruled out that its author bore a different name or that this was the work of several hands. In fact, this is almost certain.

Perhaps it is this that gives rise to the impression of incoherence of this manuscript, its incompleteness or the inconsistency of the author, with confusing narrative flows, contradictions, and ambiguities throughout this brief write-up? As some of its commentators have observed, certain periods in the author's life are passed over in silence, and just as reticent is his description of the alleged journey to Agartha. For example, in one place it has been claimed that his stay in Agartha lasted seven years. We arrive at this by adding up the dates given in the manuscript. But upon reading the manuscript, we have the impression that it was only a matter of a few days.

The seemingly missing parts were either removed or, for some reason, the author himself decided not to inform us of them. The editor of this edition has adhered to the first position: the manuscript has been subject to arbitrary interventions and significant cuts.

Anatoly M. Irishkov rejects this view, arguing that the manuscript is, in all likelihood, the work of one author, although this scholar also allows for the possibility that the manuscript has been shortened, that some chapters have gone missing, or that some shorter appendices were later inserted (which do not significantly change the course or meaning of the story):

> *A Tale of Agartha* is not a work of fantasy literature, but rather notes written down in several different periods, a kind of travel diary or literary memoir - so indeed claims their author. They were written later, as the writer indicates, on the basis of memories, not documents, on several occasions starting in 1966. At first glance, they do not seem to have a clear structure. The ideas which the author puts forward are neither consequential nor consistent. This is natural: over the course of lives, the views and ideas we advocate change. The same is true of his experience of Agartha, of which he sometimes speaks with horror, sometimes with admiration and passion. It is superfluous to seek narrative and stylistic coherence in the memories that the author recorded over different periods of his life.

Such shortcomings, he concludes, in fact speak in favor of authenticity. There are claims, which cannot be documented at this time, that Sikorsky's report existed in several different hand-written (or many-handed) versions before it was first published. It has not been possible to track them down to this day (or at least the compiler has not succeeded). Therefore, the publisher was forced to prepare this edition of the book in accordance with the already extant versions.

The first edition of this book was published in Moscow in 1994 by the publishing house "Demiurge." The other two editions - one printed in Moscow in 1997 with the addition of the alleged *Agartha Prophecies*, as well as the 2008 edition printed in Saint Petersburg - are, unfortunately, only commercial editions and cheap, sensationalist misuses of Sikorsky's account. The Petersburg edition also contains one undoubted forgery: an alleged conversation with the author, which, according to the publisher, was held in the summer of 1972 in Moscow, in which Sikorsky is, absurdly, presented as a follower of the Dalai Lama.

The mystery of this manuscript is comparable to the mystery that accompanies its author. Who really is Maximilian Rupert Dietrich Sikorsky? "I think about how, in the meantime, I have become a face without a name, as nobody has called me by my real name, the one I received at baptism, for years…We hide our real faces under the masks of alien names." As could be expected, sporadic research has not confirmed the existence of anyone with this name at all, despite that fact that in Russia, and especially in the Baltics, there are many who bear this surname. The author explicitly claims: "The names and dates in this story are false." Equally expectedly, the Sikorsky name is not included in the lists of participants in Soviet post-World War II archaeological expeditions in Mongolia.

The records of an expedition to the Mongolian Altai (which took place in 1948, not in the 1950s, as Sikorsky claims), however, attest the name of one Maximilian Jurjevich

Sidorov as one of the participants, and in a rather vague capacity. Is Maximilian Jurjevich Sidorov really Sikorsky? This recent argument is allegedly supported by the fact that Sidorov did not possess any academic title despite being an associate of a number of archaeological and geographical institutes. Sidorov died in Moscow in 1974, at an advanced age, seemingly as the consequence of a sudden heart attack. Sidorov, however, was not born in the Baltics, but (probably) in Moscow, and he was not of noble origin. What we know about him suggests that he was a kind of adventurer whose biography contains huge gaps. There are indications that he knew Mongolia very well and had already been to Mongolia on several occasions. Irishkov advocates this view. Sidorov, in his view, is Sikorsky, under a different name and with a slightly modified biography; Sikorsky-Sidorov was then an associate of the KGB, or another branch of the Soviet secret intelligence services, tasked with overseeing research and reporting to an unnamed authority at the peak of Soviet power. In fact, according to Irishkov, Sikorsky did indeed reside in Germany and the United States, and then in Tibet and Mongolia during one period of his life, and he enjoyed the protection of some Soviet secret office, at least from the moment he stepped on Soviet soil until the end of his life.

We are not aware of the grounds from which he derives this speculation, which he does not substantiate with any documentation. But we will not go further into this idea. We will let the reader draw the appropriate conclusions, bearing in mind that the facts presented in the manuscript are in the very least debatable and doubtful: the names are obviously altered, and the chronology and geography are often unreliable.

But if we assume that Sikorsky's report is true at its core, or at least in some important parts, can we really interpret his manuscript as an actual account of his stay in Agartha? And does it not contain some secret code that, as some researchers hope, could really lead us to a world hidden underground? According to the opposite opinion, this is a mere literary mystification.

The actual author of the manuscript, who presented himself under the, by all accounts false, name of Sikorsky successfully covered his tracks. According to another hypothesis, no such author ever existed. Persistent search for him in documents and historical sources has not yielded any significant results. Are they hiding, as Fadayev believes, in the dossiers of some secret service, and should we wait for the moment when they will see the light of day? (And did Irishkov have access to them?)

Attempts to trace the author in this manner are discouraging; the reader who is interested in this account, it seems, has only to pay close attention to the manuscript. But if we can approach this book as an encrypted report, then it should be borne in mind that the claims made by the author cannot be verified by independent sources, or that the information is so general that its truth is implied. This leads to the conclusion that the alleged Sikorsky manuscript is a gross forgery or simply a work of fantastic literature. An article signed by Anatoly Ismailov and published on 13 February 1987 in *Literary Russia* seeks the author of this manuscript among the popular writers of Soviet-era fantasy literature, focusing solely on questions of subject matter and literary style. In our view, this effort has also not produced results worthy of attention.

In his brief preface, the publisher of the first edition claims that this account existed in various copies and versions in Moscow sometime from the mid-1970s (or perhaps a little earlier) that circulated from hand to hand (only to then be lost or destroyed). The first print edition was based on two incongruous versions, some of which, according to the editor, had some unbelievable or seemingly impossible details.

Such claims cannot be proven, and it is possible that such really are the mystifications of the publisher or writer. "This is not my personal story", Sikorsky says at the beginning of his notes, adding that he began writing on 25 January 1966. The ensuing part contradicts this claim, since it evokes his childhood, albeit briefly, mentions some of his previous travels, and describes several events that are only indirectly related to the writer's search for Agartha.

The manuscript consists of three parts. The second part, entitled *Descent into Agartha*, which contains a description of the alleged visit to the kingdom of Agartha, was written much earlier than the rest (in 1966); the first part is really just an introduction that was subsequently added to give us some information about the author, or at least to lend the illusion that we know him. The titles of each section were added by the publisher.

The third part opens with a chapter titled "A Few Words at the Very End", consisting of abstract and rather loose considerations that form a kind of epilogue to this story. Following it are a few brief notes mainly pertaining to the author's stay in America and the period that preceded his "descent into Agartha." They were written as a follow-up review from the writer's "Moscow exile." Some commentators have suggested that death stopped the author from further writing the memoir, or that he had suddenly lost all interest in completing his manuscript. Only his sketches remained.

Let us suppose for a moment, as some interpreters do, that this manuscript is not a literary mystification or a work of fantastic literature, but is an authentic record, a memory, albeit vague, of quite real events. In that case, another question remains: what is the real role of the person posing as Sikorsky? Is he really just an "observer and not an actor", as he claims, someone who "only records and does not participate", whose mission is only to describe his visit to Agartha in order to prepare the world for a major change and for the allegedly dramatic events that he anticipates? Someone who is void of political passions, who is not interested in the ideologies or religions of our time, someone "rejecting with contempt everything that bears the mark of modernity", seeking "another foothold elsewhere"?

A participant in a Nazi expedition to the Himalayas ended his life peacefully in a modest Moscow exile. This fact should be borne in mind.

Sikorsky is a man of shadows, someone who enjoyed the protection of Heinrich Himmler and the Nazi Ahnenerbe and who carried the rank of SS officer; a mysterious emissary pursued by NKVD investigators; a descendant of the Whites, an aristocrat, and yet a loyal subject of the Soviet Union, who does not hide his sympathy for Stalin and Soviet Russia, nor his contempt for Hitler and National Socialism; an advocate of empire, of Eurasia, and someone who opposes the "free world", the "New Atlantis", the "Carthage of our age."

In the last period of his life, he was an associate of certain Soviet secret services (as evidenced by the note on the expedition to the Mongolian Altai), or someone who lived under their cover. His predictions for the future of the world are fundamentally correct. World War II did not provide humanity with lasting peace. Today, we stand on the brink of what he calls the "final battle of history", the "clash of Rome and Carthage", the impending "war of East and West." This naturally places him within certain conspiratorial and geopolitical schemes. Jean Peladan, in his somewhat bizarre work dedicated to Sikorsky and his (supposed) journey to Agartha, entitled, *Messenger of the King of the World*, proceeds from the following assumption: Sikorsky was an adept and member of some secret society or, more likely, a whole series of secret associations ranging from Europe to the United States to Russia, or the Soviet Union, including numerous para-Masonic associations and Theosophical circles in the US. The roots of such a secret society should be sought in imperial Russia, and then in the circles of Russian emigrants, the White Russians. They continued in Soviet Russia and its "occult history."

It is not clear on what basis this author links Sikorsky to the secret organization of the Baltic Barons, "Consul", and through this secret cell to the Austrian and German Ariosophists. This, through the Thule Society of a certain Robert von Sebottendorf, a completely obscure personality and an alleged confidante of Hitler, leads him to the occult circles of the Third Reich.

In any case, he is alleged to be their adept who carefully hid all such connections. The manuscript evokes one visit by the author to a Masonic temple in the United States. He is also a follower of some conspiracy theorists, Traditionalists and Perennialists like René Guénon and Julius Evola, with whose work he must have been acquainted during his time in Europe. Some of their ideas can be recognized in the fictitious history of humanity given in the manuscript by Mani. For example, he cites the "race of soft bones" explicitly mentioned by Evola in some of his books. The term "language of the birds" is also found in the works of Guénon, as well as in a whole series of his followers' works.

Finally, he is an associate of the Soviet secret services, with which he first made contact in the late 1930s in Nazi Germany after arriving from the United States and after his first Himalayan expedition (and possibly in Weimar Germany). In other words, he was recruited as a Soviet secret agent during that period. How else can we explain that a participant in the Nazi expedition to the Himalayas and someone who, at least briefly, enjoyed the protection of Himmler himself was interrogated by NKVD agents, and then continued his life in the Soviet Union and participated in several Soviet expeditions, such as the one sent to the Mongolian Altai?

According to Peladan, Sikorsky owes this protected position to his mission. He is not just a traveler to Agartha, or someone who has made contact with the underground in order to convey the full news of its existence. This fact, after all, was already well known in the circles of Russian esotericists and mystics, at least from the time of Saint-Yves d'Alveydre, whose wife was Russian, and in fact well before that: it arrived in the West through Russia. In his book *Beasts, Men and Gods*, Ferdynand Ossendowski also reported the search for Agartha undertaken by the "mad bloody Baron" Ungern von Sternberg, and subsequently many other actors in the occult history of the Soviet Union, both Red and White, would engage this idea.

Sikorsky, in his view, is an envoy conveying a secret message from Agartha; he is the real messenger of the King of the World. Moreover, he is someone who is expected to continue to convey the messages of the King of the World in the future; he is a plenipotentiary of the underground kingdom and a guardian of the secret Agartha. On another level, Sikorsky is a spokesman for certain esoteric and mystical circles expounding the "secret doctrine", he is an advocate of synarchy in the likes of Saint-Yves d'Alveydre. For this reason, he denies the role of the French esotericist Guénon.

He is also a participant in the secret history of Russia and the Soviet Union. This "secret history" of Russia (and the whole world) is supposedly described in the manuscript itself, in mythological codes, in a mythical key: through the conflict of the Firstborn and the Secondborn, the appearance of the Dark Brotherhood (and an even more secret order opposing it), through allusions to the Ancients and memory of the uprising of the Titans, and through the complex entanglements of Agartha's fictitious history.

The commentator assumes that the writer's place in the secret hierarchy was much higher than he was willing to acknowledge, and that the same person, under different names, appeared in several other decisive events in the aftermath of the Great Patriotic War. Before that, he was a Soviet agent, perhaps very influential, moving for some time in the esoteric circles of the Third Reich.

The intention of the writer of this discussion is not to issue his own judgement or to offer any interpretation. He is content to present the facts and opinions of those who have thoroughly studied the manuscript, and to leave the explanation of these obviously ambiguous and scarce facts to the reader himself.

- Vyacheslav Antonov
2015

The Reawakening of Myth

PART III:

SACRED HISTORY AND THE END OF THE WORLD

Selected Essays

SACRED HISTORY

I.[50]

History has its sacred logic. Just as there is sacred geography, which views geographical data not as "dead" or "material" phenomena and realities, but as a sacred text (written with special signs), so can we speak of sacred history. History is not only "material", it is the manifestation of the "supernatural", the invisible, the Sacred within earthly reality. Events that take place in time have their symbolic value, and history is no more than a reflection of this superior order.

Moreover, history is entirely sacred because within it even that which is not sacred but only human (or even subhuman or demonic) is entirely subject to sacred logic. History is governed by Providence. If God is omnipotent, then the whole of history is a result of his will. But even in this case there are inevitable limitations willed by God. First and foremost, there is the freedom of man, who can choose either "good", i.e. the sacred principle, or "evil", which is its direct negation. It follows that the principle of "evil" is history's active mover. History thus encompasses the negation of the sacred and its reaffirmation. The same can be transferred onto the personal plane: human life unfolds between two poles: the sacred and its complete and radical negation, the demonic. In terms of his individual existence, man's task is not to live "free from sin", but to achieve deification: to become like or even equal to God, and thus to overcome purely human existence.

---

50   Written in 2008, published in the Serbian edition of *The Return of Myth* [*Povratak mita* (Niš: Niš Cultural Center, 2010)].

Exile from Paradise, the Murder of Abel, and the Fallen Angel

Evil is the active driving force of history. Without it, history could not take place. This does not mean that the principle of the sacred manifests itself in any less active way over the course of and within history, but rather that only "evil" represents the original impulse of history, without which it could not have begun at all. In Christianity, history begins with the "Fall", the exile of Adam from paradise. The next act is the murder of Abel. In other words, the main direction of history is involution, not evolution; there is no progress, only regression and falling away from the sacred. Yet this process is neither simple nor unidirectional. There are forces which constantly, actively counteract this course. The principle of the sacred is constantly intervening in this basic course, not questioning it in essence, but also not allowing it to completely prevail. Thus it shall be until the very end of time. At that point, history will end and we shall enter the domain of eschatology. In Christianity, this fundamental drama is finally resolved by the Kingdom of Heaven, the final victory of the sacred principle within earthly reality. It interrupts the course of history and even time itself, which figures here as linear. But there are other answers to the very same question: the end of the world and the end of history can also be merely the end of one temporal and historical cycle, at the end of which the sacred principle manifests itself again in its integrality. Its manifestation in its completeness, in its integral form, at once means the beginning of a new cycle which will inevitably have the same course and meaning (degradation and regression). This is the cyclical concept of time and human being within time. History then continues through the re-emergence (or the first emergence in the new cycle of time) of the manifestation of the principle of "Evil."

In Christian theology, God is omnipotent. He is the creator of the cosmos, of everything that exists, the visible and the invisible. He is boundless, self-reflecting power, the spirit, the force that confirms itself through creation. His only limitation is the freedom bestowed upon man and ultimately every created being. Angels also possess freedom, even the freedom to rebel against the Creator himself - such is the Christian tale of the Fallen Angel. Whether these limitations are self-imposed or stem from some other cause, they remain part of the established order of the cosmos (which is order itself) as the "rules of the game" by which history unfolds. "Miracles" are steps out of this order. This does not mean that they are arbitrary. Man is also given the same power to commit an act that represents a step out of his natural, "physiological" limitations, an act which transcends the mere human condition. This confirms his likeness to God. Man is created in His image. "I said, 'You are 'gods'; you are all sons of the Most High'", reads the famous passage in Psalms.

Creatio ex Deo and *Creatio ex Nihilo*

Here it bears pointing out one essential conceptual, metaphysical difference between all the monotheistic religions, which include Islam, Judaism, and Christianity, and "paganism", that crucial difference which makes all the Abrahamic religions different from non-Abrahamic ones. On the metaphysical level, the highest category is the Absolute, "infinity", which represents a negative category insofar as it is in no way possible to determine it from the conditioned, limited standpoint of being. Furthermore, one of the possibilities of the Absolute is manifestation, and this coincides with "pure being." "Pure being" here can be equated with the manifestation of the Absolute, that is, with God's creation in the Christian perspective.

In the non-Abrahamic traditions (or religions), there is no strictly established boundary, no "barrier between the world of ontological principles and the manifest itself (i.e., the world) - a barrier which otherwise, in the creationist religions, separates them."[51] Following Alexander Dugin, we can call this perspective "manifestationism", characteristic of which is the fact that the manifested is not strictly separate and does not have a different essence from ontological principles. On the contrary, this connection is manifest everywhere and in everything, and things and beings themselves constantly have the possibility to transcend the framework of the manifest, to move vertically either towards the proto-intellect and through it ("active perfection", "liberation", *moksha*), or towards the substance of manifestation and through it into the fold of proto-matter ("passive perfection"). The manifestation of the Absolute is therefore continuous, and creation, that is creation *ex Deo*, is essentially constant, not a singular event in time.

The "creationism" characteristic of the Abrahamic traditions adopts the opposite standpoint: creation is *ex Nihilo*. The barrier that separates the principle from the manifested is therefore strict and essentially insurmountable, and creation itself, as a one-time and unrepeatable event, is necessarily related to a "voluntary self-depreciation of the Godhead", being therefore a kind of "self-humiliation" which in Christianity is called the "*kenosis* of the Father." Thus arises a completely

---

51 Alexander Dugin, *Metafizika Blagoi Vesti* [*The Metaphysics of the Gospel*] (Moscow: Arktogeia, 1996).

different attitude towards everything created, including man himself who, in a consistently creationist perspective (for example, in Judaism), is not a manifestation of the Divine, but is, like all of nature, basically "nothing", existing only thanks to God's grace, with all the ensuing consequences. However, from case to case, especially in Orthodox Christianity or Sufi Islam, this perspective ceases to be so strict and even allows for minor or major deviations from the rigid "creationist" view towards "manifestationism" in altogether different forms.

The Image that Falls Away from its Creator

In any case, man occupies a central place and significance within sacred history: he is its true center. In the earthly environment, he represents Heaven itself, the sacred principle, sifting its inherent contents, order and light. The order that peers through the created is at once a reflection of that order which is the inner content of man himself, and which is reflected in nature (which is the work of the Creator) as in a mirror. The created world, as has already been said, is subject to the destructive, corrosive happening of time. It resembles an image falling away from its Creator. (In the manifestationist perspective, this means that the very manifestation of the Absolute is "weakened" in the manifest). Man himself is inevitably subject to degradation, thus imparting sacred history with the quality of a distinct and irreconcilable dualism. In this way, man is no longer merely the guardian of everything created, but he also becomes the force that actively opposes it. Thus, he ceases to be the bearer of the sacred principle of history, but he does not go beyond the logic of sacred history. All the more, he thereby confirms this sacred history.

Sacred history reconciles two seemingly contradictory and irreconcilable things: man retains his freedom within it, all the while continuing to be, or not ceasing to be, an "instrument of Providence", wherein his role has both a ritual and symbolic character as well as the quality of active participating in history which, nevertheless, is realized to a large extent independently of his wishes. Man does not know its outcome, nor can he know the real consequences of his actions. But God requires from man not passivity and passive expectation of the resolution of the great cosmic drama, but his participation. Man is obliged to participate in an active way so as to maintain the work of the Creator. On this rests that superior ethics (not morality, which is habitual insofar as it rests on consensus) most succinctly expounded in the *Bhagavad Gita*, in which Krishna teaches and calls on Arjuna to follow his example through action: although there is nothing in the three worlds that he (Krishna) would like to acquire, he still acts in them. He acts indifferent to victories and defeats, gains and losses. He acts because if he did not act, the world would perish: "By my direction (of action), the world unfolds again and again" (*Bhagavad Gita* 9:1). Man thus imitates the gods or the Creator himself.

Man's active participation in history does not mean that he is aware of its true purpose, its "meaning", much less its sacred logic. This is especially true for that historical period which the Christian tradition designates as the "End Times" and which the Hindu tradition calls the Kali-Yuga (the last of the four regressive cycles of time). This is the time of general confusion, the time in which, as the Vishnu Purana forewarned, "Men of all degrees will conceit themselves to be equal with Brahmans" and "every text will be sacred scripture that people choose to think so" (*Vishnu Purana* 6:1).

The "End Times", which have already begun or which we have already come close to, is also the time of the complete profanation and desacralization of history (as well as all other human spheres), in which all consciousness of the higher meaning of historical occurrences fades. This general profanation of history has the consequence of reducing history to the level of purely human causes and wholly arbitrary constructions of the "meaning of history." In this period, in the final part of the cycle, the sacred principle of history becomes invisible and unattainable to people, or in the very least the vast majority of people, and sacred history completely disappears from the consciousness of ordinary people. But this does not annul its presence. The sacred principle still determines history, only this happens hidden from human eyes. Overall, archetypal principles continue to "govern" history in this time, as they are covertly contained in the most diverse ideological forms of the modern world - from technocratic ideology to Marxism, from liberal-capitalist ideology to fascist ideology or Americanism. After all, every historical phenomenon - including states, political parties and movements, prominent individuals, the actors of historical events, and even non-political institutions ranging from the financial to the cultural, artistic, and "environmental", has its role in sacred history, the true meaning of which - of which people are unconscious by nature - will be revealed later, in the dramatic denouement of the "End Times."

The proliferation of profane and arbitrarily constructed meanings of history, whether derived from philosophical conceptions of an idealistic or materialistic bent, or from political doctrines and ideologies, has yet another meaning:

such conceals the real bearers of the sacred principle, as well as the bearers of its demonic, infernal negation.

The King of the World and the Prince of this World

Christian tradition speaks of the invisible "seven righteous" by whom the world is maintained. The Apostle Paul, in his *Epistle to the Thessalonians*, speaks of the mysterious presence of the "one who withholds" (from the Antichrist and his coming). In his book, *The Mission of India*, the French esotericist Saint-Yves d'Alveydre introduced the West to the Buddhist myth of the secret center of the world, "*Agartha*", hidden somewhere in the depths of the Himalayas, India, or Afghanistan. The Polish writer Ferdynand Ossendowski speaks in his book *Beasts, Men and Gods of the "King of the World"* who, hidden in the underground kingdom of Agartha, invisibly rules the surface of Earth. According to this myth, which Ossendowski faithfully conveys, this ruler has the power to talk to God himself: "Fire appears on the altar, gradually spreading to all the altars near, and through the burning flame gradually appears the face of God."

Traditionalist thought, through the works of the esotericist and metaphysician René Guénon, provided an exegesis of this myth: at its deepest root is the idea of the supreme spiritual center, the spiritual center of humanity during the last time-cycle of humanity, i.e., the Iron Age in the traditions of the peoples of the West. As Guénon observed, numerous parallels and analogies of this Buddhist myth of the King of the World can be found across the most diverse traditions, from the Hindu and Jewish through the Islamic and Christian to the Celtic myth of the Holy Grail which was subsequently, superficially Christianized. The very name

Aggartha or "Agarttha", Guénon writes, means "imperceptible" and "inaccessible" - "and also 'inviolable', since it is Salem, the 'Abode of Peace'" - but the name of the spiritual center before the present time-cycle was *Paradesha* ("supreme country" in Sanskrit), whence the Chaldean *Pardes* or the *Paradisus* ("paradise") known to the Western traditions.[52]

Opposing the King of the World is the "Prince of this World", i.e., the Devil, Satan, the Fallen Angel of Christian theology. He is surrounded by those whom the Muslim tradition calls the *Awliya esh-Shaytan*, or the "Saints of Satan." In Traditionalist thought, this corresponds to centers of counter-initiation (as opposed to the true centers of initiation, which Guénon considered to be an obligatory precondition for spiritual realization). Counter-initiation, with its organizations and structures, is but an inverted, parodied, twisted image of the true sacred principle and its hierarchies.

The Blurred, Distorted, and Broken Mirror of Order

René Guénon adds to the myth of the King of the World the mythical theme of the "seven towers of Satan", scattered across the globe from Africa to Turkestan, the Urals, and Western Siberia. These towers correspond to the "personalities" of the seven main fallen angels. These towers emit a very real influence on the existing world, one which, of course, ruins and degrades everything that exists. This decay in fact affects man first and foremost, as he is the (symbolic and actual) representative of the celestial principle on Earth, but it also affects all of creation, including nature itself which is the mirror of the celestial order (now turned into a blurred, distorted, broken mirror).

---

52 René Guénon, *The King of the World* (Hillsdale: Sophia Perennis, 2004), pp. 49, 54.

As for the conscious bearers of the two opposing principles of sacred history, it should be noted that neither one nor the other are people in the customary sense of the word. They are distinct from "ordinary people" by their degree of spiritual realization: even the "adepts of the Devil" are people who have traversed a long way along the path of spiritual ascension only to find that they are not "allowed" to go beyond a certain level of spiritual development. Turning to head the way back down - plummeting downwards toward the demonic and infernal - they still retain certain abilities and powers that are inaccessible and even incomprehensible to the already greatly degraded people of the "last age."

These "wandering magicians" serve the seven towers of Satan. Between them and the profane world there is a whole spectrum of secret organizations and societies (again, led by those who are to greater or lesser extents conscious of their role), as well as the whole series of the seemingly entirely profane organizations of the external cultural and political world. Yet, from the point of view of sacred history, let us repeat, no phenomenon or institution in history is truly "profane", insofar as all, even the most materialistic and pronouncedly atheistic or the most "God-fighting" and "Satanist", ultimately represent only certain archetypal, sacred ideas, albeit distorted and secularized, and are fulfilling their role immanent to sacred history.

Myth is a way of presenting certain "otherworldly" truths to those who live deeply immersed in "earthly" reality. Both poles of the dualism of human and sacred history not only have their bearers among people, but also make very real contact with the "other world": in the case of bearers of the sacred principle, with the Divine, and the opposite pole with the forces of darkness, the Devil, and Hell itself.

The King of the World on the Earth's Surface

Guénon and Traditionalist thought as a whole thus understand and interpret the myth of the King of the World and the hidden kingdom of Agartha literally, as symbolizing the spiritual center of mankind. Agartha represents the center, but one hidden in the underworld: "Agarttha, it is said, was not in fact always underground, and will not always remain so. According to Ossendowski's report, a time will come when 'the peoples of Agharti will come up from their subterranean caverns to the surface of the earth.'"[53] The center, in this version, exists in a very material way and in conditions of security afforded by concealment beneath the Earth's surface.

The same thought is encompassed in Guénon's position on "regular initiation", which he alleged to be a necessary condition for spiritual, metaphysical realization and transcendence of the human state towards the divine. Sacred history is governed by the initiated (and this is true as well of representatives of counter-initiation), and the sacred principle has its "legitimate" representative in the face of the King of the World and the spiritual hierarchy that surrounds him - that which will be revealed at the very end of history, when all the reasons for his continued concealment finally dissipate.

The idea of an underground hiding place of the incarnation of the sacred, celestial principle is in itself contradictory. According to sacred logic, the seats of spiritual authority are to be found in mountains, not in the underworld

---
53   Guénon, *The King of the World*, p. 49.

which is logically and naturally connected with the chthonic, the infernal, and the hellish. These same chthonic influences are, in all probability, revealed by the idea that initiation is a precondition for spiritual realization. The relationship between God and man excludes in principle any meditation - such is not necessary for man, much less God. The manifestation of the sacred principle throughout history always remains direct, albeit shrouded in mystery, similarly to how knowledge of the sacred logic of history does not make it possible to predict specific events (prophecies, except in rare circumstances, are based not on seeing future events, but on knowing the order immanent to history).

Archetypes and ideas themselves choose their bearers throughout history, and people within sacred history, no matter however paradoxical such may sound, retain their freedom by acting in accordance with their own nature. The security and protection of the "inaccessible, inviolable place" cannot therefore refer to the bearers of the principle, but only to the principle itself, for the reason that it belongs to the intelligible, not the sensory world, to the world of eternity, not the world of change and ephemerality.

"Inviolability" can, of course, also apply to an individual, a specific person, if such is the will of Providence. This can be a hallmark of heroes that are in every way exceptional. However, in the metaphysical drama of sacred history, there is no certainty, only risk, just as there is no "good" that is self-evident.

II.

History has its meaning, and this meaning is unconditionally sacred. Such sacred meaning overrides all human, necessarily arbitrary constructs of the meaning of history. It fundamentally cannot be known to people, except in extraordinary cases. "We do not know nor do we have the right to know", says one of the heroes of Ernst Jünger's novel *Heliopolis*, "what history is in essence, in the Absolute, beyond time. We can guess, but we do not know the verdict of the Court of the Dead." To ancient historians, beginning with Herodotus, any idea and speculation on the meaning of history was foreign; they were content to record and describe historical events so that they would not be forgotten.

The God that Appears on Earth

Let us repeat in the most general terms that the sacred logic of history is predicated on the following principles: the whole created world is a reflection, an image in a mirror, of the heavenly order; creation is the manifestation of the sacred principle in the material. Man is symbolically and really the representative of the sacred principle of the cosmos, that celestial order that is embodied in the earthly environment. This was especially the case at the beginning of time. But then, in a series of cyclical shifts, a departure from the principle inevitably ensued. This shift affects both the created world and man himself, as well as the human community in general. Moreover, it is precisely the degradation of man that is the cause and measure of the distancing of everything created (nature, the earthly environment) from the heavenly order.

Cyclical degradation is inevitable, including all the way down to the point where the whole world will become a demonic negation of the sacred principle, its exact, complete opposite. At the end of the last among the descending, progressively degrading cycles of time (which the Hindu tradition christened the "Kali-Yuga" and the Christian tradition the "End Times"), at the very beginning of the new cycle of time, the sacred principle will manifest itself in all its purity. All traditions concur on this. Although they all differ on the specific details of future events, there are no significant disagreements among them on this point.

The idea of the gradual evolution of the whole world and the human community is completely foreign to all ancient religious and esoteric conceptions. Decay is inevitable and obvious, it is in the very nature of time, which necessarily has an erosive trajectory. But this course is neither straightforward nor unilinear. A whole series of causes can lead to its at least temporary halt or short-term straightening - short-term in relation to the total duration of the entire cycle and straightening in the sense of restoring what already seemed to be permanently lost.

The Coming of Christ and his birth and life on Earth show that it is possible for God to directly intervene in the course of human history: the sacred principle, of which Christ was the incarnation, thus acts altogether directly. The god Odin in Scandinavian mythology constantly comes to aid people, just as the gods of the Slavic pantheon fight alongside their followers. This idea is also known in the Hindu tradition's concept of avatars. The *Bhagavad Gita* tells of Krishna who, indifferent to losses and gains, victory or defeat, with his appearance on Earth helps "the world unfold again and again." Christian tradition speaks of two Comings of Christ (the second still being anticipated), while the Hindu tradition knows as many as nine avatars, the appearance of the tenth belonging to the domain of anticipated events.

The sacred principle, therefore, can act directly. God, for reasons and with consequences which are not always clear to people, can appear on Earth. Although these are quite exceptional events in sacred history, such acting is a model for man to follow: man should essentially do the same as God (or the Gods) and imitate him in order to become like him. This is the norm for man on Earth who, again, represents the sacred, heavenly order and principle. In other words, God (or the Gods) and man are united by the same and common goal. In the end, thus, each of us is with our thoughts and deeds a participant in invisible sacred history.

This applies as well to all other types and domains of human action and participation in history, even when they seem to be entirely profane. The division into profane and sacred is artificial and arbitrary. A number of completely profane associations and organizations of the "exterior world", without any consciousness of the sacred, have very important and active roles in sacred history. Sometimes they are "blind tools" of Providence, at other times they are merely masks under which demonic influences hide. The same is true of any historical actor: Hitler or Napoleon, for instance, were important participants in sacred history even though, as indirect evidence suggests, neither had any interest in the sacred and "otherworldly" aspects of historical events.

The Return of Matriarchy

All of this does not deprive man of freedom. Within sacred history, man remains a completely free being. He can, in accordance with his own will, act in accordance with the sacred principle or actively counteract it. The French esotericist René

Guénon called those forces opposed to the sacred principle "forces of counter-initiation."

The evolutionary notion of history is an altogether new and profane idea which contradicts all true traditional doctrines and ancient religious concepts. The created world, as we have seen, is subject to the ravages of time, and if it were at all possible to speak of any "development", then this would be a matter of faster or slower involution. The idea that the whole world, and thus human society, is progressively developing towards some predetermined goal in alignment with some meaning intrinsic to this evolution and without the acting of any higher, superior principle, as is the case in religious conceptions, from this point of view seems completely absurd.

In fact, the role and place of the sacred principle in materialist and evolutionary conceptions is merely taken over by matter itself, which corresponds to the ancient principle of Earth as opposed to the sacred principle of Heaven. The goal and meaning are hidden within matter itself and will subsequently, through evolution and material progress, be realized. Yet it is on this point that ancient traditions and teachings are not univocal. For the purposes of this essay, we adopt the division between patriarchal and matriarchal traditions or, in somewhat different terms, between Uranic and Chthonic traditions. Telluric, chthonic cults are essentially based on the deification of matter (understood in a much more subtle way than is the case in modern materialist conceptions) and its infinite mutations. The Uranic is the constant, unchanging, and eternal amidst the world of metamorphoses and continuous, aimless mutations. Uranic religiosity is the ancient Indo-European, Aryan tradition, and only it - all other traditions can be subsumed under the notion of telluric, i.e. matriarchal and chthonic.

Modern science has, similarly to contemporary art, through the deification of matter and the material resurrected ancient chthonic archetypes and patterns of thought. But such is only one segment of the great return of the matriarchal substance that characterizes contemporary culture. Today, it is already possible to speak of a great revanche of matriarchal matter and values over the patriarchal up to the point of the complete victory of matriarchy. The very same historical current includes the revival of utopian tensions, wherein the space of utopian attempts has long been not only human society, including social and political relations, fields of culture and art, but also, finally, the space of the human psyche and the human body (e.g. the androgynous utopia).

From the Golden Age to the Iron Age

Sacred history is fundamentally cyclical. The main division encompasses four descending cycles of time corresponding to four human races.

The Christian conception of time is linear. The Coming of Christ and the Second Coming are singular, unique events in history. This idea of linear progress is connected, not without reason, to Christian eschatology. The Twilight of the Gods, or rather the "Twilight of Powers" in Scandinavian mythology is, despite the death of many gods, not a singular, unique event. Although it marks the "end of the world", at the very end of this cataclysm a New Earth appears, "the eagle flies, and fish he catches", and new gods and new people will emerge, those who are the first to come out of the Forest of

Memory. In other words, it is rather a matter of restoring the diminishing divine and human powers that have been exhausted by the end of the cycle of time and history. The Christian Apocalypse, on the contrary, promises with the End of the World the descent of the City of God, the creation of Paradise on Earth. The "New Jerusalem" which is to rise over the ruins of the old order means a qualitatively new degree, something that goes beyond the usual order of time and history. Hence the expression "the end of time", the secularized expression of which is the "End of History" spoken to by thinkers such as Marx and Fukuyama.

The four basic human races - the golden, silver, bronze, and iron - testify to the progressive decline of human powers. The people of the iron race are but the "unworthy descendants of the fourth. They are degenerate, cruel, unjust, malicious, libidinous, unfilial, treacherous."[54] The people of the golden race, on the other hand, "are all gone now, but their spirits survive as genii of happy music retreats, givers of good fortune, and upholders of justice."[55] Here it is also worth introducing a certain qualification as Robert Graves saw it: "The myth of the silver race also records matriarchal conditions - such as those surviving in Classical times among the Picts, the Moesynoechians of the Black Sea, and some tribes on the Baleares, Galicia, and the Gulf of Sirté - under which men were still the despised sex, though agriculture had been introduced and wars were infrequent. Silver is the metal of the Moon-goddess"[56] - a goddess who is obviously chthonic, feminine, if not an androgynous deity.

---

54   Robert Graves, *The Greek Myths* (New York: Penguin, 2017), p. 77.
55   bid, p. 76.
56   Ibid, p. 78.

The myth of the four human races corresponds to the Hindu tradition's four ages, over each of which human and divine powers progressively diminish. As Scandinavian legend describes it, at the end of the last time-cycle even the combined powers of the gods and humans are no longer sufficient to stop the triumph of the entropic forces of chaos and darkness. Black Surtr will eventually set the Earth on fire with his sword brighter than the Sun, and Non-Being will claim victory over Being. The Earth will eventually sink into the ocean. The Bridge of Bifröst that connects Earth and Heaven will collapse under the weight of the heavenly armies. Thus, a unified army of gods and people - including all those who have ever fought bravely on Earth - will come out onto the battlefield, but this time not even this can contain the catastrophe. The world will sink into darkness, fire will swallow both earth and water. Among the gods, only Odin knows the final outcome. Odin also knows that he is to be among the first to be devoured, swallowed by the monstrous wolf Fenrir, and he knows that when the Sun shines over the Earth again, he will not be among the living. However, this does not prevent Odin from being the first to throw his spear at the crucial moment that starts the battle marking the onset of the Twilight of the Gods.

Gods or Demons

Man, as has already been said, remains a completely free being within sacred history. Threatening Heaven or Hell has no effect on him. As Swedenborg put it, demonic souls feel heavenly bliss in hell, while the heavenly environment leaves a hellish impression on them. The celestial hierarchy, in other words, becomes unbearable for those who find happiness in chaos and destruction. God's existence cannot be rationally proven, but the great atheistic movements of our time are not the consequence of a lack of faith as much as the deeds of man's open rebellion against God and the sacred principle. Even belonging to one of the institutionalized religions - among which Guénon distinguished between the esoteric, hidden and exoteric, outer circles of the great world religions - does not guarantee salvation, since all of them differ on the specific details of the expected end of the great eschatological world drama.

Perhaps, after all, this end is very close, although "no one knows the day nor the hour" of the Second Coming of Christ. By heeding this call, man in fact answers the deepest call of Being. The question that is posed before the man of the Uranic tradition is not "to be or not to be human", but rather "to be or not to be a god" or to be something lower: a man-beast or even a demon.

Time has a cyclical flow, and each of its cycles has its own quality. But the very height or depth of human possibilities does not change over them. The latter are not forbidden or inaccessible to the man of the final age, just as they were available to the people of the Golden Age. The man of the final times, after all, does nothing else but resist the current of time. He must master time and its erosive forces in order to return to the original, primordial, best state.

The man of Uranic tradition thus takes a stand "against time" or "against history", in which he sees not progress but only vain mutations and metamorphoses. For him, only that which is always immutable and one, that which is identical to himself, is of value. In history he sees not progress but regress, for over the course of history the tradition that he carries and represents extinguishes and disappears. Ultimately, deep beneath the changes of history, there always remains the same reality: to participate in history and its "processes" means choosing between the role of the executioner and the victim. What the man of Uranic tradition wants, unlike the man of the Chthonic tradition, is something much more than history with its whims and coincidences, which grant its actors either the tragedy of defeat or short-lived, illusory triumph.

Above History

History is governed by Providence. This does not mean that its outcome is predetermined, but rather that the choice between the sacred center and its demonic antipode is made outside of and above the possible outcomes of this struggle.

Sacred history remains an invisible reality by which the visible is determined and ranked. We will only be able to know History in its true meaning and sense from beyond history and time, in eternity. Uranic man has nothing to gain nor lose in this: he already has his own center, he is his own truth of Being. For Chthonic man, by contrast, only the judgement of history, of success or failure in it, of victory or defeat, confirms or refutes his "faith." Uranic man is integral and unconditional: his position is thus not only against, but also above history. "We can guess, but we do not know the verdict of the Court of the Dead."

This is the struggle waged between Being and Non-Being, between fidelity to the self and renunciation of selfhood. It cannot, therefore, end in any truce, any seeming peace, or any compromise. Uranic man therefore treats the Chthonic with contempt, since he sees in the latter only a distorted and monstrous image, a caricature of the true human being. The Chthonic, on the contrary, recognizes in his enemy, in the one who represents the truth of Being, his own inadequacy: in him he discovers what he himself is not and can never become.

***

ARCHY AND ANARCHY[57]

As a general rule, the political doctrines and ideologies of our time represent but distorted and largely or entirely secularized forms of ancient sacred concepts and ideas. They are distant, degenerate, late echoes deprived of sacred essence. Yet even in this form, they still retain their original archetypal content that is common to a surprisingly large number of people, even if such is often deformed beyond recognition.

So do works of contemporary art often preserve contents and meanings of which not only their audiences, but also their professional interpreters, critics, and even their authors themselves are unaware. Moreover, the tendency of art criticism to limit its domain to the field of aesthetics already disqualifies such attempts at interpreting works of art. The Russian scholar Meletinsky spoke of 20th century culture being subject to a "process of re-mythologization" (as opposed to the "de-mythologization" of the era of Illuminism and positivism). The evocation of ancient mythical contents is precisely one of those most characteristic features of the "historical avant-garde." The appearance of androgynous symbolism in the works of Marcel Duchamp and the Surrealists (and not only them) is a typical example of this. In fact, as Dragoš Kalajić observed in his *Map of (Anti-)Utopia*: "The whole line of the historical avant-garde, from Dadaism through abstract art all the way to Suprematism, is none other than an 'aesthetic' series of forms or manifestations of the principles and symbols of chthonic traditions."

In other words, the avant-garde is not aimed at destroying tradition altogether. The subject of their enmity is only one

---

[57] Written in 2008, published in the 2010 Serbian edition of *The Return of Myth*.

tradition, just as the historical avant-garde and even the greater part of modern and (postmodern) art of the 20th century is only the affirmation and continuation of another, equally clear and definite tradition. In this sense, one work by Marcel Duchamp is of paradigmatic significance: his "transformation" of Leonardo da Vinci's Mona Lisa, on whom he drew a goatee and mustache. According to the general conviction, such a "transformed" classical work is an expression of mockery of classical art, a sign of the rejection of and total break with the past and tradition. It is true that such a transfigured form of Leonardo's painting actually represents the symbol of the androgyne (a motif that is, after all, obsessively present in the works of Duchamp). The symbol of the androgyne belongs to one tradition of values and ideas: the artist's work does not ironize or negate but rather affirms the values of matriarchal culture opposed to the patriarchal, thus taking the motif of the androgyne, already suggested and secretly present within Leonardo's painting, to its ultimate, final expression.

Heaven and Earth

In general, the merit of 20th century art lies in precisely this radical, extreme expression and representation of ancient archetypal contents that have been more or less covertly present in the history of art and culture. Here they may be deprived of their sacred dimension and essence, but they are nonetheless given in extreme, naked form, one that does not allow for wandering, ambiguity, or misinterpretation. The above-mentioned work of Dragoš Kalajić, *Map of (Anti-) Utopia*, represents a unique attempt, tracing the content of 20th century works of art, to create a "unified morphology of culture" revealing the parallel existence of not one but two traditions, not one but two worlds of values, two different, contradictory cultures and, ultimately, two different human types. This is the contrast between the Uranic and the Chthonic. This opposition extends through all historical periods and reaches back deep into prehistory. These are two basic principles upon which civilizations and cultures are built and out of which is consequentially derived all "horizontal" development and application to secondary modalities.

From this also follows that there are two different and irreconcilable *forme mentis*, two psycho-ideologies or mentalities which appear through all times, including through what we call the "(post)modern." No compromise is possible between them, for there is no possible synthesis that could overcome their fundamental dualism. That being said, however, these two types rarely appear in pure form: Uranic culture shows a constant tendency to contaminate the elements and contents of the Chthonic, which is a consequence of the strategy of severing and mimicking the bearers of Chthonic culture. Their relationship, therefore, is a constant, although often covert, mutual struggle. Their real origin is not the sphere of culture, but the sphere of the spirit, and all the different forms in which they manifest are but secondary expressions of this basic dualism that is really of metaphysical origin. Yet it is much easier to demonstrate their existence by illuminating complexes of values, beliefs, and ideas than it is to point out their historical origins. Their origins are lost in the darkness of time. They are not available to scientific opticians, but in any case their existence is perfectly certain. To our knowledge, Kalajić's attempt was singularly unique, although it had its predecessors, on two of which we shall dwell briefly, namely, the conceptions of Johann Jakob Bachofen and René Guénon.

In his work *Das Mutterrecht* ("*Matriarchy*"), which is of capital significance, Bachofen arrived in his study of myth at the conclusion that there exist two different types of society. The first and, in this author's opinion, the older one is matriarchy, and the second, historically "younger" which has since replaced the first, is patriarchy. Both stem from religious conceptions. Matriarchy, its organized customs and value systems are based on "matter" and "Earth": the person of matriarchy "belongs to matter and a religion that knows only the life of the body, and therefore it is melancholic and desperate in the face of the eternal disappearance of everything that is born. The transience of material life and matriarchy are interdependent ideas." The other half of this despair is ecstatic surrender to the principle of infinite change, metamorphosis, and the evolution of all things that exist. The person of matriarchy, or "Chthonic man" in Kalajić's terminology, strives to conform to the current of time and the laws of infinite variability, against which any resistance is an act of arbitrariness, lawlessness, and violence. The final goal of Chthonic man is reintegration into the "primordial unity", i.e. the primordial chaos preceding everything created, for the "one everything" only partially dies and is eternal. One form of this is the Dionysian ritual of the "dismemberment of the dismembered", the "negation of the negation", which nullifies the "multiplicity of being" and returns everything differentiated to the primordial, original, and therefore ideal state of non-differentiation. Everything else arises out of these basic assumptions, including the legal principles of the organization of matriarchal society, which privileges the feminine principle (as opposed to the masculine one), the Mother as opposed to the Father. The cults of matriarchy (which does not know male deities) are the cults of the Great Goddess, the Great Mother who both bestows and ruthlessly takes life away (thus achieving the desired return to ideal unity). Matriarchy strives towards leveling (against hierarchy or firm order), for in life and before death "all people are the same" as brothers, sons, and children of the same mother. The god Teshub has no father but only a mother: wet earth, in which his tomb is also to be found.

Landscapes of Light and Landscapes of Darkness

Patriarchy is based on entirely different assumptions and ideals. In Bachofen's words, patriarchy "points towards suprapersonal life belonging to the realm of light." It is precisely the symbolism of light that is of the greatest importance, because visible light points toward higher, truly metaphysical meaning. It is also a symbol of the invisible that is above everything created, above the created world. In the words of Emperor Julian in his *Against the Galileans*: "The sun which is visible to our eyes is the likeness of the intelligible and invisible sun."[58] Or in the words of the *Chandogya Upanishad*: "Now, the light which shines higher than this heaven, on the backs of all, on the backs of everything, in the highest worlds, than which there are no higher - verily, that is the same as this light which is here within a person."[59]

Light spreads radially, and that is the way in which creation takes place, the way in which order is introduced within the primordial chaos. Light is the symbol of creation itself. The opposite of order is not some other positive principle, but mere lack of order, the simple negation of order. The opposite of

---

58 Julian the Apostate, "Against the Galilaeans", in *Cyril of Alexandria, Contra Julianum* (translated by Wilmer Cave Wright, 1923).
59 *Chandogya Upanishad* III:13:7, *The Thirteen Principal Upanishads* (trans. by Robert Hume) (Oxford: Oxford University Press, 1921).

light is darkness, which is merely the absence of light. Light, which is permanent and immutable, belongs to a completely different order than the endless metamorphoses of everything extant: light points to the world of eternity, immutability, and order, as opposed to the chaos of the Chthonic. The oneness of the "light from beyond heaven" and the "light that shines within man" points toward the oneness of the subjective (human) and objective (God) sides of reality, the human and the divine. Patriarchal man rejects the circle of necessity, the circle of constant appearance and disappearance, for the sake of what is above and beyond, for the sake of the eternal. His opposite is Chthonic man who appears out of the (earthly) dust into which he will return again. He does not shine, for earth is characterized precisely by opacity, turbidity.

Where are the true historical origins of these two conflicting worldviews to be found? Patriarchal culture and religions were brought to Europe by the Indo-Europeans, and the path of their migrations and conquests was the path by which the values of patriarchal culture were spread into matriarchal Old Europe. Patriarchy gradually claimed victory, but this struggle is undecided and long-lasting. Bachofen spoke of a shift between two basic social systems, wherein patriarchy replaced and followed matriarchy chronologically. In fact, this struggle never ends, nor can it end. Not purely patriarchal, but to a greater or lesser extent mixed societies have been created across the Eurasian continent, societies which simultaneously retain elements of both even while patriarchal institutions may have become dominant. The victory of patriarchy is only temporary. It can never truly be complete, for the ideas of matriarchy are based in a different human type and a very particular, characteristic psychology. Historically, patriarchal institutions have weakened over time, and extraneous elements have penetrated patriarchal order to the point that in our time there can no longer be any talk of patriarchal order in the true and original sense. The principles of matriarchy not only persist throughout time, but since the moment of the victory of the patriarchal principle matriarchy has waged its struggle against this different world of values, seeking out its desired revenge and the re-realization of its own ideal. The so-called "modern era" crowned this thousands-years-old process.

Patriarchal values, as we have already said, are eminently Indo-European values. We find their expression wherever Indo-European cultures and their bearers turned up, in all the landmarks of spirituality, religion, as well as social institutions. Originally, patriarchal values were not to be found anywhere else outside of Indo-European cultures, and wherever eminently patriarchal contents appeared in other and distant cultures we can think of a mediated influence of Indo-European tradition.

Joy and Melancholy

It is in the Indo-European (polar, Hyperborean) tradition that the French esotericist and metaphysician René Guénon wanted to see the "Primordial Tradition" that exists at all times and is of "truly suprahuman origin." Yet this Primordial Tradition fully existed only in the first, Golden Age (the first of the four regressive cycles of time), and thereafter was subject to gradual, ever-quickening degradation. In Guénon's conceptualization, time has an erosive flow, as a result of which there is not evolution but involution and degradation, inevitable and unstoppable falling away from the Principle. Not only man but everything created is exposed to this process up to the end of the final age, the one in which we live now. The end of the fourth age is also the beginning of a new cycle of time, a new Golden Age, when the Primordial Tradition shall reappear in its integral form.

Guénon's works were an attempt at reuniting the broken parts and fragments of this once one tradition that have been scattered across myths, beliefs, religious and metaphysical systems, and the traditions of different and diverse peoples - to reunite and merge them in their integrity in the sense of the ancient principle "Shine the light and gather what is scattered."

Unfortunately, we can only agree with Kalajić's conclusion that Guénon's attempt to restore the Primordial Tradition remains essentially unconvincing, not only because "Guénon's map of the 'Primordial Tradition' was missing many important landmarks of the Indo-European continent of spirituality" (such, as for instance, the Slavic tradition and the heritage of Orthodox Christianity), but also because "his vision is closer to some kind of modern reconstruction rather than metaphysical reality." Guénon arbitrarily included the gnosis of operative Masonry in the corpus of tradition, whereas Masonry is often merely a syncretic set of diverse, even incompatible elements taken from various traditions, the results of which were painful and often insurmountable contradictions in Guénon's works. Thus, the final outcome of Guénon's seeking was, in Kalajić's words in his "Introduction to the Works of René Guénon", "a speculative product reflecting the sunset of spiritual energies on the site of once great spiritual struggles, where only ruins remain." Joy once reigned on these "battlefields" and spiritual virility triumphed, yet in Guénon's attempt to rehabilitate tradition there is a hopeless melancholy, for this attempt managed to gather only the "ruins" or "ruins of ruins" illuminated by "lunar" light and not the light of the sun, which is the light of the very solar principle of order.

In our opinion, however, the failure or only half-success of this seeking does not call into question the validity of Guénon's intuition as to the existence of the Primordial Tradition. After all, according to Traditionalist doctrine, this tradition can be renewed in its integral form only after the end of the "Iron Age." In terms of the dualism between the Uranic and Chthonic, however, Guénon's "reconstruction" exhibited a high degree of pollution of the Uranic by the Chthonic up to the point of losing the very essence of spiritual virility. This was a consequence of Guénon's rather arbitrary reduction of all differences and dualisms to one and the same basis and starting point, often at the cost of distorting or even falsifying their original meanings and significances.

Order and Anarchy

It is clear that this "mistake" stemmed from the assumption that there existed one single tradition common to all of mankind (although Guénon did constantly suggest such to be of Hyperborean origin). The result was an essentially static and lifeless "construct" that suppresses and denies any dualism. Otherwise, Guénon's Primordial Tradition in fact contained numerous elements and doctrinal traces which, irreducible to Indo-European patterns, testify to the existence of at least one more "antipodal center or principle of the development of cultures and civilizations" (Kalajić). That we cannot precisely determine its origins, whether geographical or chronological, does not negate the fact of its existence. However, it is a fact that the cultures and civilizations that we define as Chthonic have taken shape and gravitated around the South of the Eurasian continent, while we can mark the point of origin of Uranic spirituality to have exclusively been the extreme North of the continent.

Historically, there are no civilizations that can be labelled purely Uranic. Rather, there are only spiritual landmarks or spiritual manifestations of the purely Uranic, patriarchal principle. All known cultures and civilizations represent examples of the "coexistence" or mixing to greater or lesser extent, most often through open struggles, of these two irreducible principles. The spiritual sphere and the domains of art and culture are also the site of their uncompromising struggle. Even if the institutions of patriarchal society are gradually collapsing under the blows of the revenge of matriarchy, it would still be mistaken to conclude that the very manifestations of the Uranic principle either extinguish or appear in less pure forms over time. The Uranic principle of order, which we understand here as a metaphysical and suprahistorical principle, is contained within creation itself, in the very work of the Creator. Opposite of this is the principle of chaos, anarchy, and non-order, which results in a constant increase in entropy marking the negation of God's work, the negation of the principle of order inherent to the cosmos. The continued existence of the world requires the constant restraint of the forces of chaos. An analogy to this can be found in the biological world, where the existence of life itself is dependent upon very complex organic structures, whereas their disappearance or transition from a state of order to disorder signifies the death of a biological organism. In his work *Byzantinism and Slavdom*, the Russian thinker Konstantin Leontiev extended the same idea to the social plane, noting that the loss of complex social structures and their simplification inevitably leads to anarchy and entropy, to the death of states and civilizations.

The same idea can be extended to the entire cosmos, the whole universe, which itself is an extremely complex and living structure. This concept itself is dualistic, as it is based on the constant struggle and opposition between two principles and the balance of their forces: totally overcoming one principle is not only undesirable, but also impossible - impossible before the end of time and the world. Here, Gibbs' law of entropy finds complete confirmation: "In Gibbs' universe order is least probable, chaos most probable. But while the universe as a whole, if indeed there is a whole universe, tends to run down, there are local enclaves whose direction seems opposed to that of the universe at large and in which there is a limited and temporary tendency for organization to increase. Life finds its home in some of these enclaves."[60]

Chaos is primordial to all cosmogonies. The act of creation itself brings order to primordial disorder. These are the three steps of Vishnu, who "measures the borders of Heaven and Earth." Creation results in the emergence of an island of order amidst ever-lasting chaos. Order tends to spread, while chaos tends to nullify order towards returning the world to its original state of undifferentiation. Thus begins the great cosmic drama, a struggle whose field of battle is the whole universe, including man himself, and which can in no way end. The order that results in hierarchy and structure is life-giving, life-creating, whereas the state of chaos is analogous to death. But the complete victory of the principle of order would also result in the end of any movement, in the end of this struggle

---

[60] Norbert Wiener, *The Human Use of Human Beings: Cybernetics and Society* (London: Free Association Books, 1989), p. 12.

and the end of history. Its complete triumph would lead in the end to the same outcome as the victory of chaos over order. Therefore, Uranic spirituality supports dualism: the goal of Uranic man is neither victory nor peace, but struggle itself.

Man retains his freedom here: he can adhere to either principle. The principle of order, similar to the principle of light, is one of the ways in which the principle of the sacred is expressed through creation. History is also a field of battle of this dualism that is absolute, for it cannot end with compromise or the complete victory of either the Uranic or Chthonic principle. This dualism is transmitted onto the highest levels, and just as there is light above everything created and visible, so is there darkness above the created world. There is no possibility of their reconciliation, synthesis, or unity of opposites. This dualism extends throughout all levels of existence. It is true that the principle of order can be sacralized, but so can the principle of chaos, and the latter is precisely the domain of that spirituality which we term Chthonic.

Utopia and Anti-Utopia

Throughout history, this dualism of the Uranic and Chthonic has taken the form of the dualism between the matriarchal and patriarchal principles. Closest to the ideal of patriarchal order were the Indo-European communities, the classical civilizations of Greece and Rome already representing mixed types of society in which patriarchal content was still dominant. Christianity was an eminently chthonic movement and religion (for instance, Easter holiday was initially a rite of fertility and the sacralization of fertility, which is completely foreign to Uranic spirituality), but the mature Middle Ages brought a kind of "correction" to Christianity in the direction of patriarchal values. Yet these failed to undo the deeply chthonic roots of this religion. The end of the Middle Ages, with the appearance of chiliasm, millenarianism, and the beginning of the Renaissance, marked the beginning of the great return of matriarchal values, whose culmination would be none other than the modern age. The modern world lives under the sign of the utopian incarnation of the primordial contents of the Chthonic psyche and its archetypes. Utopia, whose destination is "nowhere", embodies Chthonic man's constant need for metamorphosis, for a change which, by definition, is an endless "process." Uranic man has no need for constant change, for infinite emergence, since he is not something that arises and changes infinitely, but something that simply is. His obligation is to, against all external circumstances, manifest his own internal content, that of the principles of light and order. He also has the obligation to fight for his values against the surrounding circumstances which are fundamentally unfavorable (and tend towards further deterioration) without asking about the outcome. In short, the Uranic aim is not to win in this struggle, for victory is impossible, but to maintain this fight that cannot evolve insofar as it is an end in itself.

Since at least the beginning of the Christian era, Uranic man has not been supported in this struggle by any institutions. He relies solely on himself. With the breaking up of the family and its economic basis over the course of industrialization (and de-ruralization), he has been thrown into the very jaws of the modern Leviathan, into urban metropolises (for which the name "necropolis" is much more fitting). These are void of the very mirror of order that is nature and the created world (which is the work of the Creator himself), void of the order which is the mirror of the inner content of Uranic man himself. Deprived of support, external strongholds, and social institutions, standing alone against the people of the Chthonic masses who are human beings only externally, Uranic man now manifests himself in an extremely pure form, because the condition of surrounding darkness is necessary for the manifestation of light. Chthonic man expresses himself through utopia, whose contents are always "new" and infinitely mutable, and it is these contents that have been realized (true, in a completely different spirit than the one in which they were conceived, i.e. with their hidden contents realized) over the course of history, thus substantially contributing to the deterioration of the position of Uranic man, and man in general, to the point of hopelessness.

Over the course of the 20th century, Uranic man expressed himself in an art form called "anti-utopia." This cannot be identified or equated with the negative utopias of Huxley or Orwell, which did not go beyond the values and horizons of the Chthonic psychology and *forma mentis*. The scope of their critiques of utopia remained extremely narrow and limited, representing a kind of attempt to stop the realization of utopia at a certain "middle" point, at a reliable distance from the point of catastrophe. Thus, utopias are much closer to Uranic man than such "negative utopias" with their beckoning that everyone, including Chthonic man, strive towards the very limit of their possibilities.

Through anti-utopias, eminently Uranic values are expressed and sharpened to the extreme, albeit seemingly taking on the Chthonic form of utopia. But the role of this utopia is only viatorial: Uranic man seems to be moving towards the utopian future (whereas the obsession with the future is characteristic of Chthonic psychology) only to sharpen his own values in the present against the background of an assumed future that is necessarily worse than the here and now. By force of this contrast - dissociation from the already bad conditions to which modern man is accustomed towards even worse ones - the Uranic values of the lonely man, as opposed to the Chthonic demos, shine like the flame of a single candle illuminating a dark night.

It bears noting that in our time the Uranic principle has already been reduced to the chest space of the last, lonely - increasingly lonely - defenders. The Uranic principle pertains to a small elite, bunkered in fortified places surrounded on all sides by the noise of demons threatening destruction. This situation was masterfully described in Ernst Jünger's works *Heliopolis* and *On Marble Cliffs*, as well as in Miloš Crnjanski's *A Novel of London* and *Among the Hyperboreans*. As Jünger noted in his Paris diary (which he kept in occupied Paris in 1942-1943 while serving as an officer of the German occupation troops), this situation rests on a completely real experience, in a concrete time and space, yet:

> there is always something timeless in these situations. In this case, it's the figure of the proconsul, one of whom was Pilate. The *demos* vehemently demanded the blood of the innocents for him as they cheered the murderers on. And from afar the emperor, who enjoyed divine status, threatened with his thunderbolt. That makes it difficult to maintain the dignity of a senator... [61]

---

[61] Ernst Jünger, *A German Officer in Occupied Paris: The War Journals, 1941-1945* (trans. By Thomas S. Hansen; New York: Columbia University Press, 2019), p. 234.

In both cases, we are dealing with the top writers of anti-utopias, in the sense of Kalajić's definition, along with Hermann Hesse's *The Glass Bead Game*, Jean d'Ormesson's *The Glory of Empire*, Richard Bach's *Jonathan Livingston Seagull*, and Daniel Halévy's *Histoire de Quatre Ans*.

The Idea of the Center and the Age of Catastrophe

The line of demarcation separating utopias from anti-utopias is a line dividing polar opposites: light from darkness, order from disorder, Heaven from Earth, good and evil (although "good" and "evil" here should be understood extremely conditionally, because what is for Uranic man "good" is for Chthonic man absolute "evil", and vice versa, and with one qualification: insofar as "everything that persists in its being is good" for Uranic man, Chthonic man himself is "good" as long as he persists in being what he is). Hence, the "border lines" which separate the worlds of utopia from the worlds of anti-utopia also signify an insurmountable, indeed abyssal difference and dichotomy. It is not possible to cross, overcome, or reach through this border.

The developmental line of utopia reveals the gradual but ever-quicker degradation of Chthonic man towards ever-lower degrees of being, to the point that something can no longer be called a being. This line of degradation is like a parabola that leads down to the lower axis and then even lower. On the opposite end, the "integral man" manifests through the world of anti-utopia, the one whose ideal was created according to the highest models of tradition. This is the Uranic human type, the one capable of uniting the paths of action and contemplation as one, which corresponds ideally to the conditions of the "end times" or the age of catastrophe.

Here it is not possible to speak of any development, but only of a special manifestation of one unique human type which exists through all times and whose motto is "not to be without sin, but to be God" (Plotinus, *The Enneads*).

The worlds of utopia, that is to say the "values" of Chthonic man, have no center. His position is, by definition, "ex-centric", his life is "existing", literally "outside of being." The Uranic tradition, by contrast, has a (meta-)historical and (meta-)geographical center: the North Pole, Hyperborea. The fact that this center has extinguished today, that it does not exist (that it does not exist in the phenomenal world), does not mean that in the modern age Uranic man is really deprived of a center.

This center cannot be the Agartha of René Guénon's thought, because the idea that this center is materially secure, hidden beneath the Earth's surface, contradicts the Uranic tradition, which holds that the high, the supreme, cannot be an institution of the "outside world" or a "secret society."

Among the ruins of the world of patriarchal institutions, amidst the complete collapse of all the structures of traditional and patriarchal communities, Uranic man realizes his essential loneliness. But it is precisely in the night of loneliness that his only true center is revealed more clearly. Only then, in the deepest human night, is it revealed that the center can only be that "light which shines higher than heaven", the light from beyond "in the highest worlds, than which there are no higher." Verily, this is that same "light which is here and shines within a person."

***

THE ANTICHRIST[62]

"*I come in my Father's name, and ye receive me not: if another shall come in his own name, him ye will receive.*"
- The Gospel of John, 5:43

There is a terrifying, disturbing representation of the Antichrist in the fresco "The Sermon and Deeds of the Antichrist" in the Orvieto Cathedral, painted by Signorelli shortly after the year 1500. The Antichrist is depicted as Christ's twin brother, his double, not differing from him in external features. While preaching, he shows his hand on his heart, burning with love for mankind – resembling the sword-pierced, flaming heart of Jesus – but at the same time he listens to a demon whispering in his ear.

This is not in contradiction with the fact that he is feeble-minded, deviant and defective, thwarted in every way, except perhaps in the body, yet even in this as well, according to some opinions; despite a bodily resemblance to the Son of God, the Antichrist still carries a mark, some kind of hidden but essential deficiency. That makes him a carrier, an intermediary, a puppet, an ideal object for manipulation, who manipulates and is himself manipulated. Hence, he is supported by someone else, someone who manages him like a theater puppet; that is the horrible, grinning face of the demon, Lucifer, Satan, the serpent of Eden that tempted Christ, seduced Eve and deceived Adam. It is he who whispers in the Antichrist's ear and controls his every act – the Antichrist is, to repeat, in spite of all his external characteristics that could deceive the uninitiated, a perfect medium, an empty

---

62 Written in 2012, published in Boris Nad, *Nevidljivo carstvo* [*Invisible Empire*] (Belgrade: Metaphysica, 2016).

shell, completely susceptible but craving affirmation, pliable and unconditional worship.

He is a pop star of his time, almost bisexual, or truly bisexual, like Lady Gaga and Michael Jackson, someone who manages and governs the masses in stadiums, through television, the Internet or by some other, much more perfect technology designed precisely for him; without it his influence would not be possible, because he is, besides his resemblance to Christ, a homunculus, an insufficient and incomplete being, a blank screen with no face.

To say that he is backed by hell, by Lucifer with his demonic legions, however, means to adopt a partial, narrow view of Christianity. For some, he is the expected false Messiah who heads the Saints of Satan. For others, he is a messenger, a courier, Lord Maitreya, the true prophet of the new age, the true Messiah, the one who speaks to all races, religions, and peoples, who brings a message for all of humanity. He heralds long-awaited changes, mutations, and completely new perspectives opening previously unknown domains to humanity. He leads humanity towards a New Earth and New Heaven.

***

The Antichrist is surrounded by his diabolical servants at all times, yet he is in all likelihood not at all aware of their presence. In this respect, he resembles the devil-child from the film *The Omen*. He is an exemplary, politically correct and socially responsible law student at a prestigious university, such as Harvard or Yale, someone dedicated to social activism, one who should figure among the chosen leaders of his generation. He is the son of Hell and, at the same time, environmentally conscious and a supporter of the rights of the oppressed and the handicapped, a defender of minorities, whether ethnic, social, or sexual, a consistent supporter of gay rights, zoophiles or necrophiliacs, and there is no need to doubt the sincerity of his motives at all. But honesty here is not a virtue, because it is said that the Antichrist is merely a retarded advocate of the Devil with an angelic smile, someone who deviates from the "normal" service of Lucifer, with a naive faith in things which one could not possibly honestly believe in.

He is a believer, but at the same time he is not; he is a believer exactly insofar as it is permitted and politically correct. The devil is, in the beginning of his career, non-existent in reality, an obscure creature of the imagination. The Antichrist does not belong to any church or denomination, but has equal, lukewarm interest for all; he does not accept or understand any dogma, but interprets them in his own deeply depraved manner, in the limited mode of their time. In his mouth, the Gospel becomes but a bland, moralistic lesson, a banal set of general points, the chatterings of an idiot.

***

In his work *A Short Tale of the Anti-Christ*, Vladimir Solovyov describes the breaking-point night in the Antichrist's life. This is a moment of crisis, in which he is on his way to becoming aware of his insignificance and attempts to commit suicide; yet this is prevented by some unknown force.

This is the moment of his demonic illumination, devilish enlightenment. This is the moment in which he enters into a contract with the devil, which he signs by his own blood. Such is the turning point of his life in the words of Vladimir Solovyov:

Two piercing eyes came close to his face, and he felt an icy breath which pervaded the whole of his being. He felt in himself such strength, vigor, lightness, and joy as he had never before experienced. At that moment, the luminous image and the two eyes suddenly disappeared, and something lifted the man into the air and brought him down in his own garden before the very doors of his house. The next day, the visitors of the great man, and even his servants, were startled by his special inspired air.

His feeble-mindedness and insignificance thus take on a new and almost unexpected quality: intelligence, a devil's shrewdness, something that he did not have previously, nor could he have possessed with regard to his own personal qualities. According to Solovyov, during a single night he writes his brilliant work on the overall well-being, his own program which will elicit the recognition and admiration of all, or nearly all - which, in our opinion, is not even necessary. His charismatic, deceptive power is sufficient, and that is what the Antichrist unquestionably possesses.

The demon whispers to him. He shows him the way: political parties, secret societies, international agencies, associations for the protection of human rights and the legalization of drugs, non-governmental and governmental organizations - all now stop at his side. His blurry origin becomes an advantage, his limitations become fertile ground. The demagogue's path to world power is finally open, provided he does not live in some small and powerless country, but in a world superpower with the prospect of achieving not only planetary domination, but a real unity of the world, a single world state, which he will rule as sovereign lord.

The question of whether the Antichrist believes in the doctrine propagated now becomes irrelevant; he is not its author anyway, he is but someone who represents, promotes and propagates, although in a remarkably convincing way. The night of crisis and enlightenment for him means a substantial change; it is very likely that he has rejected all his previous persuasions, if he ever had any. He wins power, for example in the EU or the US, but he wants more. Step by step, the points of his program are realized, including long-desired world peace and the resolution of social and economic issues. The solutions proposed are excellent, sometimes brilliant. Hunger is eradicated among the peoples of the world, or at least among those who follow him.

Everything he imagines becomes a reality, even the impossible things: the lamb and the lion now truly live in peace, side by side. The Antichrist becomes a mass idol, an icon of youth on all seven continents. As his power increases, so do the demonic legions which surround and protect him grow.

***

At this moment, Solovyov introduces a new character: the mysterious magician Apollonius, half-Asian and half-European, a Catholic bishop in *partibus infidelium* who has the power to connect what is impossible to connect, such as technological inventions with magic and the achievements of modern Western science with the traditional mysticism of the East, in order to reach "disastrous results." His entry into the flow of the story at this point is more than justified - it is necessary, because he is a precursor, or more of an incarnation of the religion of the New Age. One of his tasks is to promote the Antichrist as a spiritual guru of the new age, someone who will bring a new spiritual (demonic) enlightenment to followers, a messiah who opens up a New Heaven, having already created a New Earth. He is not creating a new sect, but a sect that is beyond sects and beyond church where any existing one can find its place.

In his *Black Mummy (Apocalyptic Sex with the Antichrist)*, Dorijan Nuaj describes the Antichrist as an anti-human, the incarnate negation of human beings, as a "frail and feeble, grotesque and disfigured body, a heinous phenomenon." He was "so retarded that he was not able to live without help and constant care. He does not have any contact with anyone, because he is not able to have it. He is one empty, warped shell without a brain, with more water in the skull than brain tissue." Nuaj continues:

> I saw him lying curled up in a glass sarcophagus, in some kind of greenish, gelatinous mass, attached to various electrodes, tubes and needles that were stuck into his degenerated body. His body was mottled with scars which were actually the marks of diabolical forces. The scars sometimes bled, and that was a sign to the intelligence in his service, to various doctors and scientists to take a sample from that festering mass, because the use of these cells in the cloning process will produce a new being, representing a carrier of the force which created the Antichrist by making a sign on his skin. Thus, the Antichrist served as the Father of demons generated by and just as monstrous as him.

The Antichrist as a gelatinous mass in a glass sarcophagus, or a successful and ambitious law student at Harvard – whatever the case, he does not live, he has never lived and he will never live. He is in actuality a simple shell, an empty mask, a face without physiognomy, a handicapped being devoid of passion, except one: infinite, self-centered ambition. He is not satisfied only with respect, but requires unconditional adoration.

***

That was roughly what was going through my head as I gazed into the Christ-like face of the Antichrist through the huge video beam – or should I say the future of the Antichrist, because he was at that time only an undergraduate student, not a participant in the eschatological drama – the Antichrist who is probably presenting his views on a somewhat Faustian theme in front of some mega-corporation, his motion on legal norms pertaining to human organ transplants, with all of the legal implications, including the rights of cadavers, the dying and the living, the rights of the sick and the healthy, and the right to dispose of their bodily fluids and organs.

I remember that his presentation began with something to the tune of some "inviolable right to life of all", but then, thanks to the almost diabolical dialectic and a series of very complex arguments and even more complex counter-arguments, deducing somewhat unexpected consequences which questioned or restricted the importance of everything that had been said previously, approval was met in unison - due to, among other things, the Antichrist's indisputable, compelling charisma.

It was perfectly clear to me that I was looking into the face of the Antichrist. This was without a doubt and obvious, not a figment of my imagination, although I could not explain where I knew it from. It seemed to me that I could recognize the magus or demonic teacher named Apollonius by Solovyov, and a few others close to him as well.

Then, while they were endorsing, applauding, cheering and congratulating him, I suddenly saw something that defeated me. In the next moment, while I was sitting deeply slumped in my seat, I witnessed the act of his deification, as if watching it on a big screen or dreaming awake with eyes wide open.

***

Everything must have been happening in Jerusalem, or in a field not far from that city, because in my wakeful dream I saw first the narrow stone streets flooded by rivers of people, an almost unimaginable crowd. Small shops stretched along both sides, alongside some outlets, souvenir shops, and then chapels and basilicas surrounded by palm trees. Then I saw the mass overflowing a huge empty space, and in the distance the outlines of the minarets and cupolas of the mosques, and the contour of one wall, perhaps the one belonging to Solomon's temple, or perhaps the one just being raised by the Antichrist.

Under the canopies in the open air, food, drink and various refreshments were distributed free of charge; this gave everything a festive atmosphere, an atmosphere of a national feast, of a carnival. Priests of all confessions, Roman Catholics with white collars, among them bishops, Lutherans, Evangelicals and Orthodox with overgrown black beards, imams and rabbis, shamans and sorcerers, Benedictines and Franciscans, monks from the Holy Mountain and even Tibetan lamas in their orange robes were moving through the crowd.

Hundreds and hundreds of thousands, perhaps millions of people, had been pouring into this place from noon, standing in silence under the hot sun, under an unbearable tension, although it was known that the ritual itself would, for some reason, take place just on the eve of the evening.

Many visitors, curious people or fans came from all continents, members of all races and nations - Japanese tourists with cameras, Germans in groups with guides, Russians and Chinese, Aborigines, Eskimos, Laplanders, Amazonian tribes...

All of humanity, united in tremendous expectation, united in cramped hope, in blind faith, in fraternal embrace. In the middle of this space, a gigantic stage was raised, above it were screens that could record each and every small facial demeanor, each and every quietest uttered word, so that nobody would be deprived of bearing witness, regardless of the place they occupied.

Still, many were pushing at its base, where they were removed by the multifold security of the gathering. Those who did not find themselves in Jerusalem on that day were able to follow it throughout the whole day through a real-time holographic transmission, which allowed at least an illusion of presence and direct participation, envisaging not only the images and sounds, but also the smells - the smell of smoke, incense, the vapors of swaddled bodies, meals and drinks. Those who wanted could even touch the pontiff's garment, which had been exhibited on a pedestal from the early morning - a lavish white dress, woven with golden threads, somewhat resembling the clothes of the Egyptian pharaohs.

The whole ritual harbored a grotesque tone. I knew somehow that this was the fourth year of the Antichrist's power. During the first, he brought to mankind long-desired peace, uniting it at the end of that same year into the World State, and receiving with benevolence the imperial throne from grateful nations. During the second year of power, he carried out comprehensive reforms that seemed to have eradicated hunger and poverty forever, or at least it seemed that way, but without taking away the wealth of the rich nor completely eliminating social and economic inequalities. This provided him with stable support and permanently weakened the opposition, enabling him to reject repression and act as an enlightened dictator, as an absolutist whose power rests on the will of the people, and therefore there was no need to stain his hands with blood. To silence them, he called his opponents to the dialogue.

***

In the third year, the magus Apollonius entered the stage, accruing worldwide glory with his interpretation of the ancient prophecies of East and West, according to which the Antichrist is the "tenth and last Avatar", Kalki, the Messiah, Christ in His Second Coming, the true King of the World – this would become one of his many titles. All of this was followed by an abundance of omens, the appearance of comets and shooting stars, icons shedding bloody tears, stigmata among monks.

Apollonius became a cardinal in the Roman Catholic Church, but above all the gray eminence of the Antichrist's power, his *intimus*, his closest friend and ally. The act of deification itself was to finish what started in the first year of his rule. As he brought peace to humanity and provided it with prosperity, he now had to show that each and every person, even the most insignificant among people, would be able to gain immortality and, more than that, to become Christ, God, the Avatar, the Buddha, or someone like him, the one who showed the way to immortality, opening it to all people without exception.

The process itself, based on ancient traditions, magical and religious teachings, as well as hitherto unprecedented advancements in technology, science and medicine, was conceived by Apollonius – although it would be more appropriate to say that it was the invention of Hell, Lucifer, a deviously distorted mind. To this end, the Antichrist was subjected to special treatments for 30 days under the supervision of a council consisting of scientists, doctors and priests, undergoing the replacement of bone marrow, stem cell therapy, the transplantation of certain glands, certain genetic modifications, and physiological enhancements which would make him immortal and undoubtedly divine.

The lights on the stage flashed on with a certain delay, illuminating the naked body of the Antichrist in a position that resembled the Crucifixion. The staging was grotesque, with a multitude of symbols from the Star of David to the cross, the swastika and the crescent, symbols belonging to all known religions, including the Babylonian, Egyptian, Mayan, and Voodoo cults. In the background, angelic choirs could be heard mixed with children's voices, or perhaps female ones, though oddly distorted. The performance begins with a certain unplanned delay: the sky in the East darkens, dark clouds piled up, and the air in the distance was ripped with lightning.

***

The crowd is overwhelmed by terror, the atmosphere becomes charged, perhaps more than the cause requires. A mechanical hand descends above the Crucifix-positioned Antichrist; the first laceration cuts into his skin with the precision of a laser; the crowd drops a sigh. Needles, dozens of needles stab into his skin, into his swollen veins. One twitch moves the convulsed body. A thin stream of blood flows onto his skin. A replacement of several bodily fluids, including brain fluid, proceeds underway. This is the sacrifice the Antichrist offers for all of mankind. At this moment, Apollonius climbed onto the stage and proclaimed the following:

> Brothers and sisters, believing, united in expectation! You who believe in the coming of the Messiah and redemption. You who are touched by our word and you who are preparing the coming of the Age of the Spirit and the Death of Man...
>
> You who are the flock of the chosen ones over which your shepherds watch at the end of time. You need to know that no one in history has done more for mankind. Instead of war, He provided peace. Instead of starvation, He gave you prosperity; instead of ignorance, knowledge, instead of pain, joy, and instead of slavery, freedom. There is one more thing left: to give you immortality, not the one spoken of by Christians in the Kingdom of Heaven, but immortality here on Earth, real immortality of the body.
>
> This process, thanks to Him, is now well-known and studied. In fact, for a long time it was a well-guarded secret of certain cults and religions, but He has perfected it in such a way that it could soon be available to everyone. In a moment, He will rise in His divine but transformed body; this is the secret of the Resurrection.
>
> You will see Him in new glory, resembling Christ walking through the waters.

At that moment, the Antichrist opened his eyes, revealing a face well known to me, but which this time was miraculously changed. In his gaze there was something that could not stand objection. One movement of his hand was enough to send everybody down onto their knees. The living dead rose, there was a stream of droplets of bloody sweat on his forehead, and blood flowed in thin jets through his body. He threw back his head. All this was followed by ghostly illumination.

Millions of people were kneeling in speechless hopelessness, only a few of them continued to stand. They had to endure his terrible glance, his aggressive eyes almost blazing, multiplied by numerous screens. He was burning with love for humanity. With one movement of his hand, many more threw themselves down onto their knees. Then the Antichrist himself kneeled, and someone's hands threw a robe woven with golden threads over his shoulders. Priests anointed his head with holy oil. The New Emperor of the universe was to be proclaimed, the King of the Universe, the Emperor of Emperors, Pontifex Maximus, the High Priest of all confessions, the Messiah, the Avatar.

Torches were ignited in front of the stage. Priests, monks, shamans and teachers, imams and rabbis bowed. The rest were throwing themselves down into the dust. Only a few of the hundreds of thousands of gathered were still standing, and among them a threatening whisper began to spread: "Antichrist, false Messiah…Satan…"

Apollonius explained that all this would be available to everyone within a year, and that everyone would henceforth be able to become immortal and bear the sign of the Messiah. But the Antichrist's face started to twitch suddenly, and the whispering became louder, the incident threatened to spoil the direct transfer of deification. Unrest spread throughout the masses. The Antichrist raised both hands, tossing his head back, and his face changed to the color blue. No one noticed that Apollonius disappeared from the stage in his cardinal purple. Then a dark cloud descended so low that everything was dark, and several rounds of lightning fell on those who were still standing. Then thunder was heard and a commotion began, a wild mess, a stampede in which people trampled over others. Shots were heard echoing in the crowd. The big screen was turned off, and the transmission of the Antichrist's apotheosis ceased.

The following morning, the Antichrist published a proclamation in which he expressed regret over the hundreds and thousands of dead and the excessive use of force in the attempt to restore order, promising that none of the disturbers would be punished, that he would personally carry out the investigation and find the real culprits, pointing his finger at those who were responsible for providing security for the rally. The Antichrist, sitting on Solomon's throne, called for love and forgiveness, and for piety towards the dead. The cameras recorded him crying the very tears that flowed down the cheeks of Christ.

His opponents gathered on the sandy hills near Jericho, and when they saw a sign in heaven, they headed towards Sinai. This encouraged the enemies of the Antichrist around the world. They began to raise their voices.

The battle of Armageddon was nearing. Without a doubt, these were the events that marked its beginning.

The last flash of this vision was the face of the Antichrist in the decisive moments of the battle of Armageddon, when, in the guise of explosions, in the reflections of fire, he finally realized who he really was, what his real role in the eschatological drama was to be, with the exasperated face of a demon, the serpent of Eden, with the grimace of despair, anger, and humiliation. Looking straight into the cold, green eyes of the snake jolted me awake in the relaxed hall of the conference center.

***

POST-APOCALYPSE: TECHNOCRACY AND THE APOCALYPSE[63]

I.

"Death and suffering," Tarkovsky said, "are the same whether an individual suffers and dies, or the cycle of history ends and millions suffer and die." This is so namely from the point of view of the individual, as well as the demons that feed on the dying. With the death of any person, Ernst Jünger noted in his work *At the Wall of Time*, the world is extinguished "as his performance." One picture of the world fades, and only that which represents the ethical consequences continues, insofar as their one view of the world produces all the rest. We cannot say this of the vast majority of people for a reason. Their disappearance will not produce any visible or invisible change, but will leave behind them only a void. This will happen in the manner of a natural cataclysm which brings with it hundreds or thousands of human victims, such as an earthquake, flood, or war. Then the morning sun will rise above the ruins, rescue teams will rush to the aid of those still showing signs of life, or another long night will descend upon them in a long agony, full of cries of the dying. In the morning, bombers or cruise missiles will appear once more over their cities. The blow of nothingness will be strong, but not stronger than the preceding one. Something like light is looming over them. Neither the horror nor hopelessness will extinguish. Maybe that's how those condemned to death feel upon being thrown into a pit with lions.

---

63   First published in Boris Nad, *Postapokalipsa* [*Post-Apocalypse*] (Niš: *Undus Mundus* 38 / Niš Cultural Center, 2011).

II.

The destruction of a city, for instance of Troy, which the invaders put to torch one night, or Carthage, whose fields were sown with salt, is not the same as the passage of the "first earth and the first heaven." Rather, such is an isolated catastrophe, whereas the apocalypse affects the whole world. Moreover, the end of the world spoken of by St. John the Theologian and the first Church Fathers no longer falls within the domain of expected events. The "end of the world" is something happening before our very eyes, something that is already underway. A part of the world disappears every day, with radiation and oil contaminations, population exterminations, bombardments with uranium projectiles, and atomic mushrooms which obliterate tens and hundreds of thousands of people into dust in a matter of a few moments, only for the places of ruin to see the sprouting up of absurd monuments and technological and technocratic civilizations testifying to progress - progress only of technological hubris. Taken as a whole, with all the consequences and cumulative effects, these events verily exhibit an apocalyptic character.

III.

For a long time already we have been living in an "age of loss." We have become accustomed to this and become tied to it. Every day, some ethnos disappears, and with it a language and ancient culture. Every day, consequently, some animal or plant species disappears. Futile efforts to preserve at least some of the abundance fill only museums, academies, institutions, and libraries which more are like tombs than Noah's ark echoing the roar and voices of hundreds of species to subsequently populate the land. That grammars or dictionaries can fill the void that a language or an extinct human race leaves behind with its disappearance is an illusion. That knowledge of the DNA chain and various "genetic information" can compensate for the gap left by the extinction of a biological species is an illusion, even if science could one day enable the miracle of "resurrection" through the reconstruction of genetic codes.

Emerging out of the flames of the conquered city, the refugees of Troy carried on their shoulders, among other things, the boy Aeneas. We cannot expect anything similar from today's scientists, scribblers, epigones, and specialists of narrow fields who operate not with living bodies but corpses, with decaying bodies scattered across deserted shores which, once filled with murmurs and screams, are now but sites of dead, grave silence.

IV.

A careful reading of the Book of Revelation of St. John the Theologian reveals to us that the Christians of the early centuries did not wait with fear as they neared the end of the world. What is more, the end was an object of numerous desires and wishes, many hopes were vested in it. The procrastination or absence of the end led to despair. As Jünger wrote in his *At the Wall of Time*: "Looking towards the end of the world is the only thing that makes things bearable here."

The Lamb, the central figure of the Apocalypse, has the power to "make men kill one another." It breaks the seals, drives the forces and horsemen of catastrophe, and brings death "by sword, famine and plague, and by the wild beasts of the earth" (Revelation 6:8). The Apocalypse is the "day of the Lamb's wrath", before which shall bow, according to John the

Theologian, "the kings of the earth, the princes, the generals, the rich, the mighty, and everyone else, both slave and free" (Revelation 6:15-16).

In fact, here destruction is the goal and not merely a means, and not only of society and its structure, but also of flora and fauna, the Sun, the Moon, and the stars, all the way up to the longed-for "New Earth and New Heaven" which, Revelation promises, will finally replace the "old." The furious rhetoric and bizarre imagination of the Apocalypse culminate in a call for a veritable cannibal feast: "Come, gather together for the great supper of God, so that you may eat the flesh of kings, generals, and the mighty, of horses and their riders, and the flesh of all people, free and slave, great and small" (Revelation 19:17-18).

We cannot help but wonder: what incites so much wrath on the part of the Lamb and those who follow it, when not even the blood of millions, hecatombs of human victims and "the flesh of the free and slaves" can quench it, nor can the mere obscuration of the Sun and the stars, all the way up to when the desired end of the world, when the "new heaven" will appear, because it will pass first?

According to one interpretation, the figure of the Apocalyptic Lamb is an expression of the psychological reality in which the first Christians lived, crucified as they were between, on the one hand, their position at the very bottom of the social ladder, their exposure to persecution and longing for martyrdom, and, on the other hand, the desire for revenge, a great revanche on Imperial Rome. Hence, the very figure of the Lamb is distinguished by incredible contradictions and extreme antagonisms: humble meekness and unseen bloodthirstiness, pastoral care for the "flock", and "plague and death" for this "flock" which will not end until the Sun and stars extinguish.

This cruel spectacle of thunder and heavenly trumpets, of cruel deaths and rivers of blood, would make the Church Father and theologian Tertullian exclaim to the "unbelievers" with shameless joy:

> But what a spectacle is already at hand...that last, that eternal Day of Judgement, that Day which the Gentiles never believed would come, that Day they laughed at, when this old world and all its generations shall be consumed in one fire. How vast the spectacle that day, and how wide! What sight shall make my wonder, what my laughter, my joy and exultation? As I see all those kings, those great kings...liquifying in fiercer flames...those sages, too, the philosophers blushing before their disciples as they blaze together...And, then, the poets trembling before the judgement-seat, not of Rhadamanthus, not of Minos, but of Christ whom they never looked to See! And then there will be the tragic actors to be heard, more vocal in their own tragedy; and the players...[64]

V.

But this spectacle of destruction, it is said, is "beyond." Even St. John does not fully reveal his secrets: when the Seventh Seal is broken, there is silence, and a voice warns him not to write down everything he sees. Perhaps that is why the famous Russian director Andrei Tarkovsky, speaking about the Apocalypse, suggests that questions of interpreting the Apocalypse be ignored, that interpretations be left out in the

---

[64] Terullian, *De Spectaculis* xxix-xxx (trans. by T.R. Glover, *Loeb Classical Library*; Cambridge: Harvard University Press, 1931).

silent expectation of meeting the Absolute as the "last link in the chain" with which the human epic ends:

> Roughly speaking, we have become accustomed to Revelation being interpreted. This is exactly what, in my opinion, should not be done, because the apocalypse cannot be interpreted. There are no symbols in the apocalypse. It is an image. In the sense that if a symbol can be interpreted, then an image cannot. A symbol can be deciphered, or more precisely a certain meaning, a certain formula can be extracted from it, while we cannot understand an image, we can experience and receive it because it has an infinite number of possibilities for interpretation. It seems to express an infinite number of connections with the world, with the absolute, with the infinite. The Apocalypse is the final link in the chain. In this book is the last link that ends the human epic in the spiritual sense of the word.

VI.

The question of who the real author of the Book of the Revelation of the Apocalypse is - whether John of Zebedee, the author of the Gospel of John and one of "Christ's dearest disciples", or someone else - is not without significance. The former was the view of St. Jeremiah of Lyons, as well as Hippolytus of Rome, and then was ultimately adopted by the Church itself. The opposite opinion was held by St. Dionysius of Alexandria and Presbyter Gaius. The importance of this book is also spoken to by the fact that *apocalyptica* was a Biblical and especially early Christian literary genre, and that the Church accepted out of so many others only John's Apocalypse as a holy book and included it in the New Testament. To this should be added the symptom of the enormous interest in the

Apocalypse that is appearing in our time, when the Christian faith and interest in it are generally on the decline and the church and the doctrine it represents are nearing the margins of society. The return of religiosity that is occurring at this moment, when the scientific picture of the world is beginning to be shaken, is not a return to Christianity, but rather something that, from a Christian perspective, is more reminiscent of the religion of the Antichrist.

In the second century, the Montanist church was established in Asia Minor under the leadership of the prophet Montanus, who introduced himself as an envoy of Christ and predicted the near end of the world. The Montanist movement represented a reaction not to any "stagnation of the church", but in fact to the loss of the chiliastic tensions inherent to early Christianity, being an attempt to revive them by promising the impending, desired End of the World. Montanus' movement heralded numerous chiliastic and millenarian movements which would develop under the auspices of the church or outside of it, including up to this very day. It seems that these anticipations have culminated on American soil in altogether bizarre interpretations of Scripture by such movements as the Adventists, whose prophets predicted the exact date of the apocalypse. That the end of the world did not occur within the time they allotted has not detracted from their vigor. In a tradition whose originator seems to have been Christopher Columbus himself (as is evidenced by his words to King Juan of Spain: "God made me the messenger of the new heaven and the new earth of which he spoke in the Apocalypse of St. John... and he showed me the place where to find it"), America gained a veritable eschatological dimension. This motif is carried on to this day in the anticipations of the "Tribulation period" and the "ascension of the righteous in the rapture" of American Dispensationalists and television Evangelicals.

The Russian theologian Alexander Men argued that "expectations of such an end" are a sick phenomenon in the spiritual life of the church which contradicts the Christian worldview, and that the Apocalypse of various authors, including John, is only a "reflection of prophetic visions, not them themselves." Through such visions, in Men's understanding, true revelation no longer shines, but rather only man's imagination, dreams, and fantasies. In other words, the matter at hand is not an original teaching of Christ, but only "fantasies" mainly based on borrowings from foreign, Middle Eastern, predominantly Chaldean sources alongside numerous Old Testament symbols already largely incomprehensible to Christians, a point which explains the fierce debates within the church over the Book of the Apocalypse as well as the very fact that this book, although canonized, is not used in worship.

We could agree with Men's opinion, save for one essential qualification: it is this "sick phenomenon" in the life of the church, this chiliastic tension, and not the message of the Gospel, that represented the main driving passion and the main feature of early Christianity and ultimately ensured its triumph over all other religions, such as Mithraism, as is evidenced by, among other things, the writing of Emperor Julian (known as the "Julian the Apostate"), entitled *Against the Galileans*.

If "Christ's dearest disciple" and the evangelist John are one and the same author of the Apocalypse, then there is no split: the vision explains itself, and the Old and New Testaments form a single whole to which John's vision is harmoniously connected. If John the Theologian and John of Patmos are two different individuals, then this gives grounds to speak of two aspects or even two irreconcilable currents within Christianity, one of which is represented by the Gospel of John, and another which culminates in the Apocalypse as a continuation of the Old Testament.

VII.

The spectacle of the apocalypse is to materialize precisely so that - or only so that - this teaching about the apocalypse is to be confirmed.

The appearance of the Antichrist and the rise of a global (pseudo-)civilization under his rule (we could say that such would be the rise of a technocracy) is not only proclaimed in this prophecy, but is necessary for the very sake of the realization of the Christian eschatological scenario, whose true culmination is the emergence of a "New Earth" and "New Heaven." For this reason, victims look for their executioners, and martyrs, as in the first centuries of Christianity, cry out for suffering and bloodshed.

The terrible days of the martyrs must be repeated for the new faith, but this time on a much larger, indeed global scale that will affect all of humanity, so that the blood of martyrs and victims of faith will provoke the appearance of the Savior, the true Messiah, and mark the end of time. In this case, the Antichrist takes on the role of Judas who is aware of the consequences of his deeds and does not betray Christ for the sake of thirty pieces of silver, but for the prophecy to be fulfilled and Jesus to be sacrificed for the salvation of all people. In other words, to fulfill the words of the prophet.

VIII.

At some point, starting in the 15th or the early 16th century, something truly new was born out of the ruins of Christian civilization: a civilization aimed at endless expansion and growth, freed from the medieval burden of anticipating the imminent and impending Judgement Day, that terrible "mortgage" of the Apocalypse.

This shift was closely linked with a reorientation from land towards sea. As Mircea Eliade rightly observed in his "Paradise and Utopia: Mythical Geography and Eschatology": "It was in this messianic and apocalyptic atmosphere that the transoceanic expeditions and the geographic discoveries that radically shook and transformed Western Europe took place."[65] The real goal of overseas expeditions, however, was no longer the liberation of the Holy Sepulcher or the establishment of a Christian kingdom in Jerusalem (as was the aim during the Crusades at the end of the Middle Ages), but the conquest of colonies to provide a steady influx of gold into the metropolises, to ensure that nothing hindered the increase of power and wealth.

Henceforth, science and a new manner of social organization were to serve this goal. Citizenship takes the place of heritage and villages are replaced by cities, enabling unprecedented accumulation of knowledge and material resources. The circulation of money and financial flows gains new momentum, and banks gain unprecedented power reminiscent of the past power of the Church. Any enterprise becomes inconceivable without them, whether an expedition

---

65 Mircea Eliade, *The Quest: History and Meaning in Religion* (Chicago: University of Chicago Press, 1969), p. 91.

to overseas lands or conquest. Thus, the ban on interest had to be repealed. One after another, technological and geographical discoveries ensued and marked a dizzying change of perspective with which the geocentric view of the world collapsed. In the new constellation, God was allotted a very modest place. God ceased to be the source of royal and earthly power, his power restricted to temples and church property.

Spain and Portugal were not quite suited for the unfolding revolution, as these countries remained pronouncedly Catholic and did not have the strength to attempt a sufficiently definitive break with the Church. In France, this led to bloody conflict between Catholics and Protestants, such as on St. Bartholomew's Night, and culminated in the assassination of the king, the guillotine, and revolutionary massacres like the one committed in Vendée. A completely new faith was born on the ruins of the old.

Thus, the victories of one remote kingdom, that of bourgeois and Puritanical England over imperial Catholic Spain, were deeply logical and predictable. This kingdom's defeat in conflict with the Puritan colonists of New England was also predictable. The new Anglican Church was only nominally Christian, being in reality but an instrument of state power which, in turn, served the exclusively narrow, selfish goals of the king, the court, and the merchant class with their powerful societies and companies. The notion that earthly wealth and power are "signs of God's grace" were deeply bound to the doctrine of predestination, and with these ideas the Old Testament concept of the "chosen people" was revived.

In Puritan eyes, the New World discovered in the West was thus identified with the Earthly Paradise, the Promised

Land, Canaan, a conquest of renewal or even general salvation, and the god of England was identified in the writings of the Anglican theologian William Crawshaw with the god of Israel. The Puritans believed a New Golden Age to be on the horizon, with America as the land where "God will create a new paradise and a new Earth" (Edward Johnson).

The banner of progress was taken over by the followers of the most radical Protestant sects, this time on American soil so as to be "far from history and its delusions", i.e., to be unfettered by tradition, especially European tradition, in establishing "God's city on the hill." America thus became the land of the much-anticipated Second Coming of Christ, and numerous eschatological hopes were attached to it. This, however, could not take place in a direct way, as Protestant theologians once imagined, but only through technocracy and by way of the literal fulfillment of New Testament apocalyptic prophecies. This would soon lead to rivers of bloodshed.

Little by little, millenarianism turned into the Puritan ideology of labor and progress, according to which the "New Jerusalem" and the Earthly Paradise will be "produced by labor." Hence the American cult of progress, innovation, and youth, and in general the "American flair for the grandiose" (Eliade). Before the "City of God" is built on the hill, however, the destruction of everything old and the "world damned by God" must take place. The Antichrist will appear and exercise his rule as a weapon in someone else's hands, whether he is aware of his true role or not, as a means of provoking God's wrath, as a blind tool of the apocalypse for ruthless destruction and the Second Coming - the return of the true God to Earth.

Evidently, Satanism and the cult of Satan did not exist until the victory of Christianity (and this opinion is shared by the historian of religions Mircea Eliade). The convinced followers of Beelzebub, Satan, the Prince of Darkness, and Lucifer appeared out of the persecution and remnants of ancient pagan cults, "sorcerers", "witches", "wizards", and priests opposed to the church.

Once summoned, however, the Devil truly comes in in his own way. The mission of the Antichrist is to provoke the appearance of the Messiah on Earth.

***

THE WAR FOR THE END OF THE WORLD[66]

> "The animating energy of the American imperial project is essentially religious, not political. The ruling American mythopoetic is eschatological. It is about 'end times.'"
>
> - Arthur Kroker, Born Again Ideology

Liberal Totalitarianism

According to a nearly universal assessment, the United States of America is a pragmatic world power, a completely modern world empire whose interest in ideology - in this case in liberal ideology - is superficial, secondary, and almost coincidental. Liberalism, according to this understanding, very easily mixes with "democracy", or a political system in which everyone (at least nominally) has the right to profess any political position and in which no single one has an inherent advantage over another. In reality, the liberal conception is one that allows for the possibility of all others to exist, but they must necessarily remain marginal. Yet liberalism is not just a point of departure; it is, in reality, the only legitimate ideology of Americanism with which the eventual existence of rivals is perceived as an excess, as an incident, similar to how America experiences the existence of any potential competitor on the planetary level.

Liberalism basically uses somewhat "softer" means instead of completely open repression, but this does not mean that liberalism is any more benevolent towards its opponents. Like many others, liberalism is a totalitarian ideology, one that is firmly rooted in the American mentality whose hidden

---

[66] Written in 2008, published in the 2010 Serbian edition of *The Return of Myth*.

foundation is Protestant, Puritan eschatology. These are the reasons why over the past few decades, and especially since the fall of the Iron Curtain, Washington has acted as a true messianic center, one whose enigmatic language is based on the rhetoric of "democracy", "free trade", and "human rights." America was created as a community of "chosen ones" equal among themselves, separated from the "rest of the world" by an impenetrable wall but with hands outstretched to all of humanity, to whom it offers its eschatology and solution to the "mystery of history."

America is, without a doubt, a product of European civilization and heritage, or more precisely a very particular part of that heritage which most modern Westerners perceive as modern, progressive, and "Westernmost", as the highest point of civilizational evolution, against which Europeans, especially the Orthodox, represent a veritable deviation, an anomaly. In order to understand this, it is necessary to go back deep into the past.

Manifest Destiny

The Church Schism of 1054 was one of the most important, first-rate facts of European history. Only from that moment on did it become possible to speak of the West (initially Roman Catholic) as opposed to the European and Christian, Orthodox East. It is in "more modern" and "more progressive" Roman Catholicism that those tendencies sprouted which would reach their peak with the Reformation, i.e. individualism, economism, and utilitarian rationalism. In his study *The Protestant Ethic and the Spirit of Capitalism*, Max Weber described the birth of capitalism out of the spirit of radical Protestantism, whose basic assumption is that material wealth is a sign of God's grace. These tendencies became fully embedded in the "trade order" of England which, sometime in the 17th century, finally turned toward the sea and colonial conquests, soon to become not only the most formidable naval power, but a veritable "maritime civilization."

The maritime, liberal, mercantile, colonial British Empire was something completely different from the still deeply Roman Catholic overseas empires of Spain and Portugal. In this regard, Arnold Toynbee spoke of the "principle of technology", that is to say "technology completely severed from all the norms of (Christian) tradition." England's opposition to the Orthodox East on both the geopolitical and ideological levels soon became absolute and uncompromising. Starting in the 17th century, Russia entered the European stage most unexpectedly as a great continental power, hence the struggle of "proud Albion" against the "Russian bear", which in its mythical transposition is Leviathan's battle with Behemoth, became over the course of centuries of hostility the main motif of European political and military history.

The Reformation and the discovery of the New World were in fact simultaneous historical events. The most extreme Protestant sects headed to America, the continent in the Far West, attracted by the possibility of realizing their utopian project in the empty spaces of the New World in an obvious and concrete way. The United States of America emerged as an alliance of the most radical, fundamentalist Protestant sects convinced of their eschatological mission and Manifest Destiny or, in other words, the New Jerusalem, the City of the Lord on Earth in which, as Thomas Jefferson put it, "the wolves and the lambs live in peace, side by side." In a very short span of time, they managed to emancipate themselves from their European homeland.

Apocalyptic Scenario

In equal measure, the United States is thus the product of the vague eschatological hopes and apocalyptic expectations of the masses of believers of this new religion who made their way to the New Continent. The belief in the beginning of a New Millennium, a new Golden Age which has already begun on American soil, on the one hand, and on the other an apocalyptic scenario with torrents of blood of the "cursed" about which televangelist preachers speak today, was intended for the "rest of the world" which rejects the American resolution of history and its drama. This resolution is paradoxical and almost banal: the liberal model of societal organization, raised to the level of a religious dogma, and the absolutization of the market and "free trade" which abolishes tariffs, protectionism, and borders, not only does not imply reciprocity, but excludes the existence of any other concept, of any other force or social order, which are reduced to being misunderstandings or incidents. Without a doubt, there is a strong contradiction between this eschatological inspiration and the dry pragmatism of American society, in which, at least seemingly, everything is subordinated to business, the economy, and relentless activism. This contradiction is resolved through the special structure of the American political elite, its intellectual and geopolitical services, and through an altogether peculiar doctrine whose name is "Dispensationalism."

It is in this theological and eschatological teaching that all the important themes and obsessions of Americanism are to be found: its historical optimism, faith in continuous progress and the perfection of democracy, its obsession with apocalyptic motives, its moralistic sermons ("we are a moral people") alongside extreme amoralism whenever America and its special interests are questioned, its pragmatism alongside uncompromising idealism, which has no sense of opposition and difference, its aggressive interventionism alongside its autistic isolationism, as well as its philanthropy and faith in democracy alongside the sinister face of "democracy #1" which America shows to all who reject its solutions and its salvational model.

Time of Troubles: Tribulation

In question is a doctrine whose beginning is associated with the name of John Nelson Darby (1800-1882) and is based on an altogether extravagant interpretation of certain Old Testament prophets and the Book of Revelation of the Apocalypse of Saint John the Theologian. This doctrine flourished in the 1970s in the form of literal interpretations of the Biblical eschatological scenario, of which the most influential and popular was certainly that of Cyrus Scofield. *The Scofield Reference Bible*, which in addition to the original Biblical text contains a series of the author's own commentaries, interpretations, and prophecies, has sold millions of copies and today is the most complete edition of the Bible in English. It bears noting that in the interpretation of Scofield and his evangelist successors, the person of Christ occupies a completely peripheral place, while the central themes are the Apocalypse, Armageddon, the fate of America and, above all, Israel, and the impending conflict with King Gog in the final time of troubles or "tribulation period" as the Dispensationalists call it.

The depth of this influence is illustrated by the fact that the general public is usually not able to distinguish the original Biblical text from Scofield's inserts and additions, and that they are generally not even aware of the existence of "Dispensationalism", which is simply accepted as an integral part of Christian teaching. It is also, at least on a semi-conscious or subliminal level, very easily accepted by American atheists as a series of psychological, cultural, and ideological patterns and clichés. Indeed, Dispensationalism offers a quite coherent and rounded view of history and geopolitics, albeit understood in an eccentric, inverted spirit of Protestant fundamentalism. The vast majority of the most popular television preachers are evangelicals and Dispensationalists. For opponents of this doctrine, Dispensationalism is not a Christian doctrine but a kind of "Christian Zionism." According to the general assessment, however, this is the most influential religious and eschatological doctrine shaping the American mentality - both today as well as back in the time of the Puritan "founding fathers."

The Nuclear King Gog

Given the necessary generalization, let us look at what constitutes the very core of the Dispensationalist "myth" - a subject which is repeated by numerous authors who share this worldview with surprising consistency and persistence. The bizarreness of their content should not confuse the reader, for Dispensationalist "prophecies" sometimes obviously contain deeper geopolitical intuitions and historical insights. The central theme of this eschatology is the fate of the Church and, above all, the fate of Israel, which here means the ethnic Jews who adhere to the principles of orthodox Judaism. By the "Church", of course, is not meant the Roman Catholic one, much less the Orthodox Church, but exclusively the congregations of Protestant fundamentalists. According to this view, "white Anglo-Saxon Protestants" are the descendants of the ten tribes of Israel who did not return to Israel after the Babylonian captivity.

Towards the end of time, Israel is to be rebuilt, and this prophecy was literally fulfilled in 1957 with the creation of the Jewish state. This, however, marks the beginning of the aforementioned days of "great trouble", the Tribulation, the days in which the "empires of evil" (it is worth recalling that this term was used by Reagan and brought back into circulation by George W. Bush after 9/11) will attack the Anglo-Saxon Protestants and Israel. Let us leave aside on this point the question of the disparity of the eschatological destiny, or it would be better to say Divine Providence, of the Anglo-Saxon Protestants, which is of purely theological significance. In any case, a very strange turn is to occur at this moment: before the attack of "Gog, King of Magog", the Anglo-Saxons will "ascend" to Heaven in the "Rapture" while the sons of Israel will defeat Gog in Armageddon. The ascension of the Rapture (another extremely bizarre detail) is to take place in a mysterious way similar to flying on a spaceship or flying saucer, a point which emphasizes the importance of technology in this apocalyptic scenario: "In some contemporary Dispensationalist texts, such 'plans' are connected to the newest technological advancements, which thus gives rise to a "nuclear Dispensationalism"... Once again, Russia (and earlier the USSR) is presented as among the "forces of evil" of the "nuclear King Gog."[67] Then, according

---

67   Alexander Dugin, *Misterii Evrazii* [*Mysteries of Eurasia*] (Moscow: Arktogeia, 1991).

to this strange apocalyptic scenario, Protestants will be led by the Protestant Christ in his Second Coming to return to Earth (to Israel), and the Jews will convert to Protestantism, thus beginning the millennial Kingdom of Christ on Earth.

At the End of Time

Dispensationalism, to say the least, explains very well various "light" motives or neuralgic points of American foreign policy. First and foremost, the unconditional alliance with Israel, which most often contradicts the real interests of the American Empire. Fear of weapons of mass destruction, such as nuclear, chemical, or biological agents that could eventually come into the possession of countries forming the "Axis of Evil" (à la George W. Bush) is not merely a case of tendentious propaganda or media disinformation, but also a recurrence of Jewish, Old Testament, and Puritan fears of the destruction that is to eventually befall "God's chosen people." One characteristic example of this can be found in the Gospel of Matthew 24:14-18:

> And this gospel of the kingdom will be preached in the whole world as a testimony to all nations, and then the end will come. So when you see standing in the holy place 'the abomination that causes desolation,' spoken of through the prophet Daniel - let the reader understand - then let those who are in Judea flee to the mountains. Let no one on the housetop go down to take anything out of the house. Let no one in the field go back to get their cloak.

The significance of this doctrine to American consciousness is evidenced by the fact that at least two American presidents, Jimmy Carter and Ronald Reagan, can be labelled as Dispensationalists, while George W. Bush openly declared himself to be a "Premillennial Dispensationalist." Of even greater significance, however, is the observation that the entirety of American culture since the time of the Puritan settlers has been deeply imbued with this very eschatological and apocalyptic motif. As Arthur Kroker rightly concludes in his study *Born Again Ideology*: "The animating energy of the American imperial project is essentially religious, not political. The ruling American mythopoetic is eschatological. It is about 'end times.'"[68]

Armageddon is Near

In general, the American political and intellectual class does not reflect the diversity of the population of the North American continent, but it is the predominant "WASP" or "White Anglo-Saxon Protestant" type that is firmly rooted in Protestant fundamentalism. Translating the furious, frightening rhetoric of Puritan preachers into the precise, rational, concrete language of geopolitical and economic analysis is the task of their intellectual services. The result is a grotesque blend of Protestant messianism and the liberal model feigning tolerance and "openness to all differences" which, in the frenzy of missionaries, is offered to the "rest of the world" as the American model of salvation from the terror, obstinacy, and darkness of history. But in its very essence, Protestant fundamentalism, in which Dispensationalism has an honorable and prominent place, remains the "hidden" ideology of America that determines the thoughts, hopes, and dreams, of a huge, predominant part of the nation, including its atheists.

---

68 Arthur Kroker, *Born Again Ideology* (Victoria: CTheory Books/ NWP/ Pacific Centre for Technology and Culture, 2007), p. 24.

Barack Obama, of course, being the son of a Kenyan immigrant and a white woman and a man who bears a Muslim name while presenting himself as a "Christian", is by no means a typical representative of the American political elite or the "moral majority" of the American nation. He is not only a propaganda and marketing ploy of a failing empire, but also a sign of the deep racial and ideological divisions of America in which, since 11 September 2001 and the catastrophic financial and economic collapse, is once again seeing a revival of Puritan hopes and fears for the "end times." "Armageddon is near, hard times have arrived", television preachers thunder. The "moral majority", intimidated by terrorism, existential insecurity, the prospect of immiseration and the "war of all against all" is indeed turning into the herd of its Protestant pastors at the end of time.

Towards the Third World War

Wars are not an unconditional consequence of religious beliefs, nor are they fought solely over economic or energy resources. War is the result of a situation in which existing contradictions can no longer be resolved peacefully, but only with military force, when the horrors of peace are worse than the horrors of war which, in fact, provoke them. The depth of the crisis that is shaking the United States, and which cannot be resolved by financial or economic interventions, is irrevocably pushing the last world empire onto the war path, towards a final showdown with the "forces of evil." After all, as the Russian economic analyst Mikhail Khazin has remarked:

> In gloomy times, the psychology of society has to be changed, society has to be mobilized. The best way to do so is with a threat, a danger. This is nothing new for America. In 1898, in order to start a war with Spain, one which resulted in

America kidnapping the Philippines and Cuba from Spain, the Americans blew up their own ship, the Maine, in Havana. In 1941, Pearl Harbor happened.

Dispensationalism has ready answers for such an apocalyptic scenario. The days of the "Tribulation period" have come. The "Empire of Evil" about which Reagan and then Bush spoke, and the "hordes of King Gog from the land of Magog" are, in the Dispensationalist key and in the psycho-geography of Americans, unequivocally associated with the Russians and their allies as the Biblical, apocalyptic "princes of Rosh, Meshech, and Tubal" (wherein Rosh is interpreted to mean Russia, Meshech Moscow, and Tubal is an ancient name of Scythia). In the case of America, however, the final showdown assumes altogether particular features: otherwise progressive, philanthropic America also has its sinister aspect, the face of the Apocalypse itself, intended for those who reject its (farcical) Gospel. This is the face of the "Angel of Mercy" which has already destroyed Serbia, Afghanistan, Iraq, and, who knows, perhaps tomorrow Syria, Iran, China, or Russia.

The "battle for the end of the world" against King Gog, against Prince Rosh and the "Axis of Evil" has already begun - it started in 1995 in Republika Srpska and Krajina and then in 1999 in Serbia, when the "Angel of Mercy" showed itself in such scenes as American soldiers writing grotesque messages for Serbs on deadly projectiles loaded with depleted uranium or cluster bombs, and in the bombings of Fallujah, Basra, or Baghdad. In the background of these explosions echoed the gospel of American political leaders on the "nation driven by moral hope" and the "world's most moral power."

***

ROME AND CARTHAGE[69]

Preceding the various particularized, narrow definitions with which geopolitics operates is the division of global-scale geopolitical categories: the division into thalassocratic and tellurocratic states, naval powers and continental empires, maritime and land civilizations respectively. States which base their power on land, the "eternal" empires which represent the element of Land or Earth, as a general rule emerge within the depths of land, most often from the very center of a continent. Islands and coastal areas, by contrast, usually pertain to the opposite, thalassocratic field and represent the true homeland of trade and commercial powers whose dominant element is Water (Sea). As Carl Schmitt underscored in his description of the English re-orientation towards the sea in the 17th century, transitioning from one element to another is of essential significance and means a fundamental and radical conversion.

Both of these two fundamental categories - Sea and Land - are considerably older than geopolitics as a science itself. They have been known not only since the earliest times, for example, figuring throughout a number of mythological and theological conceptions, but have also played a significant part when it comes to traditional states, their interests, alliances, and (foreign-)policy orientations. Geopolitical categories have always formed a reality which cannot be neglected or ignored. It also seems to be the case that the most basic forms of state creations have changed little throughout history: the example of Carthage as a particularly thalassocratic, colonial-trading power is a form which has essentially been repeated

---

69 Written in 2000, published in Boris Nad, *Vreme imperija* [*The Time of Empires*] (Belgrade: Rivel Ko, 2002).

up to our time. Rome represented the opposite example of a pronouncedly imperial, continental, tellurocratic power.

Leviathan and Behemoth

In considering the history of the world as a conflict between two opposing, irreconcilable forces in the likes of "the war of Sea against Land" and "the history of the struggle of sea powers against land powers and land powers against sea powers", Carl Schmitt resurrected an old and fruitful tradition. This German thinker reminded us of a medieval Kabbalistic myth presented by Rabbi Isaac Abravanel (1437-1508) which represents one of the most famous descriptions of this "elementary confrontation of Sea and Land." As Schmitt notes, the conflict between Leviathan (the sea monster) and Behemoth (the land beast) spoken of by Rabbi Abravanel, evokes a basic motif of world history and is actually a mythical transposition of the blockade of land powers by sea powers seeking to break the former's supply lines: "The Kabbalists say that Behemoth strives to tear Leviathan apart with his horns or teeth, while Leviathan keeps shut the land animal's muzzle and nose so that he cannot eat or breathe."

This same motif, renamed in somewhat different terms, will reappear in the works of a number of geopoliticians, such as the great founder of political geography, Friedrich Ratzel, who pointed to the importance of the antagonism between maritime and continental powers. This Land-Sea dualism also lies at the heart of Mackinder's geopolitical model, which in many ways was fundamental to all later geopolitical doctrines (Mackinder can rightly be considered the "father" of the Atlanticist strategy of this century), as well as the tradition of continental geopolitics, whose key concept is that of a continental bloc opposed to the colonialism of naval powers.

For many authors, however, these elementary categories of sea and land signify not merely two different principles on which state power rests, but two contrasting modes of human existence. Alexander Dugin recognizes in them "two fundamental aspects of (human) existence", as these two elementary concepts are at once the foundations of the human experience of planetary space. Ultimately, they imply two opposite conceptions of the world, among which the continental is hierarchical and vertical. The notions of soil and space are qualitatively, completely different from those of sea, which is always perceived as a spontaneous element. How, then, could we avoid associating the notion of Land (Earth) with space as such, with continuity, while the category of Sea (Water) is usually identified with time and transience?

The Dualism of Atlantis and Eurasia

Although both of these forces possess their own fields of predominant influence and their own gravitational fields, attempting to determine their geographical boundaries can only have an approximate and conditional value. Borders and dividing lines have changed throughout history. However, the fact of the matter remains that the great tellurocratic empires have formed in the depths of the Eurasian continent (and they have been connected with the central steppe, the planes, rather than forest or mountainous areas). Thalassocratic powers, meanwhile, have been tied to the Atlantic Ocean, to the islands and land gravitating toward such. "Thalassocracy and Atlanticism", Dugin notes, "became synonyms long before the expansion of Great Britain and the Portuguese-Spanish conquests." Throughout history, their conquests have taken their points of departure from "centers in the Atlantic zone", that is "from Gibraltar to the Middle East, and not the other way around."

Without even questioning this basic division, this picture is furthermore complicated by the discernment of other, different spatial areas, geopolitical zones and blocs. Between Russia's central land and island complex - which in the case of Britain consists of Australia, Oceania, and the North American 'island' "at the service of naval and trading forces" (Halford John Mackinder) - stretches a kind of interzone, a zone of peripheral countries representing a domain of mixed cultures. Germany, as the central European hegemon and the central European power, has the same significance for Europe that Russia bears in relation to the entire Eurasian continent: it anchors Europe as a continental bloc. In the European Far West gravitating towards the Atlantic, we find several powers whose interests can be identified with those of the overseas West - the United States of America. Indeed, the United States with its naval power is the ideal example of a modern thalassocratic power. The many Balkan peoples and countries, in the final analysis, signify more or less precise analogues of greater geopolitical entities. Serbs, with their traditional pro-Russian orientation and Orthodox and Byzantine heritage, obviously represent the Eurasian component. Byzantium, the Second Rome, throughout its history exhibited many features of a true Eurasian power.

However, this series of secondary divisions clearly points towards a deeper, fundamental antagonism, the geopolitical and cultural antagonism between Atlantis and Eurasia, which in turn relativizes the (real or presumed) dualism of Europe and Asia or West and East.

The Return of Eurasia

For Mackinder and his followers, Europe and Asia are as different from one another as are hostile entities: "European civilization", Mackinder thought, "is, in a very real sense, the outcome of the struggle against Asiatic invasion." Thus, according to this author, the first great cultures and civilizations, such as Babylon and Egypt, found themselves in irreconcilable opposition to the way of life of the steppe peoples and in constant danger of invasions by nomadic peoples from Central Asia, in which Mackinder saw only "hordes of ruthless horsemen without an ideal." This, however, was only a new geopolitical formulation of the Atlanticist theory in sharp opposition to what could be called the Eurasianist doctrine. Various known historical facts, as well as careful historical and archaeological inquiry, can call this opinion into question. Mackinder, for example, proceeded from the assumption of a racial unity of the steppe peoples of Eurasia, but the Scythians were Indo-Europeans while the Turkic peoples of Siberia are not a homogenous people in a racial sense. Moreover, Genghis Khan's empire possessed its own imperial ideology.

If we are to understand the concept of Eurasia and the genesis of the Eurasianist idea, then it is necessary to recall, in the briefest terms, certain key events in Russian history. Following liberation from the Tatars and the disintegration of the Mongol state, within Muscovite Rus emerged the idea of Moscow the Third (Last) Rome, which, in a later period, would become the basis of Russian imperial ideology. But already at the time of regaining independence, Russia was, in a certain sense, turned away from the West. From the Eurasianist point of view, the period of Tatar occupation was historically fruitful, insofar as Russia's closeness to Asia enabled the Russian synthesis of influences from East and West. In this sense, the conquest of Siberia bore, in the very least, the same significance as the Mongol-Tatar invasion - and Siberia is the "sacred ground" of the Russian Empire.

Consequently, in a cultural-historical sense Russia possesses both European and Asian features, being a third continent that "links elements of both and draws them into a certain unity" (Petr Savitsky). All subsequent rapprochements with the West, such as that undertaken by Peter the Great, could only strengthen its European component, but could not render it an integral part of Europe. The periodic oscillations between these two poles that is so typical of Russian history is a consequence of this essentially Eurasian character. In Russian imperial consciousness, Russia is the heir of the imperial tradition of Genghis Khan's empire, the "heir to the great khans, the successor of the cause of Genghis Khan and Timur, the unifier of Asia" (Petr Savitsky). Another equally important component is the Byzantine heritage common to all Eastern Christian peoples.

All of these facts, together with the geographical position of Russia, have determined Russia's leading place among the countries of Europe and Asia and its wielding of a continental mentality. Historically and geopolitically, these lands are opposed to the island countries of the Atlantic bloc led by the United States of America, the "modern Carthage" (Konstantin Leontiev), the United States representing an oceanic civilization of a neo-Phoenician type, albeit, as Leontiev pointed out, in a simplified and caricatured form.

In other words, if Russia is Eurasia proper, symbolically and truly representing the interests of all Eurasian peoples, then the United States, on the contrary, is the modern society of Atlantis, the new geopolitical center and stronghold of Atlanticism and Atlanticist ideology.

Towards a Eurasian Alliance

Does this Eurasian mentality not have, after all, its deeper archetypes and "collective unconscious", just as it has its own precise historical analogies which we can trace since the earliest past of the continent?

For some geopoliticians, Russia is the modern bearer of Turanism, an imperial-nomadic mentality of a supranational character which predates not only the empire of Genghis Khan, but also the very settling and ethnogenesis of the Slavs. In this case, the first traces of the geopolitical dualism between Atlantis and Eurasia must be sought in a much earlier period than even ancient times. From the Eurasianist point of view, however, the meaning of Russian history lies in that Russia has managed to rediscover the common heritage of Eurasia and is thereby restoring the lost unity of the Eurasian peoples.

We can add to this line of thinking another argument, namely, that the oldest cultures were not maritime, nor did they originate in the peripheral zone but, on the contrary, as is confirmed by numerous archaeological studies, originated precisely in the central part of Eurasia, in the Urals or to the south of them, on the territory of present-day Mongolia and in Eastern Siberia. It is here, by all accounts, that the center of the migrations of the Indo-Europeans is to be sought, the starting point from which the Indo-European cultures spread from East to West.

Thus, the Eurasianist "resolution" rejects the simple dualism between East and West, seeing in the traditions of the peoples of Europe and Asia, linked by the experience of historically inhabiting this common space, a potential unity rather than an irreconcilable antagonism. On the other hand, the modern domination of the West is represented by the hegemony of the pronouncedly Atlanticist United States of America, which treats the common heritage of the peoples of Eurasia as a foreign body. Let us recall that the concept of the West originated in America at the beginning of the last century, not as a name for the common space of Europe and the "New World" but, precisely to the converse, as a designation for American uniqueness in relation to Europe.

The resolution for which Eurasian-oriented geopolitics strives is therefore directed towards Eurasian consolidation, towards the creation of a continental alliance along a Berlin-Moscow-Beijing-Tokyo axis, based on pragmatism as well as on the convergence of the historical and national traditions of Eurasia.

***

THE SECRET OF THE EAST AND THE CRISIS OF THE WESTERN WORLD[70]

One distinctive feature of the modern world observed by the French thinker and esotericist René Guénon in his work *The Crisis of the Modern World* (*La crise du monde moderne*, 1927) is the schism that has taken place between East and West. This division is warranted and "seems beyond doubt."[71] It is true that there have always been numerous different civilizations which have developed in their own ways. "Difference", however, does not mean "opposition": there can be commonalities between different civilizations "so long as they are all based on the same fundamental principles - of which they only represent applications varying in accordance with varied circumstances."[72] On the level of fundamental principles, therefore, there is no fundamental opposition between the Chinese, Islamic, or Russian-Orthodox civilizations. This is the case with all civilizations that can be called "normal" or "traditional." And this is precisely what justifies the validity of the contemporary division between "East" and "West." Between East and West there is one fundamental and insurmountable opposition: Western civilization, "common to (Western) Europe and America", does not recognize any supreme principle, but "is in reality based only on a negation of principles" and is "by this very fact ruled out from all mutual understanding with other civilizations."[73] Indeed, Western materialist civilization is a singular anomaly in world history.

---

70 Written in 2020, previously unpublished.
71 René Guénon, *The Crisis of the Modern World* (Hillsdale: Sophia Perennis, 2004), p. 22.
72 Ibid, p. 21.
73 Ibid.

The Western and Eastern Spirits

The latter conclusion could be countered with the argumentation that today the "global civilization" that has been established is based on "Western values", and that all the societies of the traditional East have, to greater or lesser extents, already undergone "Westernization", thus becoming essentially identical to Western society and part of the one "Western Civilization." But this is primarily a delusion of the West, which generally does not understand the East (or "understands" it completely erroneously and insufficiently, as is evidenced by so-called Orientalism). Such is also the delusion of some "Easterners", those who have accepted "Western deviations", abandoned their tradition, spread confusion in their countries, and who have been convinced that "the West wins in all fields", that the West as a civilization is "superior", and therefore the East must unconditionally submit to the West. This is typical of all those who "negate principles", instead always remaining on the material and "external" level, on the level of technological development and superficial influences. Such people are "Easterners" only by origin and should be considered "Westerners" even when they are politically opposed to "Occidentalism" and advocate "nationalism", which is contrary to the truly traditional spirit. Such "Easterners" are marked by an essential "ignorance." They are "loud", while "true Easterners" are "silent", just as the heart of the traditional spirit is "silent" and "withdrawn into itself", not at all trying to get to know the West. However, there are also those among them who have decided to temporarily accept "Western methods" in order to free themselves from foreign (Western) domination, to accelerate the inevitable Western downfall after which they would reject these methods, just as they would reject their own ostensible "Westernizing."

That which has made its way to the East was at its source "modernization": the East has had to accept competition with the West, even in those fields and ways which are not integral to it, such as technology and the economy, with the aim of freeing itself from the West and the latter's penetrations, so that "the East could preserve its very survival." The West, meanwhile, has spread with seemingly great ease and rapidity through colonization, military occupation, "capitalism", "democracy", and "hard" and "soft power", but this expansion has remained only external and ostensible. The "confrontation" between East and West has therefore not disappeared: on the contrary, it has grown stronger and more important with time. Thus, even today there remains a fundamental opposition between the "Western spirit" (the significant shift, the real pivot having occurred over the past several centuries in the Western world, with which began the so-called "modern age") and the "Eastern spirit" (the "other", relatively original spirituality that has survived only in the East). "These two terms, then, express nothing more than an actual fact."[74] On one end always remains the West with its specific development, while on the other has remained the "planetary East", i.e. those civilizations which, despite what has unfolded on the surface, have not deviated from the norm.

Approaching the "End of the World"

This fundamental schism between East and West is constantly deepening, because the West "does not stop moving away and changing", while the East (despite all the

---

74   Ibid, p. 23.

changes on the surface), "roughly speaking, remains more or less the same." The West is "marching", while the East remains "immobile." This divergence can be represented by a diagram in which the East is the axis, and the West is "a line starting from the axis and moving further and further away from it."[75] The process through which the West has passed ever faster and faster has already been deemed "creative destruction": the West has constantly destroyed its own traditions, including its own religions, and subjects everything to doubt, including even the very principles upon which Western (European) civilization was constructed. At the same time, the West is not building up anything: although it is a product of or deviation from European tradition and civilization, it is not Europe, but rather a negation of traditional Europe, an Anti-Europe. For a long time already, it has been not Christian, but anti-Christian, developing into the anti-Christian (Western) spirit. The consequence of this development is a distinctly "materialist civilization": the consumer society composed of atomized individuals in which no superior principle matters and in which everything is allowed to be "doubted" except "doubt" itself. In fact, this is a matter of inner disintegration and deep spiritual crisis, of dissolution which creates nothing, instead only moving aimlessly, a crisis still awaiting its outcome. Such societies are very unstable and fragile on the inside: the fact of the matter is the internal disintegration of (Western) society itself. For some time now, the West has emanated premonitions and forebodings of the end of this very civilization.

Until altogether recently, the West firmly believed in one dogma: infinite development, infinite "progress" towards

---

[75] René Guénon, *Introduction to the Study of the Hindu Doctrines* (London: Luzac & Co., 1945), p. 33.

one all-obligatory goal which can in no way be stopped. All others have simply "lagged" (and in time, presumably, will accept "Western superiority"). The root illusion is the conviction that Western civilization has a "privileged place in the history of the world." As early as the beginning of the 20th century, however, if not earlier, there appeared certain individuals who "perceive, though in a vague and confused manner, that the civilization of the West may not always go on developing in the same direction, but may someday reach a point where it will stop, or even be plunged in its entirety into some cataclysm."[76] Consciousness of this crisis has in itself been essentially a favorable development, a sign that these chimeras and illusions have begun to dissipate. Ultimately, there have appeared those who have anticipated and predicted or wished for the "end of the world": "It is certainly no accident that so many people today are haunted by the idea of the 'end of the world.'"[77] This wrongly grasped idea, with all of the deviations it can lead to, is undoubtedly a sign of the spiritual confusion of our age, but also something greater: "the vague foreboding of an end - which in fact is near - works uncontrollably on the imaginations of some people."[78] Some individuals have increasingly clearly apprehended an end "without being able to define exactly the nature or extent of the change they foresee"[79], considering such to be the approaching "end of the world" precisely because they do not see anything outside of this one civilization and one cycle, hence their identification of its otherwise inevitable end with a veritable "end of the world."

---

76 Guénon, *The Crisis of the Modern World*, p. 2.
77 Ibid, p. 4.
78 Ibid.
79 Ibid, p. 5.

Consciousness of this crisis shows that the West is reaching the "critical phase", "that a more or less complete transformation is imminent", or even its very disappearance, and that "a change of direction must ensue - whether voluntarily or not, whether suddenly or gradually, whether catastrophic or otherwise."[80] We are now approaching the denouement, and this itself sheds light on the unnatural state of affairs that has been proceeding for several centuries. History is accelerating and events are succeeding one after another evermore rapidly. The culmination has yet to arrive. Yet when it comes to determining duration and timeframes, Guénon adds that one should be cautious: "the crisis is not yet ended and it is perhaps impossible to say exactly when, and in what manner, it will end. It is always preferable to refrain from prognostications that cannot be based on grounds clearly intelligible to all, and that therefore could be misinterpreted, adding to the confusion rather than relieving it."[81]

Protecting the West from Itself

The crisis is here, but, again, it has not yet seen itself through. Etymologically, "crisis" is, among other things, the hour of decision: "The phase that can properly be termed 'critical' in any order of things is the one immediately preceding a resolution, be this favorable or unfavorable - in other words, one in which a turn is taken either for the better or for the worse."[82] Yet it is far from the case that the possible outcomes of the crisis will be arbitrary or accidental. The chaos of the modern world is also illusory. It is governed and ruled by definite cyclical laws. What appears to be disorder and anomaly

---
80 Ibid, p. 2.
81 Ibid, p. 3.
82 Ibid.

is, in fact, a necessary, constituent element of a higher order; the "totality of disorder" constitutes the order in the world. In a way, things actually remain in balance, because they are affected by the action of opposing forces, none of which can disappear. The crisis in question can only end in a "way out of the dark age," the end of which we may already be witnessing. And this, in Guénon's opinion, is indicated to us by many signs.

In general, the trajectory of human history and the history of every civilization is "fall", "decline", involution. But everywhere and always, two complementary forces, two opposite directions, impact events on the whole: one descending, the other ascending, one centripetal, the other centrifugal, in the sense of either moving away from the principle (the center) or approaching the principle, an operation which is comparable to a heartbeat or the movement of breath. In the general movement of the world, a downward movement may sometimes involve a special action in the opposite direction, a "divine influence" or manifestation leading to the establishment of an (always temporary) balance. Then there is a "partial ascension", when the fall seems to be temporarily stopped or neutralized. In the case of the West, even this possibility cannot be completely ruled out. "Ascension" is always possible, but it implies a "renewal of tradition", and this not only excludes any "aversion to the East", but also the cessation of the "opposition to the East" which stems from none other than the Western deviation vis-à-vis tradition in general. Nearing the East would mean the return of the modern West to itself; the distance of the modern West from the East is the measure of its decline.

It is even clearer that those who today speak of "defending the West", meaning "defending from the East", really do not know of what they speak, for today it is the West that "is threatening to submerge the whole of mankind in the whirlpool of its own confused activity", whereas the East never attacks, as "the true East has no thought of attacking or dominating anybody, and asks no more than to be left in independence and tranquility - surely a not unreasonable demand."[83] The East is not on the attack, but "the West really is in great need of defense" - not against the East, "but only against itself and its own tendencies which, if they are pushed to their conclusion, will lead inevitably to its ruin and destruction."[84] In other words, the West cannot win its "battle against the East", for victory or defeat is decided on the higher, spiritual level: the "victory of the West" would bring defeat to all of humanity and a real end - the "end of history", which would in actuality not be triumphant at all, but the "end of the world." Instead of "defense", it would be more appropriate to speak of a "transformation of the West." The matter at hand is really one of return: the return to the spiritual East. Is there enough time left for this as modern Western civilization is taking large and decisive strides towards its own final catastrophe? Regardless of the outcome of these exertions, action cannot be in vain, because such provides the factors that could survive the flood and become the germs of the future.

Can the East help the West?

Can these seemingly quite abstract considerations following Guénon provide some kind of signpost amidst today's confusion? The ostensibly sturdy and immutable "international liberal order" established by the Western powers over the past few decades is now proving to be extremely unstable, or

---
83   Ibid, p. 31.
84   Ibid.

simply a mere illusion, and the same can be said of the internal structure of many Western countries. The crisis of the Western world is spreading uncontrollably, worse than any epidemic, in all fields and spheres, and appears to be exacerbated and deepened by what may seem to be insignificant reasons, but which may reach the point of real catastrophe.

The confrontation of East and West has perhaps reached its peak today. The West is not only in deep crisis, a point which is no longer denied even by the most ardent, persistent, and consistent "Westernists", but, at the same time as this crisis, the East is re-emerging and gaining strength. Just yesterday predictions of such were still denied and refused by the West, convinced as it was of the permanence and superiority of its own models and the very idea that history has reached its pinnacle with "Western Civilization." Now it is worth recalling Guénon's warning: the Western world is genuinely in mortal danger, not because of the East, but due to "its own errors which it itself advocates."

No virus or pandemic caused the current crisis. The crisis of the West has long been in development, its effects are only finally becoming cumulative. This crisis is spiritual, civilizational, political, cultural, social, economic and financial, a crisis of health, migration, and an environmental crisis all at once, and this whole series of crises has but one outcome - one which could turn into a devastating tsunami that would sink one civilization and shake the whole world. Moreover, the West is not even in a position to help itself at all, and aid, such as medical aid now, is unselfishly coming from the East, only to be accepted by Western officials with suspicion, mocked by the so-called public opinion in its searching for the culprit for the West's own troubles in the "hostile East." The contemporary pandemic was neither created nor accelerated by China, but by the West itself, which created the ideal conditions for infection, accelerated the spread, and increased its consequences. Metaphorically speaking, "the West was the first to be infected", and the infection therefrom "spread throughout the world", for it, the West, "plays the role of the historical mold", and the virus itself destroys that which is already weakened. If the warning posed by this situation is not heeded, then the present pandemic will certainly not be the last. After all, it is enough to catch sight of the differences in the reactions to the current "corona crisis" between East and West. As Pepe Escobar has noted: "the Asia triad of Confucius, Buddha and Lao Tzu has been absolutely essential in shaping the perception and serene response of hundreds of millions of people across various Asian nations to Covid-19. Compare this with the prevalent fear, panic and hysteria mostly fed by the corporate media across the West."[85] The point is the East's fundamental cultural difference from the West, a difference of culture that is deeply rooted in tradition practiced in everyday life.

If, on the contrary, it is not too late, then the fate and future of the West directly depends on the state of its intellectual elite and their ability to transform the West. The present situation does not provide much ground for optimism. The true elite only "still exists in the Eastern civilizations", while "in the West on the other hand the elite no longer exists" (existing only as an aspiration and an insufficiently shaped movement), "and the question may therefore be asked whether or not it will

---

85 Pepe Escobar, "Confucius is winning the Covid-19 war", *Asia Times* (13/4/2020).

be reconstituted before the end of our epoch", that is whether "certain Western elements would have to bring about this restoration"[86], obviously with support and effective aid from the East as the only source of "living tradition." The West can no longer "cure" or transform itself by its own forces, but only with external help. The possibilities for this, no matter how small, still exist. The first precondition for avoiding catastrophe is recognizing and accepting the fact that the modern West, regardless of its high technological achievements, has always represented an inferior civilization in relation to the East, and that its hitherto superiority has been based only on "brute force, subjugation, and pillaging." It cannot hide behind its "more or less hypocritical veils", nor any of its "moralistic pretexts, none of the humanitarian declamations, none of the wiles of propaganda." [87] The West will first and foremost have to forget its prejudice over its own superiority and, at the same time, will have to give up its aggressive "proselytism which cannot bring itself to admit that it is sometimes necessary to have 'allies' who are not 'subjects.'"[88]

***

---

86 Guénon, *The Crisis of the Modern World*, p. 109.
87 Ibid, p. 100.
88 Ibid, p. 113.